TAKING TIME SERIOUSLY: JAMES LUTHER ADAMS

John R. Wilcox

University Press of America™

Copyright © 1978 by

University Press of America, Inc.™

4710 Auth Place, S.E., Washington, D.C. 20023

ISBN: 0-8191-0600-3

Library of Congress Catalog Card Number: 78-61391

TABLE OF CONTENTS

iii

PREFACE

The thought of James Luther Adams has impressed
itself deeply on my thinking. In the pages to follow,
this fact will become increasingly evident. I have
found that we share a communal perspective on theology,
and, in bringing my personal questions to the research
and writing of this paper, I have discovered that Adams'
approach to ethics has much to offer me in the way of
answers and newly framed questions.

A discussion of my theological and personal perspectives will clarify the contents of this book for
the reader. I find the late 1970's, in which I am
writing, very different from the early and mid-1960's
when I began my theological studies. Until recently,
I pursued my studies within the context of a religious
community, leading the apostolic form of monasticism so
prevalent in the so-called "active" communities of Roman
Catholicism. Life within my religious community, as
well as in the church, underwent a vast restructuring
process in keeping with the "renewal" called for by the
Second Vatican Council. A spiritual as well as a sociological endeavor, "renewal" depended in large measure
upon religious and theological thinking and thus gave
birth to an enthusiasm for theology. I found myself in
the enviable position of having my educational and personal interest in religion and theology applauded by
academic colleagues and community members as well. Indeed, the Roman Catholic church as a whole, seeking to
revitalize the religious education of its members, joined
in the applause.

My interest in theology was undoubtedly brought to
the fore by a rather generalized, but nevertheless prevalent, community interest in theology. In two courses,
introduction to the field, one in sociology of religion
and the other in Christian ethics, I began to see the
close relationship between social structures, culture,
and religion in any society and to value the societally
supportive structure of the religious community. At the
same time, dramatic changes were taking place within the
religious congregation. A more consensual decision-
making structure replaced a previously hierarchical one.
Theological study and community restructuring brought
about a greater degree of individual growth as well as a

v

demand for a more personal sense of relationship within the community, both in the context of religious faith. The democratizing reform of the congregation's structure and an attendant religious personalism paradoxically helped me to leave the community despite, or perhaps because of, my concern for community.

I find myself writing this book, then, within a context which has changed considerably. The recent concern for religion and theology which seemed to pervade not only the atmosphere of the church but also the secular world has diminished. While more people are involved in theological education than in the past and members of religious communities receive a more sophisticated introduction to religious thought, the enthusiasms of the recent past are gone. This is not necessarily to be regretted. Charisms are important but they are not the staff of daily life. Significant changes have been effected in religious community life, but the task of renewal continues. Enthusiasms do effect change; however, everyday life and its evaluation are more important and more difficult to focus on.

As I reflect on my enthusiasm for restructuring religious community upon a theological base, I am perplexed by my own narrowness of perspective. As I see it, I failed to act with equal concern for the great social and ethical issues in the larger community of the world. Though aware of the civil rights movement, the Vietnam war, the plight of the farm workers, I did not become involved. And I still have not become deeply involved. As this book is concluded I come to the end of my rope -- and my excuses.

The relation of the above to James Luther Adams is probably evident already. Concern with the nature of the religious community led me to areas of Christian ethics which dealt with the aspect of man in community. Studying Christian ethics, I came to see this specific concern within a wider perspective. As part of the widening process, I read a _Festschrift_, Voluntary Associations, written in Adams' honor; the book contained a biographical and bibliographical section which stirred my interest. Adams' emphasis on the social nature of man, his use of sociology and the typology of the voluntary association were congenial to my vocation and the bent of my studies. Adams' thought reinforced my growing understanding of revelation as a continual process; I saw my communal vocation as broader than a call to a particular religious

vi

congregation. Then, too, I found a jarring conflict between my congregation's emphasis on personalism and my own inability to live out deeply human personal relationships within the congregation. Encountering my spouse, who brought the personalism to fullness, changed a negative reason for departure from the congregation into a positive one.

Adams' writings thus answered some of my existential questions and widened my perspective. I am still pondering the issue of man in community, now within the context of marriage and a teaching career. Of interest to me personally as well as professionally, Adams has provided great insight into the structural nature of community, the value of democracy, and the voluntary association as a means of fostering and preserving the attainment of justice and mercy in society.

One might find it strange that all this has been said within the context of a book. It has to be said since James Luther Adams became an integral part of the process of personal growth and development. Profound change occurred in my life as I researched and wrote this work, and these changes are both cause and effect of this paper.

The goal of this book is the exposition and interpretation of James Luther Adams' Christian ethics. Adams is uniquely important as a Christian ethicist. He has related theology to the social sciences, to voluntary associations, and to social action. The contribution which he makes can be attributed to his comprehensively social orientation. Allied to and at the root of this orientation is an element that is exemplary for others doing the ethical task; it is the dialectical and tension-filled nature of Adams' thought which leads him to a stance of constant interaction with his environment. Historical-social analysis is the methodological tool he finds adequate to accomplish cognitively what he encourages experientially of himself and others.

One of the things I asked myself time and time again was why Adams has not written more extensively. There is no doubt in my mind that he has the information, the insights, and the methodology. I think I know the personality of the man sufficiently to understand his ability to make keen judgments about interconnections between religion and culture. But his strength seems to me to be more in the verbal expression of the insight through intense conversation, teaching, and the writing of essays than in the systematic application of his understandings to writing and publishing. I see this as the reason Adams has influenced so many students and fellow theologians throughout his life. This approach, however, limits the circle of his influence and the impact he could have on ethical thought today.

In saying the above, I must also add that the very way he does ethics offers food for thought to others involved in this task. Concern for context by its very nature leads to the approach Adams has. He seeks relevancy and attacks diverse problems, both necessary facets of interpreting a pluralistic society. Nevertheless, even as I defend him, I still must say, "Jim, write it down."

Finally, I wish to thank several people who have been an important part of this project. My wife, Suzanne, has been my main emotional support throughout the writing of this book. I cannot thank her enough for that. She has also been an important critic of this work and most helpful in forcing me to show greater clarity and conciseness of expression.

Appreciation and thanks go to the Marist brothers, the religious congregation in which I began this work. Without their spiritual, emotional, and financial support, I would not have undertaken this course of study. In particular, I wish to thank several members of the local religious community in which I began the book: Sean Sammon; Anthony Miserandino; John Malich; Peter Ostrowski; Michael Kelley; Joseph Lederer; Patrick McMahon; Ronald Pasquariello.

Guidance in and criticism of this work came from Roger Shinn and Beverly Harrison. I have learned much from them in the process. Dr. Shinn served as my advisor, and I wish to thank him, in particular, for his reading of several drafts. His criticisms and comments were always to the point and I have gained much professionally and intellectually because of his concern. Beverly Harrison has twice read this book bringing several important criticisms to my attention. I want to thank her also for her time and assistance.

The author of the first dissertation of James Luther
Adams, James D. Hunt, has been very helpful. His bibliography on Adams provided an important starting point for
much of my own research. He has sent me many texts of
Adams' lectures that were not otherwise available. The
Adams bibliography compiled by Ralph Potter, Jean Potter,
and James D. Hunt, and which appears in the Adams Festschrift, Voluntary Associations, has also been valuable in
directing early research.

My colleagues at Manhattan College are to be thanked
for their support, in particular, the chairman Brother
Albert Clark, F.S.C. Mrs. Mary Vaughan, the departmental
secretary, typed many of the pages of this book. I owe
her a special debt of gratitude for her concern and interest, especially in the typing of the first draft. Kathreen
Brewer, Irene Granovsky, Colleen Meyer, Sara Nicoll and
Alice Warwick were responsible for the final typing and I
thank them for that. The production of the final copy
would not have been possible without the assistance of
Neil Fabricant, Esq., Director of the New York State
Legislative Institute, Baruch College, who graciously
provided the facilities of the Institute for the final
typing.

A final note for the reader: All footnotes, unless
otherwise stated, are from the corpus of Adams' works.
Furthermore, developing a fairly complete bibliography
of Adams' works has been a goal of this project. As a
result, the bibliography at the conclusion of the book
is more extensive than the actual references in the body
of the text.

CHAPTER I

JAMES LUTHER ADAMS: BIOGRAPHY

<u>Introduction</u>

The task of Christian ethics is embodied in the
person of James Luther Adams, who situates it within
the context of American society by combining reflective
action with active reflection. How can we delineate this
task to which his life is dedicated? Perhaps an image
will serve to emphasize its contextual character, the
image of a tapestry in which the dominant figures of
scriptures, tradition and the sense of community are
highlighted by the subtle background hues of culture
and history. Harmony and hence beauty emerge from the
successful blend; negating any element would destroy the
aesthetic impact of the completed work. But by combining
the specifically Christian with the necessarily secular and
cultural aspects, a "thing of beauty" is produced, pleasing
as such to the eye of the beholder and the mind of the
maker. The beholder views the tapestry of ethics either
from within the church as a member of the Christian community, or from without, as one searching for a cohesive
value system.

Thomas Luckmann would place our tapestry in his "mar-
ket place of value systems" as a concrete expression of
Christian community to the world at large as that world
seeks to make sense of itself. The threads familiar to
all observers would be those of the secular background,
the behavioral and social sciences, for Christian ethics
relies as much on these fields as it does on that of
philosophy. The Christian ethicist relies on the sciences
not only as background material but as part and parcel of
his self-understanding.

The continuous work of James Luther Adams is to
weave the tapestry of Christian ethics in constant interaction with the life of society. His manner of doing the
ethical task is by no means accepted by all theologians or
Christians. But Adams, a Christian ethicist for our times
and our country, chooses to enrich his rootedness in
Christian scriptures, tradition, and community with the
insights of contemporary sociology, psychology, philosophy,

political science, and history. His choice of this methodology serves to underline the eminently practical character of his work.

Adams, as an American ethicist, stands in the tradition of openness to the secular disciplines, a tradition noted by Langdon Gilkey:

> American theology in the last half-century has, then, received substantial help from a number of secular disciplines ranging from the physical sciences through the social and psychological sciences to the humanities and the arts. These bewildering changes of intellectual partners reveal, however, one continual characteristic of American theology and its relation to its "sources." They show that American theology has been socially involved first with regard to intrinsic concern, and then, as a consequence with regard to the formation of its own fundamental categories of thought. The evidence indicates that the intellectual shape of recent American theology has been determined in each decade by the character of the crises then current in the wider secular milieu.[1]

Adams stands as a practitioner of Gilkey's two basically American theological themes, the close relationship of the secular and the religious and the social involvement of the religious in the secular. He stands, likewise, as confirmation of James Gustafson's view that Christian ethics in the American theological tradition has sought to have practical effects on public and private morals. "It is far more characteristic to find theoretical work developed out of practical moral concern than it is to find extensive treatises seeking to resolve theological and philosophical questions in the abstract."[2]

It is the contention of this book that Adams stands in this tradition, even though Gustafson does not include him among the leading exponents of this peculiarly American approach to Christian ethics. A "practical moral concern" characterizes Adams' approach to the ethical task.

---

[1]Langdon Gilkey, "Social and Intellectual Sources of Contemporary Protestant Theology," in Religion in America, ed. William G. McLoughlin and Robert W. Bellah (Boston: Houghton Mifflin, 1968), pp. 161-62.

[2]James Gustafson, "Christian Ethics," in Religion, ed. Paul Ramsey (Englewood Cliffs, N.J.: Prentice-Hall, 1965), p. 287.

His writings, far from being abstract treatises on other worldly happenings, are really spin-offs from his personal involvement and concern. Without taking away from his close intellectual and spiritual ties with European thought and church life, I contend that the currents of American life and thought moved Adams. He not only responded to this history, but helped shape it. In my view, an analysis of Adams' biography and writings in the context of social events from the late 1920's to the present might well concretize a way of doing ethics for a new generation of theologians in this country.

As I analyze the Adamsean corpus in this book, I wish to evaluate his methodological approach to ethics and, in doing so, his insights about the twentieth century religious situation. Let me briefly review the stages in which I will approach this task in the paper to follow. A biographical sketch of James Luther Adams introduces the man -- thinker and doer -- while it contextualizes his writing. Basic in my mind to any deep understanding of his thinking is the next chapter which examines his lifelong reformulation of religious liberalism, in which context Adams' insights about man become clear. These lead him, and consequently me in the next chapter, to devote some time to his theology. Chapter Four, by elucidating the characteristics which are basic to Adams' ethics, reveals how he weaves insights about man and about God into a way of doing ethics. A study of the voluntary association and power then demonstrates how he puts his ethics to work. In the final chapter, I examine his contribution to Christian ethics.

James Luther Adams: Early Years and Theological Formulation

Although Adams came to be a champion of liberalism, his family background prepared him hardly at all for such a role. His father, James Carey Adams, was a Baptist country preacher, a premillenarian who later became a Plymouth Brother, and a man whom Adams recalls as extremely other worldly.[3] Letta Barrett Adams, his mother, was also a devout believer.

---

[3]James Luther Adams, "Taking Time Seriously," in Taking Time Seriously (Glencoe, Ill.: The Free Press, 1957), p. 11. This book is a collection of essays by Adams. The above essay also appears under the title "How My Mind Has Changed," The Christian Century, LVI, No. 36 (1939), 1067-70.

It is perhaps to his educational experiences that
we must look to find the roots of his liberal thinking.
The college campus of the University of Minnesota, to
which Adams went in 1920, provided a milieu in which
Adams repudiated his strict religious upbringing. "My
new law was in the scientific humanism of John Dietrich
and my new prophecy was in the anti-Rotarianism of H. L.
Mencken."[4]

However, it seems in retrospect that his railing
against religion was simply a turbulent eddy catching
the eye but hiding the deep currents of a profound religious sense. Upon graduation in 1924, Adams entered
Harvard Divinity School and, as Max Stackhouse states,
he was influenced by "the tradition of social responsibility in Unitarianism and of pluralism ('the uses of
diversity') coupled with the historical, critical methods
promoted at Harvard."[5] Adams' lifelong involvement with
the field of sociology began here due to the orientation
provided Harvard by Francis Greenwood Peabody, who had
offered the first course in social ethics in an American
seminary. He laid the groundwork for future developments
in sociology at the school and showed a deep interest in
Negro education and racial questions -- not a general
characteristic of the social gospel at the time.[6]

Adams' years of higher education (1920-1927) were a
time of transformation in society in general and Protestantism in particular. Modern technocratic America
was coming of age. The religious crusade that was World
War I, the debacle of Prohibition, the symbolism of the
Scopes trial, and the reality of the Depression, mark the
twenties as a period of crucial change for American Protestantism.[7] During these years of radical change, Adams

---

[4]"Taking Time Seriously," p. 12.

[5]Max Stackhouse, "James Luther Adams: A Biographical and
Intellectual Sketch," in Voluntary Associations: A Study
of the Groups in Free Societies, ed. D. B. Robertson (Richmond, Va.: John Knox Press, 1966), p. 340. Max Stackhouse
was a student of Adams at Harvard and is presently convener
of the Department of Religion and Society at Andover Newton
Theological School.

[6]Sydney Ahlstrom, A Religious History of the American People (New Haven: Yale University Press, 1972), p. 795.

[7]Donald Meyer calls Post-World War I America an age of de-

4

was studying at Harvard whence we must look to discern the genesis of his theological education and ethical perspective. There Adams was influenced by Irving Babbitt's literary humanism with its stress on ethical standards and conversion. In retrospect, Adams came to see that there was actually little difference between Babbitt's contribution to his formation and that offered to him in the theological and historical disciplines of the divinity school at Harvard.[8] Nevertheless, while he affirmed other influences besides Babbitt, he emphasized the role Babbitt, in particular, had played in helping him understand the Christian doctrines of sin and grace. It was Babbitt, moreover, who developed in Adams a skepticism with regard to the romantic liberal conception of human nature.[9]

It was also at Harvard that he discovered the shortcomings of such a humanism, calling it an "individual psychology of self-culture." Marxism and Anglo-Catholicism, with their emphasis on community, provided him with a necessary complement. Contrasting Marx and an understanding of the church with literary humanism, he saw that the latter "did not, except in the schools, elicit participation in the processes by which a more just social order and even a humanistic education are to be achieved."[10]

Upon graduation from Harvard Divinity School in 1927, Adams spent the summer in Europe where he became familiar with the writings of Paul Tillich. He was in Nuremerg at the time of the Nazi festival. In the course of the festival, the interference of a young German prevented Adams from being physically beaten as the result of an argument over the merits of Nazism. Dinner at his rescuer's home gave him a first hand picture of the German situation.

---

feat and complexity for American Protestantism. "A single general fact lay behind this and provided the context for everything else: Protestantism could no longer easily, even to itself -- and this was the nub -- count upon its historic position as an accepted, senior partner in the national culture." Donald B. Meyer, <u>The Protestant Search for Political Realism 1919-1941</u>, (Berkeley: University of California Press, 1961), p. 10.

[8]"Taking Time Seriously," p. 13.

[9]<u>Ibid.</u>

[10]<u>Ibid.</u>, p. 14.

It was an experience which grew more significant in his
memory as the years went on.[11]

Returning from Europe in 1927, he married Margaret
Ann Young, was ordained a Unitarian Minister and became
pastor of the Second Church in Salem, Massachusetts.
During his pastorship, he taught English at Boston University while doing graduate work at Harvard in philosophy
and comparative literature. While a graduate student in
philosophy and comparative literature at the beginning of
the 1930's, he was a member of the Harvard Glee Club,
where a conversion experience deeply affected him -- sing-
ing Bach's St. Matthew's Passion. Through his involvement
with the music, he wondered if he had a right to enjoy
what Bach had given him. "I wondered if I was not a
spiritual parasite, one who was willing to trade on the
costly spiritual heritage of Christianity, but who was
perhaps doing very little to keep that heritage alive."[12]
This was an authenticating experience, forcing Adams from
a spectator position into an "existential" attitude.
In terms of his developing individual and social self-
understanding, the question became "what am I doing in
relation to my ideas and the role I play within
Christianity?"

Characteristically, Adams answered his own question.
One of the ways in which he did so was to act as mediator
in the Salem industrial strike, a situation which brought
home for him the existential meaning of ethics. His involvement at Salem confirmed his fear that churches find
it profitable to remain aloof from situations of social
conflict, "that those churches claiming to have eternal
foundations for their faith are also subject to the dangers
of culture-religion, justifying the ways of their con-
tributors."[13]

---

[11]"The experiences in Germany during that summer, I say,
became crucial for me, but they did not assume full sig-
nificance in my consciousness until, in the middle Thirties,
I spent some months in the so-called 'underground' movement
of the Confessing Church in Germany." "The Evolution of My
Social Concern." Address at the annual meeting of the
American Association for Teachers of Christian Social Ethics,
Louisville, Ky., 1961, p. 3. (Typewritten.)

[12]"Taking Time Seriously," p. 15.

[13]Stackhouse, "James Luther Adams: A Biographical and
Intellectual Sketch," p. 343.

Another of Adams' efforts to clarify his role within Christianity was his association with several other Unitarian clergymen in 1927, an association which persisted even beyond his call to become pastor of the Wellesley Hills First Unitarian Parish where he stayed until he was named Professor of Psychology and Philosophy of Religion at the Meadville Theological School in Chicago. The association, of which he was one of the original members, came to be known as the Greenfield Group.[14] They thought of themselves as "a study group for the purpose of working out together a critique of liberalism and also of searching for a remedy."[15] Daily personal and communal disciplines, the works of the church, communal readings -- all became an integral part of the members' lives.[16]

Adams describes his involvement in the group as a "vigorous year-round discipline of reading, discussion, and the writing of papers."[17] A key element was the nature of the reading -- theology, Scripture, liturgy, and prayer were combined with a study of secular disciplines such as philosophy and sociology.[18] The communal reading of Troeltsch, along with the writings of Reinhold Niebuhr and Karl Mannheim, were formative for Adams.

The developmental growth of the Greenfield Group, as described by Frank O. Holmes and Robert H. Schacht, Jr., has no small bearing on Adams' personal search.[19] In the beginning, each member presented a paper of his own choosing. This proved to be too individualistic; the discussants failed to appreciate the reader's point of view, and

---

[14]Even though Greenfield was not given to the group as a distinctive name until 1934, for clarity's sake the group will be called Greenfield at all times. See Frank O. Holmes and Robert H. Schacht, Jr., "The Greenfield Group--Its Beginnings and History," The Christian Register, CXXVII, No. 5 (1948), p. 45.

[15]"Taking Time Seriously," p. 16.

[16]It is interesting to note that among the communal readings was that of Ernest Troeltsch's Social Teachings of the Christian Churches, influential on Adams' thinking.

[17]"The Evolution of My Social Concern," p. 4.

[18]Ibid., p. 4.

[19]"The Greenfield Group," pp. 45-48, 63.

the result was intellectual anarchy. The solution was achieved by building up a background of commonly understood ideas and vocabulary developed through a basic bibliography which all read. This was a time-consuming and painstaking process, yet one that was crucial to Adams' self-development.

Holmes and Schacht regard the era during which the group met as a major factor in its success. Pre-Depression days were not a time of keen religious interest. The churches' appeals for high moral living received small response.

> The coming of the depression in 1929 with its attendant baffling social and economic problems of the early 1930's, brought an increasing conviction among people that neither the practical nor the intellectual problems of the time could be solved by individual effort alone. There was an increased sense of need for group experience and group thought.[20]

The times themselves play a decisive role in Adams' individual and social self-understanding. The Greenfield Group reinforced this development.

While Reinhold Niebuhr and the developing Neo-orthodox critique of religion were influential in the group's thinking, it must be remembered that the group was seeking to understand "the content and objective of liberal faith." However, such concern was directed toward the institutional aspects of Unitarianism. "The Group has always attempted to balance its interest in ideas and scholarship with a concern for the immediate problems of parochial leadership which every minister faces."[21]

A number of Unitarian ministers also formed groups aimed at developing certain disciplines for the devotional life. The local New England group to which Adams belonged was called the Brothers of the Way. He says that the group, being

> . . . suspicious of the sort of devotions which aim at a cloistered virtue, included within its

---

[20]"The Greenfield Group," p. 45.

[21]Ibid., p. 46.

disciplines weekly visits of mercy to the
needy, a "general" discipline of active
participation in some secular organization
of socially prophetic significance, and an
annual retreat where we participated in discussions of social issues and in the sacraments of silence and of the Lord's Supper.[22]

Adams' quest for identity became increasingly interrelated with his concern for group participation, responsibility, and discipline.[23] And yet he himself would say
he was not yet taking time seriously. "Still I only
vaguely apprehended the relation of all these things to
the history that was in the making."[24] Von Hugel, like
Babbitt, had given Adams a sense of the past in relation
to the present, but Von Hugel had no theology for social
salvation.[25] It would be his 1935-36 year abroad that
would bring a convergence of these multiple concerns.
That is jumping ahead, however.

During the period of Adams' participation in these
group experiences, he continued his graduate courses at
Harvard in the fields of comparative literature and
philosophy. Whitehead's concern for a metaphysic,
Babbitt's attack on the Romantic conception of man, Von
Hugel's search for theology, spirituality, history, and
institution in Christianity abetted Adams' questioning
of the basic tenets of liberal American Protestantism.[26]

Against the backdrop of the Depression, the early
years of the New Deal, and an un-ideological interest in
Marx, Adams came to know as pastor the economic problems
faced by the country: unemployment; strikes; the
growth of labor unions. These

. . . then conspired to develop a social concern, both theoretical and practical, which
had previously been only peripheral. At the
same time the awareness of the fissiparous

---

[22]"Taking Time Seriously," p. 17.

[23]"The Evolution of My Social Concern," p. 5.

[24]"Taking Time Seriously," p. 17.

[25]Ibid.

[26]"The Evolution of My Social Concern," p. 3.

individualism and the unprophetic character
of conventional middle class humanitarian
religious liberalism served to increase my
concern for the nature and mission of the
church and especially for the _ecclesiola in
ecclesia_ as indispensable for the achievement
of significant and costing consensus relevant
to the historical situation.[27]

Here, I contend, is the genesis of Adams' associationalism and the basis for his reconstruction of
liberalism.

When his call to Meadville, the Unitarian Seminary
in Chicago, came in 1935, Adams prepared for his future
teaching by spending the year 1935-36 in Europe. His
diversity of interest and his developing theology are
apparent in the several different activities in which
he became involved. Adams researched the sources of
Bishop Hurd's literary criticism. He studied at the
Seminary of St. Sulpice and consulted with a Roman
Catholic priest for spiritual direction. He also investigated the liturgical movement at the Benedictine monas-
tery of Maria Laach in Germany and pursued the further
study of liturgy at the University of Strasbourg. He
became acquainted with the French Protestant religious
socialist and member of the Chamber of Deputies, Andre
Philip.[28] While in Germany he studied the relation of
religion to fascism and democracy. He interviewed Nazi
and anti-Nazi leaders and observed the underground movements. During this German stay Adams was detained by
the Gestapo for some of his activities. He traveled to
Germany and France in 1938 and was again detained by
the Gestapo. Needless to say, the impact of these trips
was profound.

Adams' prewar German experiences led him to support
the Allied cause in the war, a war which he understood as
related to a wider issue: the linkage between the totalitarianism of the Axis and social inequalities in the

---

[27]"The Evolution of My Social Concern," p. 4.

[28]See "Taking Time Seriously," p. 18, as well as Stackhouse, "James Luther Adams: A Biographical and Intellectual Sketch," pp. 346-347.

United States. "The total war for democracy must in-[29] clude the struggle for democracy within democracies."[29] The strength and vitality of his religious liberalism (see Chapter Two) and the constant interplay between principles and events are evident in his critique of all parties in the war.

James Luther Adams:
The Career of the Teacher-Scholar

Adams' Interaction with Events
and Societal Problems

In a series of actions, Adams lived out what he felt should be the ministerial role vis-à-vis history on the move. Returning from the days in which he was able to observe the prewar situation in Europe at first hand, Adams began a teaching career at Meadville Seminary in Chicago. Teaching has provided a forty year framework for Adams' career and is the context for his scholarship and ethical concerns. Briefly stated, his calling as teacher led him from Meadville to the Federated Theological Faculty of the University of Chicago (1943-1956). While teaching at Chicago, Adams completed his graduate work in theology with a dissertation on Paul Tillich's Philosophy of Culture, Science and Religion (1945). He joined the Harvard Divinity School faculty in 1956 where he remained until 1968.[30] Since then Adams has held Professorships at Andover Newton Theological School (1968-1972) and at the University of Chicago, where he once more is teaching, lecturing, writing, serving on advisory boards, and completing translations of Ernst Troeltsch's works.

Adams came to grips with history in the university world of which he was so much a part. His academic career, however, has been and still is complemented by his membership in a vast array of associations, both

---

[29]"The Axis is Longer Than You Think--The Anti-Negro, Anti-Semitic, Anti-Labor, Anti-Progressive Axis," The Protestant, IV, No. 5 (1942), p. 28. See also "Emancipation Proclamation--1941," The Protestant, III, No. 12 (1941), 14-20.

[30]During this period of time he was an official observer at the Second Vatican Council. See "Report from the Vatican Council," The Unitarian Christian, XVIII, No. 2 (1962), pp. 13-14. His involvement updated his dialogue with Catholics which began in the 1930's.

religious and secular. Involvement with the International Association for Liberal Christianity and Religious Freedom and the Unitarian Universalist Fellowship is balanced by his membership in such secular groups as the American Civil Liberties Union. In speaking of his own life in the late 1930's and 1940's, he says: "I joined newly formed acquaintances in the founding of the Independent Voters of Illinois, and I began to learn at first hand about <u>Moral Man and Immoral Society</u>."[31]

Thus, one consistent way in which Adams interacted with events and societal problems, thereby fleshing out his teaching and writing, has been through associational activity.[32] Such activity has been for Adams the means whereby "the Christian can carry back to the church experience, significant fact, informed concern, insight demanding interpretation at the hands of the <u>koinonia</u>."[33]

No significant event or deeply experienced societal problems passed his notice. Nazism, the arms race, racial struggle, East-West dialogue, even the challenge of growing old -- each became a focus for his own ongoing dialogue with event.

His attacks on Nazism and positive support of many aspects of Marxism led to his being investigated by the Broyles Commission of the Illinois State Legislature (1947-1949). Nothing ever came of this investigation but a deepening desire on Adams' part to follow the heritage of the Left Wing of the Reformation.

Following World War II, Adams regarded with concern the dialogue with the Communist world and the arms race. While viewing the frustrations of the former, he felt that "only through some such discussions may we expect to achieve a self-critical attitude as well as mutual understanding."[34]

---

[31] "The Evolution of My Social Concern," pp. 16-17.

[32] See the Appendix, pp. 207-214.

[33] "The Evolution of My Social Concern," p. 22.

[34] Letter to the Editor, <u>Comprendre</u>, No. 12 (1954), p. 55.

In a letter dated August 27, 1945 addressed to President Truman[35] and circulated at the University of Chicago by Adams, Charles Hartshorne and others, he called for American penitence in the hour of victory and for immediate consideration of the future of atomic weapons within the United Nations.[36] Ten years later on August 3, 1955, Adams was among forty leaders in education and public life who signed a letter to The New York Times demanding an immediate end to the arms race and "repentance and confession" on the part of the United States. "Let us realize once and for all that no people has a moral right to drop H-bombs on another people at any time or for any reason and let this realization become the basis of national policy."[37]

In a letter to the editor of Comprendre on the feasibility of East-West dialogue, Adams recognizes the complexity introduced by secrecy. Yet, he adds,

At the same time one recognizes that in our kind of world situation, secrecy is indispensable as a means of policy. Our awareness of this fact only deepens and darkens the dilemma. . . .[38]

Racial dialogue comes under Adams' gaze in the context of his own church and of the Black Caucus within that church. He finds the Black Caucus making the white membership aware of its racism. The black is forming a new self-image, but the white must do the same thing. A critical and creative spirit should enliven both races.

---

[35]Letter, James Luther Adams, Charles Hartshorne, et al., to President Truman, August 27, 1945. Personal collection of James Luther Adams. (Typewritten.)

[36]Letter to the Editor, The New York Times, August 3, 1955, p. 22. On this question, see also "Changing Frontiers: Vanishing and Emerging," Address to the Unitarian Christian Fellowship, May 1957. Published in the Supplement of the Unitarian Christian, October, 1957. Also in The Unitarian Register, CXXXVI, No. 6 (1957), 10-12, 45.

[37]"Changing Frontiers: Vanishing and Emerging," p. 22.

[38]Letter to the Editor, Comprendre, No. 25 (1962), p. 226. See a similar theme in Adams' "Forward" to Ellis H. Dana, The Real Meaning of Communism (Madison, Wisconson: Brochure, 1962).

What we all seek is a new and common self-
identity that is inclusive and that can be
shared. . . .
. . . that unfinished business of American
democracy obviously calls for the recognition
of guilt, but more than that it calls for new
works that are meet for repentance, in short,
for new beginnings.[39]

As white people must reevaluate their stance toward blacks, so too must the aged in society find some
meaning. Adams points out in a recent article, "Aging:
A Theological Interpretation,"

In principle . . . every age-group possesses
its own unique quality and dignity. . . . A
theology of aging asserts, then, that each
age-group (and each person) has its own in-
imitable rendezvous with the coy mistress, the
meaning of life.[40]

He couples the uniqueness of the older person's place
in and contribution to society with the continued growth
and creativity related to faith in God and life's
possibilities.

Adams' interaction with events and societal problems fits into what he himself calls a prophetic understanding of faith which

. . . asserts that God through Jesus Christ
is the Lord of history and culture. . . .
In response to the Lord of history this community of faith takes time and culture seriously, so seriously as to hold that political
and social institutions, the arts and the
sciences, as well as the individual believer
have a vocation from on high.[41]

---

[39]"Our Unconquered Past," The Unitarian Christian, XXIII,
No. 3 (1967), p. 5. See also "The Shock of Recognition:
The Black Revolution and Greek Tragedy," The Unitarian
Christian, XXIV, No. 4 (1969), pp. 4-9.

[40]"Aging: A Theological Interpretation." The Unitarian
Universalist Christian, XXVIII, No. 2-3 (1973), p. 11.

[41]"Forward." Dimensions of Faith, ed. Walter Kimmel and
Geoffrey Clive (New York: Twayne, 1960), p. 11.

Philosophical-Theological Basis for
Adams' Interaction with Events

Diversity of interest and concentration on problem
areas characterize Adams' work throughout his career.
As I shall demonstrate, it is this consistent focusing
on the social context of these interests and problems
that contributes to Adams' uniqueness in the field of
ethics. We must consider what intellectual influences
Adams felt in his development as Christian ethicist.
His early sensitivity to the movements of history and
his adherence to a redefined liberalism prepare him for
dialogue with others. However, Adams' student days at
Harvard, his experience in Europe, his Unitarian Fellowship, important though they be, were only the beginning.

Adams studied process thought under Whitehead and,
as a result, developed a concern for ontology and comprehensive thinking.[42] This orientation was reinforced
by Adams' contact with Paul Tillich's theology.[43]
Whitehead and Tillich were at odds over the basic issue
of the nature of God from an ontological perspective,
but as Max Stackhouse observes: "Both Tillich and the
'process philosophers' had a sense of the ontological
roots of man in the nature of being and the pertinence
of that problem to the human situation in history."[44]
Such an approach utilized by the process philosophers
and Tillich, likewise has its impact on Adams.[45]

As we have seen, Adams' interest in Tillich even-
tually took the shape of a doctoral dissertation.[46]
Their mutual interaction had yet another dimension, that
of Adams' impact on Tillich. The latter himself remarked

-----

[42]Adams also encountered process thought among colleagues
in Chicago: Charles Hartshorne; Henry Nelson Wieman;
and Daniel Day Williams.

[43]Adams came in contact with Tillich's writings on his
first European trip in 1927.

[44]Stackhouse, "James Luther Adams: A Biographical and
Intellectual Sketch," p. 351.

[45]For instance, see below, Adams' "Ontological Foundation
of Mutuality," pp. 46-48.

[46]James Luther Adams, Paul Tillich's Philosophy of Culture,
Science and Religion (New York: Harper & Row, 1965). This
dissertation constitutes Adams' only full-length published work.

that "he [Adams] has studied my thought so thoroughly
that I have sent to him all those who wanted to know
about it, because he knows more about my writings than
I do myself."[47] And he observes that "I have learned
from him [Adams] . . . the emphasis on the practical,
social as well as political, application of the principle of agape to the situation of the society in which
we live."[48]

Both Tillich's and Whitehead's emphases can be
traced in Adams' approach to theology and, in particular,
to religious ethics. In his affirmation that mutuality
in community is rooted in an ontological understanding
of reality,[49] we hear echoes of the two thinkers cited.
And while Adams denies any ontological theory of pre-
established harmony, he is careful to delineate the
parameters of progress within human history.[50] History
is, in fact, a key and operative category in Adams; it
is no accident that he edited Henry Nelson Wieman's The
Directive in History (1949) as well as translated Paul
Tillich's The Protestant Era (1948). In his own life,
he developed in dialectical interaction with thinkers
and events, constantly shaping and reshaping his thought.[51]
Stackhouse observes:

> He thinks vis-à-vis other minds, external
> evidence, or objective events. . . . The
> variety of approaches, the conflicting ways
> of looking at a problem, the historical set-
> tings of various alternatives, . . . these
> are the issues that are crucial to him.[52]

---

[47]Tillich, "Foreword," in Voluntary Associations, p. 5.

[48]Ibid.

[49]See below, pp. 46-48.

[50]Ibid.

[51]Adams describes this process: "I suppose you would say
that it's almost second nature and a habit in lectures when
I encounter a new figure to deal with in the course of the
lectures, then I'll make a digression and lay out half a
dozen different points of view that have to be taken into
account. . . ." Taped interview, XII, with James D.
Hunt, August 14, 1964. Transcript, pp. 16-17.

[52]Stackhouse, "James Luther Adams: A Biographical and
Intellectual Sketch," p. 334.

Adams' earlier allusion to Reinhold Niebuhr's seminal work, Moral Man and Immoral Society,[53] highlights the influence of American Neo-orthodoxy, especially in the form of realist theology, on him. There is no doubt that the rise of Neo-orthodoxy helped stimulate Adams' reformulation of liberalism, thus making it much more dialectical and sensitive to the Christian understanding of sin and evil. Max Stackhouse speaks of the influence of such thinkers as Niebuhr, Walter Marshall Horton, and John Coleman Bennett on Adams,[54] but we have evidence especially of Adams' dialogue with Niebuhr. He defended Niebuhr against Unitarian and liberal attack, especially in the 1930's and early 1940's.[55] Moreover, his impressive review of The Nature and Destiny of Man (Volume I) indicates appreciation of Niebuhr's prophetic voice as well as criticism of Niebuhr's emphasis upon man's sinfulness.[56]

Adams' constant involvement with the events of history is and has been a product of his rootedness within history seen as "a struggle in dead earnest between justice and injustice looking toward the victory of the good in the promise and fulfillment of grace."[57] Sensitive to an understanding of history within the prophetic tradition, his view is deeply Christian yet open to secular historical understandings and eschatologies.

Sensitivity to history and eschatology can be traced to the impact of Rudolf Otto's influence on Adams through personal contact between the two during Adams' European stay of 1935-36. Otto's Kingdom of God and Son of Man also played a role in sharpening Adams' eschatological sensitivity.[58]

---

[53]See above, p. 12.

[54]Stackhouse, "James Luther Adams: A Biographical and Intellectual Sketch," p. 344.

[55]James D. Hunt, "James Luther Adams and His Demand for an Effective Religious Liberalism." Unpublished Ph.D. Dissertation, University of Syracuse, 1965, pp. 289 ff., 391 ff.

[56]Review of The Nature and Destiny of Man, Vol. I, Christendom, VI, No. 4 (1941), pp. 576-80.

[57]"Unitarian Philosophies of History," Journal of Liberal Religion, VII, No. 2 (1945), p. 106.

[58]See Adams' review of this book in Alumni Review (Presbyterian Theological Seminary of Chicago), XIII, No. 4 (1938), pp. 236-37.

The Christian roots of his historical sense strike
me as biblical in origin, for the revelation of God
through event is Judaeo-Christian if it is anything at
all.[59] However, the peculiarly Adamsean character of
this Christian view of history cannot be ignored.
Adams underscores the incipient danger of seeing God at
work in history, for such a revelation may be misinter-
preted. God may become equated with the status quo.
Faith, in Adams' view, "struggles against the idolizing
of any creature, whether the creature be 'religion,' the
words of Scripture, tradition, doctrinal formulations,
the church, the social system, race, or nation."[60] A
creative and critical capacity is essential.

Adams' concern for man's historicity interpreted
within a theological context leads him to emphasize the
work of the Spirit in history. In this he differs from
Niebuhr who chose to center his approach on the place of
Christ in history. Adams' sense of the Spirit flows
from his fascination with the eschatologists of the
Christian tradition from Joachim of Fiore through the
Radical or Left Wing of the Protestant Reformation and
to its high point with the English Puritans.[61] His appreciation of religious eschatology is complemented by
Adams' affirmation of secular eschatologies. He regards
Augustine, Paul, Joachim, Karl Marx, William Channing
and Emily Dickinson as proclaiming their faith from

---

[59]Adams points this out himself in a talk given in Tokyo
in 1960. "Contributions of Occidental Religions to Cultural Understanding," Proceedings of the IXth International
Congress for the History of Religions (Tokyo: Maruzen, 1960),
p. 730. See also, minutes of meeting of study group on The
Biblical Doctrine of Man in Society, at Seabury Western
Seminary, May 26-28, 1954. Adams made a significant contribution to the discussion of man's historical nature as found
in Scripture especially through his use of sociological categori

[60]Ibid., p. 732. See also "The Uses of Diversity," Harvard
Divinity School Bulletin, XXIII (1958), pp. 47-64. Pagination
used here follows brochure edition of article, p. 9.

[61]See especially "Our Responsibility in Society" in Taking
Time Seriously, pp. 59 ff., for an indication of the in-
fluence of Radical Reformation scholarship on Adams' thought.
On this see also "The Prophethood of All Believers," in
Taking Time Seriously, pp. 21 ff.

different perspectives but speaking a common "optative mood."[62] Such an approach, moreover, recognizes the validity of art, sculpture, dance, and music as revelatory in their own right.[63]

It is the role of the minister, operating within the diversity of the church,[64] to bring culture under judgment in the name of that which stands over and beyond culture.[65]

> But the ultimate ground and goal of diversity are not necessarily evident in the institutional arrangements required by the concepts of checks and balances or by the ideal of equality. . . . From the Judaeo-Christian point of view, the ground and goal of diversity are not in our control. They belong to the divinely given creative and redemptive forces to which the Old and New Testament bear decisive, if not exhaustive, witness, forces that grow not old and that elicit a living faith that is not attached to temporal "securities."[66]

---

[62]"Unitarian Philosophies of History," p. 106.

[63]Adams takes pains to emphasize this point in "The Arts and Society," paper prepared for The Theological Discussion Group, Washington, D.C., November 4-6, 1955 and "Music as a Means of Grace," Crane Review, X, No. 1 (Fall 1967), pp. 42-45. See also "From Psyche to Society," Perkins Journal, XXVI, No. 1 (1972), pp. 17-24 in which Adams discusses the relation of sculpture, particularly the work of Alberto Giacometti to ethical issues. This lecture is also published in On Being Human Religiously, ed. Max L. Stackhouse (Boston: Beacon, 1976), 139 ff.

[64]"The Uses of Diversity," pp. 13-15.

[65]The Social Import of the Professions, Address at the 21st Biennial Meeting of the American Association of Theological Schools, June 17-20, 1958. Printed as brochure, p. 12.

[66]"The Uses of Diversity," pp. 4 and 5.

The influence of metaphysicians such as Tillich and Whitehead on Adams is counterbalanced by the strong historical sense evident in his biblical prophetic awareness and his analysis of the Left Wing of the Protestant Reformation. Concern for man in society and history consistently leads him to the field of sociology. While that influence will be discussed in Chapter Four, it must be noted that Ernst Troeltsch, Max Weber, Karl Marx, Karl Mannheim, and Ferdinand Toennies have profoundly affected Adams' interpretation of social ethics and the historicity of man. Parallel with the concern for sociology is the fact that "much of what JLA has presented in the history of Protestant social ethics he has viewed in connection with the work of jurists from Althusius through Frederick Julius Stahl and Otto von Gierke to Rudolf Sohm."[67]

Man's associational propensity, another aspect of his historical nature, is an important concern of Adams. Theorists and critics of associationalism, particularly of voluntary associations, have had their impact on Adams.[68] Max Weber, Thomas Hobbes, F. W. Maitland, William Ellery Channing, Ernest Barker, A. D. Lindsay, J. N. Figgis have all had a strong influence on his thought.

---

[67]Stackhouse, "James Luther Adams: A Biographical and Intellectual Sketch," p. 336.

[68]See "The Geography and Organization of Social Responsibility," Union Seminary Quarterly Review, XXIX, Nos. 3 and 4 (1974), pp. 245 ff., wherein Adams develops his understanding of the value of voluntary associations and the theorists he considers most important. See as well "'The Protestant Ethics,' with Fewer Tears," in In the Name of Life: Essays in Honor of Erich Fromm, ed. Bernard Landis and Edward S. Tauber. (New York: Holt, Rinehart and Winston, 1971), esp. pp. 185 ff. Also "Voluntary Associations in Search of Identity," in Journal of Current Social Issues, IX, No. 6 (1971), pp. 15-22 and "The Voluntary Principle in the Forming of American Religion," in The Religion of the Republic, ed. Elwyn Smith (Philadelphia: Fortress, 1971), pp. 217 ff.

20

The Relevance of Adams' Biography
for the Christian Ethicist

The following points must be made:

1. Christian faith and spirituality, as well as church participation, are clearly evident in Adams' biography. This aspect of his life has implications for anyone doing Christian ethics. The affirmation of a transcendent, personal God creates a frame of reference for Adams which differentiates him from the atheist or agnostic. He thus reminds us that Christian ethics is not an academic issue but involves a life decision. In his ethical stance, Adams couples church involvement with faith.

2. The theory and practice of Christianity go hand in hand in Adams' ethics. This interactional motif appears, likewise, in his approach to learning and scholarship. Adams reads not only Augustine but also Marx, and he applies sociological categories to the religious practice of Christians. The daily newspaper is a key ingredient in his religious ethics. Thus, his ethical theory can be called dialectical in that it incorporates religious and secular thought. It is dialectical in another sense, in that theory must be informed by constant attention to what is going on in the world. The Christian ethicist can learn much from such an approach. Adams affirms that the validity and vitality of Christian ethics depends not only upon the religious tradition but also upon nonreligious thought, social scientific investigation, and the events of daily life.

3. Adams' involvement in the Brothers of the Way and the Greenfield Group points to the need for the contemporary Christian ethicist to perform his task with a sense of community. Not only is Adams' demand for community lived out in church involvement, but his ethical thought is also worked out within a communal context. This context is also a religious one, and both the intellectual and religious nature of this community context are elements the contemporary ethicist needs to incorporate into his own approach to Christian ethics. Ethics deals with action arising from diverse individual insight and motive in combination with social forces. Since viewpoint and social analysis are difficult to understand and perceive alone, a communal setting for ethical thought is most appropriate. Moreover, the very nature of Christianity calls for a communal interpretation of God acting in history.

21

4. Adams as teacher-minister was given new direction and self-understanding by his involvement in the Salem mill strike, his several confrontations with the Nazis, and his relations with the underground churches in Germany. These experiences gave a realism and relevancy to Adams' ethics which anyone seeking a role as ethicist should evaluate carefully. Can the contemporary ethicist really do ethics without first-hand involvement in contemporary crises, whether this be on the international or domestic scene or in dealing with individual ethical problems? A resounding no comes from Adams.

5. The voluntary activity of Adams, seen in his biography, likewise points to an activist posture for the present-day ethicist and also offers a concrete modality for the fourth point above. The scholarly context of his ethics must be informed by a vitality flowing from the voluntary association, secular or re-ligious, as the means of effecting ethical change on various levels of human life. This is not to deny the validity of political involvement, an involvement some-what evident in Adams and absolutely consonant with his understanding of politics as integral to man in community.

6. Finally, we see Adams as a man of his times. Sensitivity to the historical situation does not mean unthinking or mute acceptance of fate. It means, ra-ther, a painstaking effort to understand the personal and social forces in human existence, seeking to avoid the ever-present pitfalls of ideology through a con-sistent concern for principles of love and justice. Adams calls the Christian ethicist to be a man or woman of his or her times, seeking to react to and be respon-sible in history, by using a dialectical approach and a continual sense of revision within the Christian tra-dition. The response to and responsibility for the times does not mean co-optation. Rather, it is the overcoming of ideology through an activist search for God's continuing revelation in history.

CHAPTER II

JAMES LUTHER ADAMS:

REFORMULATOR OF RELIGIOUS LIBERALISM

Historical Background

James Luther Adams is clearly identified with the tradition of religious liberalism not simply because he fits into the mainstream of that movement but because he redefined it. At the basis of this redefinition is his understanding of the dialectic between the individual and the group. The sociality of individual identity is, therefore, a prime ingredient of his reformulation. Obviously, for a movement such as religious liberalism which was characterized by a strong individual bias, such a reinterpretation was indeed a radical one.

The reinterpretation of liberalism developed by Adams in terms of the social grounding of identity highlights another important theme which I see in Adams, that of theory and practice.[1] The incompleteness of man and the centrality of community or mutuality demand a continual review of theory and its impact upon social structures. Adams' demand for an awareness of (1) the relative nature of human answers and (2) the centrality of man in community, focuses the problem of theory and practice even more sharply. No theory can be accepted as final. The search for new theories is grounded in the consequences of theory, consequences which are most clearly manifested in the social realm. Adams believes that the actions of the individual or church tell you what they really believe. Theory always has pragmatic consequences which reveal much about the theory. It is, therefore, easy for me to see why Adams finds sociology with its social emphasis more congenial than psychology with its stress on the individual.[2]

---

[1]Adams himself does not use the expression "theory and practice" to any extent. However, the import of this category is evident in his doing of ethics.

[2]I am sure Adams would agree with Peter Berger when the latter affirms that "the notion of projection becomes

23

As a dominant motif in Adams' theology, religious liberalism must be seen in terms both of the age from which it emerged and the age in which it developed. The liberalism which James Luther Adams came to know as part of the Unitarian tradition had its roots in the nineteenth century, the "Golden Age of Liberal Theology" as Ahlstrom calls it. Based on a profound openness to the secular sciences, it was greatly influenced by Darwinism: stability and the static yielded to flux and the dynamic. "History and Becoming emerged as dominant categories of thought."[3] Nineteenth century liberalism emphasized pluralism, rationalism, liberation from dogma and the concept of sin, the triumph of the human will, and man's natural goodness. An optimism based on a particular reading of evolutionary literature saw the Kingdom of God in this world as the result of a natural historical process. "As Bushnell had argued, the natural and the supernatural were consubstantial, observable in almost all forms of being."[4] As if by coincidence, America was entering a period of burgeoning industrialism, accelerated immigration and a limitless frontier expansion. Such activity reached a frenetic level after the Civil War, as if it were the way to forget. It seems, however, more than coincidence that theological optimism and national expansion flourished contemporaneously. Do we not see here the tandem development of liberal theology in a dynamic society?

As the country widened its horizons, so too did the theologians of liberalism. Intense optimism and visionary idealism were embodied in a theology which became increasingly secular and practical. Liberal thinkers, among them Walter Rauschenbusch, William James, Josiah Royce, and Borden Bowne introduced into American Protestantism elements of modern science, scholarship, and philosophy.[5]

---

much more plausible in its sociological rather than its psychological form, because the former is simpler and more readily verifiable in ordinary 'conscious' experience." A Rumor of Angels (Garden City: Doubleday Anchor, 1970), p. 32.

[3]Ahlstrom, A Religious History of the American People, p. 771.

[4]Ibid., p. 781.

[5]Langdon Gilkey points out, in speaking of twentieth century developments, that "in American theological writing, the influence of 'secular' categories has been direct, almost

In a sense, the naive optimism of the earlier liberals was corrected by the twentieth century liberals' continued seriousness with regard to the secular realm and acceptance of a more scientific and empirical way of thinking. But historical event and intellectual erosion were to have their effects on this liberalism as well. During World War I, the idealism nurtured in the relative peace reigning in Europe since the Congress of Vienna was destroyed by the total disillusionment that came with tanks, trenches, and overturned lives. This European disillusionment impacted as well on the American theological scene.

An orientation in Christian ethics toward practical problems has been a recurring note in American church history and thought. This intellectual foundation had its roots in German theological and English philosophical idealism. Newman Smyth's Christian Ethics (1892) and Walter Rauschenbusch's A Theology for the Social Gospel (1917) are examples of such influence.[6] The dissolution of this intellectual foundation took place in the 1920's and 1930's because the complexities of a developing technological society produced problems that could not be dealt with by the above-described idealism. Such optimistic idealism could not grapple with either the Depression or the rise of European totalitarianism, both of which were economic and political realities to which Adams was heir.

Adams' Dialectical Approach to Liberalism

The social activism of Adams' liberalism must be viewed by us, as it has been continually by him, against and in constant interplay with, a deepening spirituality and a growing self-understanding. Sperry, Dean of Harvard Divinity School and a mentor of Adams, introduced him to

---

blatant. Marxist concepts, Freudian images, and sociological structures appear on the surface, lying on the page next to Biblical and traditional notions, or replacing them by some mode of translation." "Social and Intellectual Sources of Contemporary Protestant Theology," p. 162.

[6]The thesis behind such intellectually based ethics is that "Ethics had to do with ideals and their actualizations. . . . The task of the Christian community, then, is progressively to realize the Christian ideals in the actual conduct and affairs of the human community." Gustafson, "Christian Ethics," pp. 288-89.

devotional literature through which he enriched his
own prayer life and studied the great spiritual directors,
especially St. Francis de Sales. Adams' concern for the
spiritual life received institutional expression in the
Greenfield Group and the Brothers of the Way, groups of
Unitarian ministers who had similar interests.

An individual and social self-understanding, placed
in tension, are seen as equally vital to Adams' form of
religious liberalism. Where did Adams root individual
and social self-understanding? Adams found this rootedness in an understanding of religion, but a religion
which "requires the declarative as well as the imperative
mood."[7] The imperative quality of religion -- its hopes
and demands -- cannot be divorced from "facts about man
and especially about the resources upon which he is dependent for growth and re-creation."[8] These metaphysical concerns are essential to his "declarative" description of religion. "Humanism," Adams declares,
"in eschewing metaphysics, presupposed an unexamined
metaphysics, and I decided that an unexamined metaphysics was not worth having."[9] Moreover, religion for
Adams combines a living community possessing concrete
historical tradition with individual self-understanding.[10]
Thus, the tradition of Christian spirituality is as essential to his dialectic as is Marx's social theory.

Adams' religious liberalism endures largely because
of the vitality he has injected into it by his dialectical
process. Far from an artificial juxtaposition, this process developed from his personal disenchantment with the
liberalism which he inherited. The competitiveness and
atomistic individualism which characterized early liberalism, its doctrine of pre-established harmony and laissez-
faire philosophy, were alien to Adams' way of understanding
himself. To correct what he saw as an erring doctrine,
he inserted a dialectical approach into the liberalism he
espoused -- an approach which encouraged openness to experience and to the social sciences.[11]

---

[7]"Taking Time Seriously," p. 14.

[8]Ibid.

[9]Ibid.

[10]Ibid.

[11]See "The Evolution of My Social Concern," pp. 3-4. See

The writings of Ernst Troeltsch, Reinhold Niebuhr, Walter Marshall Horton, John Bennett, T. S. Eliot and Rudolph Otto aided him in his reconstruction of liberalism. However, it was Paul Tillich, above all, who clarified Adams' dialectical understanding of religious liberalism. Interpretations of categories such as the Kingdom, the divine and demonic, sin and grace were related by Tillich to historical realities such as nationalism, the economic order and the churches. In describing Tillich's influence on him, Adams had this to say:

> In Tillich's view of the dialectical nature of reality, of revelation, of God, of the Kingdom, of man, and of history, I find an interpretation and an application of Christian doctrine which are far more relevant to the social and divine forces which determine the destiny of man than in any other theologian I happen to know about.[12]

An Overview of Adams' Religious Liberalism

Reviewing Adams' writings on liberalism in the light of World War II and of the vacillating Protestant stand relative to events in Europe, I am struck by the consistency of Adams' prewar thinking. He is sensitive to the perversity of human nature as experienced in the war, balancing it with a deeply-rooted metaphysical hope in man. Both perspectives on man seem necessary to me for an adequately defined religious liberalism.

---

also "The Changing Reputation of Human Nature," Journal of Liberal Religion, IV, No. 2 (1942), pp. 59-79; No. 3 (1943), pp. 137-60. Pagination is from the article reprinted as brochure.

[12]"Taking Time Seriously," p. 20. Tillich describes the dialectic as entering into the realities with which it deals. It participates in their inner tensions. "The tensions may appear first in contrasting concepts, but they must be followed down to their roots in the deeper levels of reality. In a dialectical description one element of a concept drives to another. Taken in this sense, dialectics determine all life-processes. . . . The description of tensions in living organisms, neurotic conflicts, and class struggles is dialectical." Paul Tillich, Systematic Theology, Vol. I (New York: Harper & Row, 1967), p. 90. Tillich identifies life

Given the political climate of the late 1930's, during which Adams wrote a great deal on liberalism, I consider him quite courageous in his defense of a liberalism which seemed irrelevant to many people. Adams, however, was not the only one coming to grips with religious liberalism. In fact, it is necessary to examine the relationship between James Luther Adams, reformulator of religious liberalism and Neo-orthodoxy, the predominant theological mind set of the late 1930's and 1940's. Neo-orthodoxy was a movement inclusive of many disciples, not all of whom were in agreement with each other. Few, if any, ever used the term of themselves. This was true in Europe and likewise in America, where, Ahlstrom says, Neo-orthodoxy came together "piece-meal."[13] On neither continent was Neo-orthodoxy a movement easily defined.[14] Rather, it is characterized by an urgency in terms of religious commitment and a critical viewpoint on the world situation, both filtered through many denominational perspectives.

In America, diversity of origin went hand in hand with the pluralistic intellectual foundations of Neo-orthodoxy: Christian and Jewish thought, Greek tragedy and modern atheism. Doctrinal diversity was also evident, but varied confessions never surrender to a common creed. Neo-orthodoxy was not a simplistic ecumenism. Because of this diversity, Ahlstrom can include Tillich, the Niebuhrs, Walter Marshall Horton, Edward Lewis, and George W. Richards, in this country. In Europe, where similar diversity prevailed, he groups as members of the Neo-orthodox movement the following: Karl Barth; Emil Brunner; Friedrich Gogarten; Albert Schweitzer; Rudolf Bultmann; Karl Holl; Werner Elert; Anders Nygren; and William Temple.[15]

---

in conflict with itself and driving to a post-conflict stage as the arena of "objective or real dialectics." Ibid., Vol. III, p. 329. As we shall see, this understanding of the dialectic is related to Adams' conceptualization of reality as dipolar. See below, pp. 37-39.

[13]Ahlstrom, A Religious History of the American People, p. 938.

[14]Ahlstrom sees four separate European dimensions: crisis or dialectical theology, renewal of biblical exegesis, the Luther, Calvin Renaissance, and a new urgency in "social Christianity." Ibid., pp. 933-37.

[15]Ahlstrom, A Religious History of the American People, p. 943, 934-37.

What bound such diverse thinkers together was their critical sense of the world situation and the inadequacy of liberalism in face of contemporary problems. The heralds, doubters, political analysts, philosophers, theologians, and biblical scholars identified under the umbrella of Neo-orthodoxy rejected the naive optimism and doctrine of progress that characterized liberalism. While liberalism provided a focus for their reevaluation of religious thinking, one must remember that not all liberals were equally subject to their criticism. Adams was most sympathetic to their concern for the centrality of God in the evaluation of human destiny. The Neo-orthodox "sense of urgency and demand for moral and intellectual humility"[16] characterized Adams as well. The problems that troubled them troubled him: "social injustice, political and churchly utopianism, routine complacency, and ecclesiastical passivity."[17]

Adams gives evidence of the same dialectical mood that prevailed among the diverse strains of Neo-orthodoxy. In concern with Neo-orthodox thinkers, Adams regards familiarity with and participation in secular developments as an important element in the religious enterprise. The integrity of knowledge includes the methods and findings of the natural and social sciences. Many Neo-orthodox thinkers could agree with Adams when he says:

> Literature, the fine arts, and philosophy offer him [the liberal Christian] interpretations and criticisms of life which contribute to self-understanding and must be evaluated. They are media through which the meaning of existence and the frustration of this meaning are clarified and interpreted in their interrelatedness. The liberal Christian holds that he can better gain a sense of the full import of his faith by confronting the insights and questionings that are provided by all of these disciplines.[18]

---

[16]Ahlstrom, _A Religious History of the American People_, p. 951.

[17]Ibid., p. 938.

[18]"The Liberal Christian Looks at Himself," Foundations of Liberal Christianity Lectures. All Souls' Unitarian Church, Washington, D. C., 1955, p. 10 (mimeographed).

Adams could not be classified with those liberals attacked by Neo-orthodoxy because they left men spiritually naked. Adams demanded the existential commitment the Neo-orthodox sought, but he was never as suspicious of metaphysics as some, although not all, Neo-orthodox were.[19] Adams is comfortable with the autonomy that is man's when created goodness is manifested in rational thought and criticism. He expresses this, for instance, in an openness to natural law theory.[20] In this sense Adams might well be characterized as a Pneumatological thinker.[21] Max Stackhouse makes this point very clearly in his evaluation of Adams:

> Adams, in the final analysis, is not a Christological thinker. He is what Christian theologians sometimes call a Pneumatological theorist; that is, his emphasis is on the Holy Spirit . . . . The dynamic, Holy Spirit, understood as the power of life that moves where it will in human experience -- bringing new meaning and wholeness -- is the theological core and decisive critical principle of Adams' thought. It appears among peoples and in groups not consciously Christian.[22]

The central task of theological liberalism, beginning in the nineteenth century, has been the establishment of a meaningful dialogue between the Christian tradition and modern thought. Neo-orthodoxy continued this tradition and served notice to liberalism to put its house in order and Adams is an example of one liberal who took the imperative seriously.

The late 1930's saw pacifism and hopes for world democracy grow dim and, as Ahlstrom says, "the American dream was increasingly interrupted by nightmares."[23]

---

[19]H. Richard Niebuhr was not, yet Karl Barth and Emil Brunner were.

[20]See below, Adams' second liberal principle, pp. 37-39. This is not to say that Adams endorsed all natural law theories as we shall see in Chapter Four.

[21]At the same time his Christological sensitivity is clear. (See below, pp. 81-86.) But he is not a Christomonist or a "Unitarian of the Second Person," a position H. Richard Niebuhr criticized.

[22]Max Stackhouse, "Editor's Introduction," On Being Human Religiously, by James Luther Adams (Boston: Beacon Press, 1976), p. xxiii.

[23]Ahlstrom, A Religious History of the American People, p. 937.

Neo-orthodoxy with its central elements of humility, urgency, a dialectical mood and a sense of historical relativism, sought to aid man in this situation. Liberalism, it appeared, left man confused, while Neo-orthodoxy absorbed the positive spirit of the New Deal and never counseled passivity and resignation.[24]

Ahlstrom points out, however, that "Neo-orthodox theologians have been justifiably accused of putting down only a very thin sheet of dogmatic asphalt over the problems created by modern critical thought."[25] Adams alerts others to this problem in those young Barthians whose violently-assertive position "bespeaks an inner uncertainty and a compensation in the form of pseudocertitude."[26] They are, in reality, skeptics with regard to man's ability to know the truth and act on it. Gordon Kaufman sees the aftermath of World War I and the other crises of the twentieth century as creating an atmosphere which viewed salvation by the God and Father of Jesus as the solution.[27]

In face of this appeal to a leap of faith, Adams sees liberalism as "the only effective resistant to ultimate skepticism and despair on the one side and to blasphemous claims to authority and suppressions of criticism on the other."[28] Adams calls for decision, conversion, commitment, faith in God, as did the Neo-orthodox, but he maintains a basic faith in man which a "leap of faith" could well diminish.

Faith in man, for Adams, is a belief in his ability to deal with religious questions by means of research and investigation. This approach is not a reduction of

---

[24]Ahlstrom, A Religious History of the American People, p. 946.

[25]Ibid., p. 947.

[26]"Why Liberal?", Journal of Liberal Religion, I, No. 2 (1939), p. 7.

[27]Gordon Kaufman, "Theological Historicism as an Experiment in Thought," The Christian Century, LXXXIII (March 2, 1966), p. 268.

[28]"Why Liberal?", p. 6.

religion to rationalism since faith in man is united
to a faith in God in Adams' view. While open to the
findings of the social sciences, he does not reduce
religion to a purely functional level. Function (i.e.,
the role of religion in maintaining social stability)
and substance (i.e., the God question) cannot be separated in Adams' thinking. Furthermore, his characteristic trust in human understanding gives him a decided
advantage today because of the religious questions that
have arisen recently. Issues such as cultural relativity
or Christianity's relation to other religions, in a word,
hermeneutical problems surrounding contemporary interpretations of the religious symbol system, presently
have priority among theologians. These issues, as Gordon
Kaufman notes,[29] could be ignored during the crises of
the recent past when Neo-orthodoxy was in vogue, but
they have surfaced once more in the present age. The
liberalism Adams espouses is congenial with the present
situation, since it possesses a basic openness to areas
of learning such as the social sciences. The latter
provide much enlightenment for understanding these religious questions.

Robert Miller echoes many of the sentiments expressed
by Adams in his continual redefining of religious liberalism. The reaction of the Protestant churches to the
events of the 1930's was, according to Miller, "pathet-
ically confused, halting, divided, and uncertain. It is
a heartbreaking record of alternating deep despair and
naive optimism, of timid vacillation and blind dogmatism."[30]
A dogmatic Christian pacifism on the part of the churches
provided an atmosphere for the Fellowship of Reconciliation.
And Ahlstrom holds that beneath this dogmatism were contradictory assumptions: "that civilized nations would not
again resort to war, and that the United States could with
a clear conscience ignore the aggressions of the dictators."[31]

---

[29]Gordon Kaufman, "Theological Historicism as an Experiment
in Thought," p. 268. In this article Kaufman calls for
attitudes of openness, respect for pluralism, tentativity.
Ibid., pp. 269-70. These are attitudes that Adams sees
as part of his liberalism.

[30]Robert Miller, American Protestantism and Social Issues
(Chapel Hill: University of North Carolina Press, 1960), p. 334

[31]Ahlstrom, A Religious History of the American People, p. 930.

For Adams, American liberalism faces a subtle enemy in the form of indifference to moral values and a "cynical anti-intellectualism." Whether it be municipal corruption, indifference toward the Japanese treatment of the Chinese, or our neutralist policy which makes this treatment possible, the American people read about it all with "well-fed equanimity."[32]

Beyond this weakening of moral fibre, Adams sees a developing irrationalism, a relativism derived from a theory that says "thinking is a laryngeal itch twitching up from the unconscious and providing only an index of one's class and vested interests."[33] This relativism is the real source of the skepticism he finds in this decade. Adams sees liberalism as the middle ground between "unconditioned heteronomous authority" and the skepticism of the sophisticated relativist. The sources of insight in the liberalism Adams reformulates are to be found in commitment to diversity, self-criticism and openness.[34] Revelation is never sealed for the liberal whose mission stands in contrast to the pseudo-orthodox. It is "the task of achieving relevance in a new situation -- a mass society that corrupts the church. Translation, like reformation, must continue."[35]

In the liberal Christianity Adams describes, there is always "a tension and even a disparity between its local articulations and its enduring genius."[36] However, the excesses of diversity and secularization in terms of providential harmony and rationalized autonomy are counteracted by Adams with an understanding of sin and redemption. The task of the liberal is to integrate diversity, secularity, and sin with creation, redemption, and sanctification in the light of the secular needs of his day, as Adams did, for example, in face of the events and movements of the 1930's and 1940's.

---

[32]"Why Liberal?", p. 7. See also on this Adams' review of J.S. Bixler, Religion for Free Minds, The Christian Century, LVII, No. 18 (1940), p. 578.

[33]"Why Liberal?", p. 8.

[34]Adams believes "the coming to terms with the scientific outlook is a permanent contribution of the liberal in religion." "After Liberalism," unpublished notes, c. 1940, p. 2.

[35]"The Ages of Liberalism," The Journal of Religious Thought, XIV, 2 (1957), p. 117.

[36]Ibid.

Does Adams' redefined religious liberalism respond more adequately to the problems created by modern critical thought? This question must be answered later in this book. For Adams, however, these problems can never be divorced from the problem created by individuals and groups interacting within the human community. For, after all, is it not this skill which will give Adams relevance for the modern ethicist, his ability to solve problems created both by modern critical thought and by society?

Religious Liberalism:
Criticism and Reformulation

Adams' brand of liberalism is clearly delineated in his work, On Being Human - The Liberal Way,[37] in which he outlines four principles of liberalism: humankind's incompleteness; the dignity of human nature and the primacy of mutual consent; community; and the ontological foundation of mutuality.

In Adams' thought, each one of these principles presumes the underlying presupposition that man is socially grounded. "I" consciousness and "we" consciousness are not terms which exclude each other. The influence on Adams of Karl Mannheim gives us a clear indication of one important source behind Adams' reformulation of religious liberalism. According to Adams, Mannheim, in his sociology of knowledge, presupposes "the belief that man can achieve meaningful freedom only by detecting the ways he and his fellows are biased through social conditioning and interest."[38] Adams clearly affirms this pivotal presupposition when he states that "the older liberal doctrine of man was egregiously deficient in so far as its theory of freedom viewed the individual as an atomic datum, choosing his goals quite freely and setting out to achieve them."[39] Freedom for Adams is "freedom

---

[37]James Luther Adams, On Being Human - The Liberal Way (Boston: American Unitarian Association, Tract No. 359, no date). James D. Hunt assigns the year 1940 as the date of publication. "Writings of James Luther Adams," in Voluntary Associations, A Study of Groups in Free Societies, p. 377

[38]"Freud, Mannheim and the Liberal Societies of Man," Journal of Liberal Religion, II, No. 3 (1941), p. 109.

[39]Ibid., p. 110.

with," not "freedom from." It means common institutional life and participation "which provides criticism, guidance, and group support."[40] For this reason, liberalism must give clear attention to the effect of social structures on the individual.

As we shall see, the social grounding of the individual has implications for the way in which theory and practice are understood by Adams. In the first place, the givenness of this social grounding is not passively accepted as a single sociological datum. For Adams, the dialectic between individual and group requires active, conscious participation through personal and associational activity. The dialectic is not to be left to fate but must be willingly and willfully entered into by individuals and groups to bring about the achievement of goals such as equality and justice. As a result, Adams denies the validity of the liberal principle of pre-established harmony.

In the second place, this social/individual understanding indicates an awareness that action must flow from theoretical analysis. Ethical thinking is not sufficient in itself since social change is effected by action in conjunction with, or flowing from, theory. As we shall see in Chapter Three, this understanding is further elaborated in his belief that the meaning of any theory is understood in terms of the consequence of the theory. Theory/practice exist dialectically for Adams.

In the third place, Adams himself demonstrates the nature of social/individual grounding in his own life by his active participation in many voluntary associations meant to effect social change.[41] The voluntary association as a means of effectively coping with social/individual tension will be dealt with in Chapter Five. Ultimately, a discussion of power must ensue since the social/individual dialectic, theory and practice, and the voluntary association imply the use of this element.

---

[40]"Freud, Mannheim and the Liberal Doctrine of Man," p. 110.

[41]See the Appendix, pp. 207-214.

Humankind's Incompleteness

Adams' first principle is that humanity means lack of completeness or perfection. Knowledge itself, a human product, is incomplete, subject to criticism and certainly to constant change. Not to recognize either of the above is to assume a pretentious posture, clearly exemplified by that of the orthodox claim to infallibility. For Adams, political and religious authoritarianism have much in common: distrust in one's own mind and overconfidence in truths which are said to originate from without the human order. However, for Adams, truth in its theoretical form originates from within the human community. Human action is the great correlate of truth. Only in the former is the latter understood and thereby evaluated and reformulated. Theory and practice must continually interact in Adams' liberalism.

Adams would reverse the trend toward idolatry in religion, especially within liberalism. He calls for religious and political commitment of a "real" sort, denying pretentions to divinity. He advocates an ever-renewed skepticism, constantly attacking ignorance and idolatry.[42] This idolatry can permeate visions of reality from varied perspectives: that of the scientist who says only truths emanating from the elect should be tolerated; that of the Academy of Arts which would determine rigid guidelines for artistic awards; that of the "rugged individualist" who urges that no one on relief should be allowed to vote; that of the communist who supports dictatorship because of a far off democratic event. Religion very often gives spiritual sanction to these forms of idolatry, thus bestowing on them the status of infallibility and divinity.

In the 1940 essay, On Being Human - The Liberal Way, Adams holds that tyranny is held in check in the United States because the main forms of idolatry are in more or less open competition, but that there is no assurance that one form will not gain ascendancy over other idolatries. He sees the liberal spirit as the only way to abjure idolatry. This requires knowledge and critical acumen. In fact, Adams wonders which is the greater enemy, idolatry or ignorance, since they usually go together.[43]

---

[42]He calls this a "higher skepticism . . . that will call in question the pronouncements concerning man, God, and the world that are offered to us by some of the churches and by the political and economic dictators, and also, we might add, by the pseudo-scientists." On Being Human - The Liberal Way, p.

[43]Ibid., pp. 10-11.

The Dignity of Man and
the Primacy of Mutual Consent

Adams' second principle of religious liberalism
is that man, although incomplete, is enormously capable
of growth and change. A dialectical sense pervades his
understanding of human nature. Rational though not
self-sufficient, responsible for his decisions, yet re-
liant on divine authority, man grows by interaction with
forces external and internal.[44]

In so doing, man reveals his own dignity. "Though
nothing in this world is complete or perfect, this is a
growing world, and human nature must be relied upon to
determine the kind of change that makes for growth rather than decay."[45] Human nature, in search of standards against which to measure growth, does so in a
reality which Adams views as dipolar.[46] One pole
(the anthropocentric) is man's capacity for truth and
growth and the other (the theocentric) is the physical,
spiritual, social and personal environment. Man's
capacity for growth is not self-actualizing; man becomes man as he struggles toward growth in tension with
that pole of reality known as theocentric.[47]

---

[44]On Being Human - The Liberal Way, p. 16.

[45]Ibid.

[46]"Some Practical Applications." Adams' contribution to the
discussion of "The Religious Content of Liberalism" (also
called Greenfield Papers). Presented at the Unitarian
Ministers Institute, Greenfield, Mass., Sept. 11, 1934,
p. 31 (mimeographed).

[47]The influence of both Tillich (the sense of the dialectic)
and of Whitehead (process thought) can be noted here. Adams'
use of dipolarity is clarified by looking at an article Charles
Hartshorne wrote in the July-August 1934 issue of The New
Humanist, entitled "Redefining God." (Adams was preparing his
Greenfield Group paper during that summer.) Hartshorne, a process theologian, describes the nature of God as being dipolar.
Following Whitehead, he says that God's nature has a primordial
(changeless) aspect and a consequent (successive) aspect. God
is not to be confused with the whole of existing things (p. 320).
Yet God is imminent in all things "for the consequent nature of
God at any given time is just God as at that time embracing
in himself the then existing creatures" (pp. 320-21). Hartshorne's description of the consequent nature of God converges

There is no doubt that an atheist interacts with this total environment but such a person would not call it the theocentric pole. That Adams names it such flows from his faith interpretation. He sees the same total environment that the atheist sees, but in the former case vision is informed by theism and in the latter by a nontheistic interpretation. Thus, the total environment is the arena for God's revelation and interaction with humankind in Adams' view. Furthermore, Adams does not intend a radical disjunction between God and man when speaking of reality as dipolar. This capacity for truth and growth on the person's part comes from God as well, even though it is placed in contrast to the theocentric pole. "Dipolar reality" is a heuristic device used to promote Adams' sense of contrast and dialectic, not division and opposition.

Adams understands reality in interactional or di-polar terms. I see this as reinforcing a vital sense of theory and practice as a consistent facet of his ethics,

---

with Adams' understanding of dipolar reality. Hartshorne concludes that what is at a maximum in God must be present to some degree in every creature. "Hence, if God creates, then every creature is in some degree creative." (p. 322). The consequent nature of God implies an open future for God, that is to say, additional values can be realized. This "does away with the last vestige of excuse for the alliance between theism and a reactionary attitude toward social problems." (p. 320). Man's call to creativity and concern for social problems is fundamental to Adams' religious liberalism and ethics. This thinking is seen in Adams' "Some Practical Applications" and On Being Human - The Liberal Way.
   Adams did not read the article at the time it was written. Both Hartshorne and he studied under Whitehead, and Adams sees that connection as the source of common influences on Hartshorne and himself. (Conversation with author, March 22, 1977.)
   The Hartshorne article as cited appears in Contemporary American Protestant Thought: 1900-1970, ed. by William R. Miller (Indianapolis: Bobbs-Merrill, 1973), pp. 315-22.

in which the individual or social happening occurs in
tension with the total environment. This reinforces
his understanding of theory as eventuating in practice.
Just as man's capacity for truth and growth alone is
not reality, so also theory in itself does not affect
or change reality. Capacity must interact with environment for there to be reality; theory must eventuate in practice for change to occur. Certainly the
impact of reading Marx and incorporating his understanding of theory and practice is evident in Adams'
redefining of liberalism. Marx would be the first to
agree with Adams that change is brought about only
through the altering of social structures.

For Adams, the religious liberal, reality is the
arena of revelation. Revelation[48] "the disclosure and
awareness of ultimate concerns," comes about in man's
interaction with dipolar reality. Even here, the per-
sonal-social dimension of human existence influences
his understanding of revelation. It is socially
grounded. In the history of the prophets as well as
in our growing knowledge of man and nature, God reveals himself.

The anthropocentric pole confers dignity upon man.
"Human nature must be relied upon to determine the kind
of change that makes for growth rather than decay."
This responsibility bestows upon human nature, then,
an inherent dignity. What are the processes by which man
carries out his role? Persuasion, and mutual consent,
surely not coercion, are prime means, for coercion is the
antithesis of mutuality. Yet even coercion, as we shall
see, is not ruled out completely by Adams. But he
negates unbridled freedom as a proper means by which man
can carry out his role with fullest dignity. The liberal
regards seriously the need to restrict individual freedom,
to demand compulsory education, and to reduce concentra-
tions of wealth.[49] Further consideration of Adams' understanding of human nature will emerge in the discussion of
his third principle, community.

Community

Adams, through his sense of the dialectic and dipolarity, relates individual to group in an ongoing process

_____

[48] _On Being Human - The Liberal Way_, p. 17.

[49] _Ibid._, p. 16.

of personal and social self-understanding and identity.
Hence, his third and central principle of community.
To understand why community is important to Adams, we
must remember his definition of religion, one adopted
from James Bissett Pratt, "a serious and social attitude
towards the Determiner of destiny."[50] The differentiation between religions depends upon what is taken seriously and what is considered the truly social attitude.
The religious liberal, according to Adams, takes time
and history seriously. Thus liberal religion is mater-
ialistic since it affirms the unity of matter and spirit.
"It is a religion for the man who takes life in this
world seriously, seriously enough to want to change himself and it."[51] A sense of theory and practice interact
in his thinking. "Religious" people who do not take the
world seriously are accused by Adams of escaping reality
or of offering an ideology based on a "future life."
They develop a "pure spirituality," objecting to religion's being concerned with social and political questions.

The religious liberal finds, as the center of his
community, a faith classically expressed in the Old
Testament prophets and "in the being, character and
mission of Jesus."[52] Thus, his religion is clearly
rooted in a tradition and transcendent frame of reference. But there is more to religion than this. The
church in its individual members and as community is a
context for resolving personal problems as well as social and institutional ones. Adams holds that "every
personal problem is a social problem and every social
problem is a personal problem."[53] In this Adams utilizes the distinctions Troeltsch makes between subjective
and objective virtue. Concern for the individual in his
personal relations and concern for the structures of
society must go hand in hand in liberal thought.

Thus, we begin to see the ramifications and scope
of Adams' sense of community. He understands community
not simply as intimate interpersonal relationships but
more broadly as man's interrelatedness with other humans

---

[50]On Being Human, p. 18.

[51]Ibid., p. 20.

[52]"The Liberal Christian Looks at Himself," p. 11.

[53]"Social Ethics and Pastoral Care," in Pastoral Care in
the Liberal Churches, ed. James Luther Adams and Seward
Hiltner (New York: Abingdon Press, 1970), p. 199.

on both a personal and societal basis. The individual
is not only responsible for his or her family but for
the wider human community and the context and structures
within which that community functions. In terms of behavior, people must work at community, not only in the
family but also in voluntary associations (i.e., political parties) and nonvoluntary ones (i.e., governmental
work) in order to foster love and justice. Community,
for Adams, is "where there is a deep concern for social
salvation and where the material and human resources are
intelligently employed."[54] Social salvation means taking
time and history, the everyday conditions of humans, into
account. Social salvation involves the sharing "with free
consent in the goods and especially in the necessities of
this life. . ."[55]

For Adams, then, liberal Christianity rejects a
pietism[56] of the strictly inner life and a communist
faith in salvation through institutional reform.

> Liberal Christianity can cope religiously (that
> is, effectively) with social problems only if it
> can corporately and also through its individual
> adherents maintain the fear of God and His
> judgments in institutional as well as personal
> life and at the same time yield to the grace,
> the form-creating Spirit that effects the fruits
> meet for repentance, the fruits that constitute
> a community of integrity and justice.[57]

An important means for achieving a harmony between
personal and social ethical concerns in Adams' thought
is the small group or ecclesiola in ecclesia. In a 1938
or 1939 address he describes the methods employed by
European and American liberals for development of the

---

[54] On Being Human - The Liberal Way, p. 20.

[55] Ibid.

[56] A pietism which confines "itself to personal and interpersonal obligations [and] fails to observe collective responsibility for the character of society. . ." is found
wanting by Adams. Adams does not find this pietism consistent. "Willy-nilly it brings preferences regarding public policy in through the back door, and thus incurs the
responsibility of morally justifying these preferences."
"The Geography and Organization of Social Responsibility," p. 259.

[57] "Liberal Christianity and Modern Social Problems," in The IARF:
Its Vision and Its Work (The Hague: The International Association
for Liberal Christianity and Religious Freedom, 1955), p. 24.

spiritual life as "daily devotions, ministerial and lay
retreats, voluntarily accepted disciplines among small
groups of kindred minds or spirits."[58] He himself
was an active member of the Greenfield Group, the Brothers of the Way, and the Prairie Group, all Unitarian
ministers' groups which sought a correlation between
personal and social aspects of religious liberalism.

Much of this emphasis can be traced to Adams' understanding of the religious fellowship in liberal
Christianity as a "place where the members respecting
each other in mutual confidence, will hear from each
other (and will test) what the Holy Spirit prompts;
thus the fellowship and also each member of the fellowship were to be enriched."[59] Adams believes that the
individual is enriched in a group context and acts
more fully than he does in isolation. This is related
to his belief that "we are all members of one body, and
this body includes the body politic."[60] The body image
is allied to his affirmation of the covenantal fellowship wherein each congregation is endowed with local
autonomy. He emphasizes the dialectical point that "in
this fellowship the so-called minority position was to
be protected in the very name of the Holy Spirit."[61]
Community is central to Adams' liberalism because the
individual achieves meaning and identity only within
this context. A voluntaristic theory, freedom, discipline and tradition, and the liberal doctrine of progress will clarify the role community plays in his thinking.

Community and Voluntaristic Theory

An analysis of Adams' third principle, that of community, would be incomplete without some reference to
his theory of voluntarism. For Adams, the will is decisive in human nature. It is ambiguous in character.
Adams' voluntarism stresses the dynamic and contradictory
in human existence.[62] At once the source of creativity

---

[58]"Small Groups in the European Churches," c. 1938-39,
p. 1 (typewritten).

[59]"The Liberal Christian Looks at Himself," p. 3.

[60]"Liberal Christianity and Modern Social Problems," p. 24.

[61]"The Liberal Christian Looks at Himself," p. 3.

[62]"The Changing Reputation of Human Nature," pp. 14, 35.

and tragedy, man's will allows him

> . . . a freedom to exercise the infinitely
> higher power of human nature in terms of
> creative love, and a freedom to waste them
> in mere lassitude and triviality, or to per-
> vert them for the sake of a will to power.[63]

While eighteenth and nineteenth century liberalism
viewed history as product of a pre-established harmony,
Adams' liberalism places history in man's hands, or
rather in men's wills. A far different reading of
events thus emerges. Science and technology are seen
as forces of mobilization and civilization, but of in-
stability and alienation as well. Revolution is followed
by a reign of terror. The growth of big business in
America domesticates freedom and true liberation. World
War II, says Adams, was Fate's gift to the naive liberal
who simplistically espoused pre-established harmony
while the events of history cried out for critical analysis and the correction of injustice.

Adams faults the liberal with a failure to maintain
the necessary emphasis on both sides of human nature.

> Indeed, one may say that an understanding of
> the metaphysical implications of the derived
> dignity of human nature (the doctrine of _Imago_
> _dei_) requires a correspondingly metaphysical
> interpretation of the universal perversion or
> frustration of man's essential dignity (the
> doctrine of sin).[64]

Implicit in the doctrines of sin and redemption, says
Adams, is a balance between pessimism and optimism. The
community of mankind can be held in no greater esteem
than the esteem in which the sum of its members is held,
with their individual propensities for evil as well as good.

Freedom within Community

Nor can the community be more free than its members.
In reviewing Maritain's _Three Reformers_, Adams criticizes

---

[63]"The Changing Reputation of Human Nature," p. 35-36.
The entire essay is valuable for an understanding of
voluntaristic theory.

[64]_Ibid._, p. 36, see footnote in Adams' essay.

Maritain's emphasis on the Catholic Church as solution
to the problem of individual liberty. For Adams,
"sound autonomy" can never be the "heteronomy" of a
divine institution under human control. What does
Adams seek? "Certainly the 'modern' must discover and
impose upon himself a standard less fluctuating and
'angelistic' than his reasons or his feelings about
himself, whether he be a humanist or a religious man
or both."[65] Adams envisions a type of freedom which
will unify the fluctuations of feeling and reason with
a standard which is not heteronomous.

He sees God as the proper source of freedom or
control in the church, not only the minister and congregation. "We believe we are bound to adjust ourselves not only to each other, but also to God, to
something higher than society or human nature."[66] This
triadic relationship involves a disciplined inner life,
discipline checking temperament, mood and even desires
for one's own rights. "The true liberalism defends
freedom only as a method and not as a goal."[67] The goal,
rather, is the health of the body of Christ, the church,
and such health is in evidence when there is a sensitivity to religious and moral issues and an acting upon
the truth as the Church members are brought to see it.

Adams would replace the traditional controls within
Christianity with an inner control by means of which
Christians assume responsibility to develop standards of
joint conduct.[68] Freedom, then, is far from an expansive
or emotional escape from bondage. It is "a concentrative
rational loyalty to those principles which underlie distinguished living, social justice, and worship."[69] Again
we see the focus on theory and practice. Such strenuous
discipline does not exist for its own sake. The final

---

[65]Review of _Three Reformers_ by Jacques Maritain, _Hound and Horn_, III, No. 1 (1929), p. 120.

[66]"The Tyranny of a Free Minister," _The Christian Register_,
CXI, 31-32 (1932), p. 470. This understanding of Adams
bears a strong resemblance to H. Richard Niebuhr's ultimate
third in _The Responsible Self_.

[67]_Ibid._, p. 470.

[68]_Ibid._

[69]_Ibid._

test is a pragmatic one: "By their fruits shall ye know them." Yet this pragmatism is constrained by disciplined freedom and principles such as mutual love and forbearance.

Discipline, Tradition, and Community

Writing about religious liberalism in 1934, Adams is pressed by the historical events of his day to demand of Christians communal work and communal identity. The shock of the Depression and the hope of the New Deal, though not specifically mentioned in Adams' Greenfield paper that year,[70] does not lead Adams to conservatism or orthodoxy as solutions. Rather, he holds fast to a liberalism constantly criticized and held in tension.

Institution, discipline, and worship are part and parcel of the liberalism he calls forth in the churches. The religious spirit, it seems to him, needs the stimulation, the fellowship and the standards which exist only in a religious institution.[71] It needs as well the tradition which is the heritage of institution.

Within the Unitarian tradition, for example, a communal effort to perceive divine elements in everyday life will lead to growth in religious attitudes as well as secular involvement. It is a religious obligation for man to know God's reality in as many ways as possible, and this means through all that the sacred and secular orders have to offer.[72] The supreme test of the liberal church's effectiveness will be the kind of individuals and society produced. This will be a constant theme in Adams' writings.[73]

The discipline by which a community seeks out God's reality in events will bear fruit in "the truth which can be acted upon cooperatively." Perhaps Adams' case for a disciplined search for standards is best summarized in

---

[70]"Some Practical Applications," which was Adams' contribution to the discussion of "The Religious Content of Liberalism," presented at the Unitarian Ministers' Institute, Sept. 11, 1934, Greenfield, Mass. (unpublished).

[71]"Some Practical Applications," p. 34. See also his article "Liberals and Religion," The Christian Register, CXII, No. 8 (1933), p. 118, which deals with this same issue of the relation of church to religion.

[72]Ibid., p. 41.

[73]See also "Liberals and Religion," p. 118.

one of his statements concerning the Greenfield Group:

> Time does not permit us to speak now of the
> group's utter agreement as to the imperative
> demand for a social philosophy and a program
> that may unite us [the Unitarian Church], of
> our conviction that the church must make a
> definite impact upon local and national econ-
> omic and political life, of our belief that
> we must effect a strenuous cooperation between
> liberal elements in other denominations or
> other groups that are working towards vital
> social integration.[74]

Liberals must, then, come to some agreement upon content.
"The open mind is praiseworthy because it finally closes
on sounder ideas and not because openness is an end in
itself."[75] Good will must involve "a discovery of standards applicable to the individual and social life."[76]

While Adams as liberal opts for standard-setting in
the context of community, he remains firm in his commitment to freedom, democracy and human experience.

> The freedom of the congregationalist reaches
> even to the doctrines that articulate the
> common faith, for he asserts the freedom to
> discuss the doctrines of the faith as against
> being told what to think. . . Each new in-
> sight into Nature which science brings us,
> each new experience of the human heart, each
> new discovery of the intellect, each new ex-
> periment in the social process, and each new
> movement in history may add to the revelation
> of the Divine.[77]

---

[74] "Some Practical Applications," p. 43.

[75] "Assailing the Liberal's Defense: Its Symptoms But
Not Its Essence," The Christian Register, CXII, No. 12
(1933), p. 181.

[76] Ibid., p. 194.

[77] With James Bissett Pratt, "The Congregational Idea."
Essay prepared for conference of Congregationalist and
Unitarian Representatives, 1932 or 1933, pp. 4-5 (mimeo-
graphed).

The Ontological Foundation of Mutuality

Adams' fourth principle of religious liberalism is that mutuality or community has an ontological foundation: "existence demands mutuality."[78] Since reality is dipolar, communal interaction places man in the real world.[79] Thus, the very structure of existence not only demands but, at the same time, supports mutuality and introduces an ontological element into Adams' conceptualization of religious liberalism and his developing ethics in which "isness" precedes "oughtness." This demand/ support is for Adams the divine element in reality.[80] Vested interests (individualism, laissez-faire economics, authoritarianism) militate against this mutuality, but liberalism, functioning within institutions, can win the day. The means at its disposal are education, prophecy, and action within the liberal church. To make use of them, the religious liberal must act in relation to structures, for "men cannot respect religion and neglect its forms."[81]

The fact that reality supports mutuality does not imply the automatic development or progress of the human community. Adams wants to make clear that his mode of liberalism has little in common with the naive earlier liberalism which saw progress as inevitable, the product of a pre-established harmony in the world. In his view, man, with his individual free will, can make choices in opposition to the mutuality which is his proper ambiance. Adams stresses the fact that man in making his choices must have "a recognition of the fact that all human achievement and meaningfulness are asserted only in the teeth of obstruction and of ever possible perversion."[82]

For Adams, to overlook man's potential for sin and coercion is to deprive his freedom of meaning. And yet, he cannot be called a pessimist in his estimate of man. He criticizes those who expound the doctrine of sin but who cannot state "the paradox of the human condition without giving the impression of having surrendered to black and bleak pessimism."[83]

---

[78]See above, pp. 37-39.

[79]On Being Human - The Liberal Way, p. 24.

[80]Ibid., p. 25.

[81]"The Changing Reputation of Human Nature," pp. 40-41.

[82]Ibid., p. 41.

Man exists as a child of God and has ever-present possibilities of repentance and regeneration. Thus, faith points beyond tragedy without denying tragedy's reality. Reinforcing this, Adams refers to George Tyrell's concept of ultimate optimism and provisional pessimism. Certainly, this thinking is not alien to the Neo-orthodox sense of the tragic in life and the eschatological victory of God.

Adams equates growth with human involvement which, in his mind, has as its primary function to bring positive change rather than decay. Adams does not express an implicit faith in "growth," as an a priori not to be questioned. His is far from the roseate optimism of a naive religious liberalism. He clearly states his sense of realism when he says: "If we do not act, and act in accordance with the demands history and community make upon us, the day will come sooner or later when we can no longer be active, can no longer meet these demands."[83] This world is the theatre of salvation and damnation, and the individual is trapped unless he is in a socially salvific environment.

Following Troeltsch, Adams holds history to be alogical, the product of both necessity and freedom. History generates novelty and cannot, frequently, be rationally explained. Man, maker of history, is fated but free. Thus, the demand/support for mutuality is not automatic but dialectically related to man's choice. He is conditioned by historical processes and his psycho-physical organism, yet he is compelled to make decisions. "For he can transcend his situation and in some measure he can freely change it; he can even change himself."[84] Fate places him in history as an individual and as a member of a group, but does not eliminate his ability to be creative in history.

The Relevance of Adams' Religious Liberalism to the Christian Ethicist

What bearing does Adams' reformulation of religious liberalism have on the Christian ethicist's way of approaching moral problems?

---

[83] On Being Human - The Liberal Way, p. 20.

[84] The Changing Reputation of Human Nature, p. 25.

48

1. Adams' method of reformulation itself merits
the ethicist's attention. His orientation is forcefully
dialectical, focusing now on community, then on the individual, now on God, then on man. Adams' dialectical
sense fosters a willingness to engage in the task of
translating ethical formulations for a new age, yet
cautions the translator that new understandings are not
the final answer. Thus, vital reformulation results
only if theory and practice exist dialectically. They
do in Adams primarily because no answer is final and
because community facilitates discernment of the interaction between theory and practice. As we shall see in
the following chapter, the pragmatic theory of meaning
reinforces this emphasis on theory and practice. In
the four principles of religious liberalism shaped by
Adams for twentieth century America, we find more specific guidelines for the ethicist.

2. Adams' affirmation of man's incompleteness gives
us a new perspective on his understanding of history and
time as dynamic processes to be taken seriously. Neither
theory nor past solutions to problems achieve a status
which is beyond question. Theory may be correct, but the
litmus test is application to the present situation and
reflection upon the interaction of event and theory.

Adams' emphasis on incompleteness in man is a re-
minder of the incompleteness of ethical answers. Standing
within humanity, the ethicist must avoid a posture of infallibility; he must steer clear of authoritarianisms
and idolatries as ways to overcome his basic incompleteness. A sinful being himself, the ethicist must maintain
a constantly self-critical stance as corrective for his
rationalizations and misinterpretations. Given a constantly critical attitude toward his work, the ethicist
must nevertheless take firm stands. His open-mindedness
ought to lead through discipline to doctrine. This pro-
gression calls for a seriousness toward time and history
from the ethicist.

3. Adams urges the ethicist to hold his sense of
incompleteness and imperfection in tension with a sense
of dignity and trustworthiness. The ethicist must rely
on human nature to bring about positive change. In this
process, persuasion should be the ordinary means but
others must be considered since the multi-dimensionality
of problems could point to other solutions. Adams found
coercion rather than the persuasion of pacifism necessary
in dealing with the Axis. He thus encourages the ethicist

49

to remember that principles are to be reevaluated in the light of changing times and circumstances and that varied tactics are to be employed in communicating them.

4. If Adams' sensitivity to history leads us to appreciate the interaction between theory and practice, his sense of community is the means whereby this interaction is carried out. An emphasis on the individual can easily lead to rationalization. An affirmation of community provides the context for discerning the practical results of theory. Without doubt, a group can be swayed as can an individual; community provides no automatic answer to problems. Adams, however, sees community as providing the arena for developing a vital and workable ethics, for here God's message is revealed.

5. Adams would encounter the problems of relativism in doing ethics by an emphasis on discipline, tradition, and community. He presents the Holy Spirit as protector of minority rights, thus mitigating dogmatic tendencies in ethical processes. Moreover, he stresses that Christian ethics must involve an openness to God's reality which is found in both sacred and secular orders. Such a stance fosters sensitivity to change and reevaluation but never guarantees the same. The ethicist should seek a freedom having its source in God and its manifestation in a balance between feeling and reason. But freedom is not an end in itself. The goal is the health of the body of Christ, which is the church. The community as the context for the Christian ethicist provides a framework wherein the Holy Spirit moves in fostering consensus and insight, thus facilitating a vital interaction between theory and practice.

6. Adams points to an ontological element as a factor in Christian ethics. "Isness" precedes "oughtness" since reality supports mutuality. His ethics relies on an "ultimate optimism" justified by the wealth of human and divine resources available for meaningful change. And yet he would counsel the ethicist to remember that an understanding of human activity in time and history forestalls any immediate optimism. Tentativeness about humankind will allay any sense of automatic harmony or progress in ethical thinking. Such thinking overlooks the tragic element in history. God's kingdom is transcendent and, as such, is to be distinguished from man's kingdom. Ethics demands a faith which points beyond tragedy and which seeks conversion and commitment.

Adams' liberalism has a distinctiveness which is relevant for the twentieth century ethicist. However, an understanding of this liberalism must be related to the theological presuppositions which inform his liberal thinking.

CHAPTER III

JAMES LUTHER ADAMS:

THEOLOGICAL PRESUPPOSITIONS GOVERNING HIS ETHICS

James Luther Adams is a Christian ethicist and certain theological presuppositions, therefore, form the basis for his ethical position. To analyze Adams' theological understanding it is necessary to study the role sociological categories play in his thinking. I have already discussed in Chapter Two the importance Adams gives to the interrelationship between the individual and the group and the way in which theory and practice exist dialectically in his approach to religious liberalism. These interests point in the direction of a sociological concern, a concern which will be demonstrated even more clearly in Chapters Four and Five.

At the base of Adams' theological presuppositions is his use of the sociological categories of sacred/secular and structural analogy. Connected to the latter is his employment of a philosophical theory, the pragmatic theory of meaning, a prime factor in his sensitivity to theory and practice. To these sociological concerns I must give first attention since they are basic to his theology.

Primary among Adams' theological categories which mold his ethics are: revelation; authority; church; God; Kingdom of God. It is to these that I will devote lengthy treatment in this chapter.

The Impact of Sociological Categories
on Adams' Theology

The Sacred and the Secular

As can be seen in Adams' biography and defense of religious liberalism, he finds the secular modes of thought congenial to his own thought and a source of God's revelation as well. Nevertheless, his openness to the secular is by no means unrestricted since the secular is in tension with the sacred. The dialectical relationship Adams sees between them is evident in his four principles of religious liberalism.[1] Thus there is no split between theological and sociological categories in Adams' thinking.

His openness to Marx is counterbalanced by an affirmation of the reversal of values demanded by Jesus' ethic.[2] Yet "its [Christianity's] true appeal will always be in the fact that it inspires us to be and to do what the world in the bottom of its heart will always concede is the finest and best in character and conduct."[3] The dialectical note is present. There is a reversal of value in Christianity's ethics, but it inspires much that this world really knows to be of value. Christianity has an objective dimension, rooted in the concept of a transcendent God, a God whose meaning, however, strikes a deep resonance in human nature, which Adams always posits as socially grounded, and which is created in God's image.

Adams' appreciation of the dialectic between sacred and secular is evident, then, as early as 1927 when he criticizes equating religion with sociology. For Adams, from these earliest days, active social involvement is the outward manifestation of a disciplined inner life engaged in loving God.[4]

Forty-six years later, in his presidential address to the American Theological Society, Adams spoke along the same dialectical lines. The intrinsic character of theological perspectives means that theology cannot be collapsed

---

[1]See above, pp. 34-48 . Tillich's influence on Adams' understanding of the interpenetration of the sacred and the secular is evident in Paul Tillich's Philosophy of Culture, Science, and Religion, Adams' major work on Tillich, especially in the first chapter, "The Need for a New Language." See also "Tillich's Concept of the Protestant Era," Adams' concluding essay in Tillich's The Protestant Era (Chicago: The University of Chicago Press, 1948), for an insight into Tillich's influence on Adams' understanding of the interrelation of the sacred and the secular.

[2]Untitled student sermon, unpublished, c. 1925 or 1926, p. 6.

[3]Ibid., pp. 6-7.

[4]"Service of God, First Task of Religious Man," The Salem Evening News, February 28, 1927, p. 3.

into ethics; yet, in terms of theory/practice interaction, "The theology that does not examine the social
consequences of belief is in this respect meaningless
from the point of view of the sociological pragmatic
theory of meaning."[5]

Structural Analogy and Pragmatic Theory of Meaning

Adams uses a principle of structural analogy to
deepen his understanding of the social order: "the basic
structure of one area can be used as a key to the pattern
of other areas."[6] Thus, within the Christian West, the
symbol of the kingdom has served, by way of vertical and
horizontal analogy, as an integrating image for society
and as a collective representation of God's intention.

The category of structural analogy, therefore,
demonstrates the relationship between theological symbols and social structure. It is likewise a consequence
of Adams' conviction as to the social grounding of the
individual and all human activity. But Adams also relates ideas and social realities by the pragmatic theory
of meaning, drawn from the philosophy of Charles S. Peirce.
"An idea becomes clear only when we determine the habits
of behavior that follow from it."[7] The religious-ethical
understanding of agape is clear once the personal and
institutional habits flowing from it are examined. Thus,
Adams would state as general principle that

> . . . the meaning of "God" for human exper-
> ience, and the meaning of response to the
> power of God is to be determined in large
> part [my emphasis] by observing the insti-
> tutional consequences, the aspects of insti-
> tutional life which the "believers" wish to
> retain or to change.[8]

---

[5]"The Use of Symbols," On Being Human Religiously, ed.
Max Stackhouse (Boston: Beacon Press, 1976), p. 125.

[6]"Some Uses of Analogy in Religious Social Thought,"
Proceedings of the IXth International Congress for the
History of Religions (Tokyo: Maruzen, 1960), p. 469.

[7]"Our Responsibility in Society," p. 48.

[8]Ibid., p. 49.

It should be noted here that Adams is not a complete pragmatist.[9] He qualifies his acceptance of consequences when he says "in large part." Adams' metaphysical sensitivities are responsible for that proviso.[10] A socially-concerned church is not necessarily a sign of authentic religion. An affirmation of God's transcendence must be joined to social action in the pragmatism Adams advocates. In other words, knowing what God means for people in terms of practical consequences of belief is not the same as what God should mean theoretically. Adams sees a tension between norms and theory on the one side, and practice on the other. Norms and theory are discovered through practice. But Adams, the metaphysician, understands the former as attaining an existence independent from the latter, though not unrelated to the latter.[11]

Thus, the pragmatic theory of meaning buttresses Adams' use of structural analogy, and these two elements are evident throughout his thinking. For the behavioral consequences of belief (pragmatic theory) are related to patterns of symbols and to the social order (structural analogy). Belief is expressed in patterns of symbols. (My belief in God holds fast to the symbol of God, which I have integrated to the symbolism of God the Father, Suffering Messiah, Holy Spirit.) This belief, if it has real meaning, will have behavioral consequences. (A growing emphasis on interpersonal relationships, an identification and close relationship with suffering humanity, or a commitment to prayer and spiritual development.) For Adams, one of these behavioral consequences is the restructuring of society based on beliefs about God and man.

Thus structural analogy and pragmatic theory as major concerns of Adams show themselves in his belief that:

. . . The forms of authority determine or express distinguishing features of the ethos of

---

[9]See below, pp. 92-93 for a full discussion of Adams' qualified pragmatism.

[10]See below, p. 61 for another example of Adams' qualified pragmatism.

[11]On this, see below, p. 66 for his understanding of ethics and metaphysics. I wish to point out that Adams has not developed an explicit ethical theory nor an explicit set of principles and norms for doing ethics. This has been one of the major problems I encountered in writing this book. When these terms are used, it is I who am applying them to Adams.

a society. . . . The esteemed types of
leadership thus provide the cultural forms
through which the society achieves an awareness of its own identity.[12]

By the same token, religious symbols, in an analogous fashion, reflect the society from which they eman-
ate. Although symbols may be drawn from nature (the body
of Christ) or history (war between good and evil), the
more important and comprehensive ones in the Bible are
the political symbols. Adams maintains that "the concept
of vocation that ensues takes seriously the historical
dimension of our existence; that is, it imposes obligations that have to do with group life, with the past,
present and future of communal, institutional existence."[13]
Biblical symbols such as the covenant become powerful
means of focusing the structural analogies of religious
belief and organization in relation to the non-religious
domain. Thus, analogies from the finite, transferred to
the infinite, are returned to the finite. Likewise, a
pragmatic theory of meaning relies on symbolization for
its elucidation, as for example the biblical image of God
as it is related to demands for human justice.

Adams views doctrines of God, man, and salvation as
symbolizing the unity of a group, but the real impact a
system has upon social policy is seen in ecclesiastical
organization. "An instructive index to the meaning of a
theological system is the kind of community developed or
desired by the faithful."[14] A good way of summarizing
Adams' approach to the problem of God would be the following statement: "Tell me how you do things and I will
tell you what your God is like." A theological doctrine
is not fully understood if only its metaphysical dimension or personal implications are grasped. "Its social

---

[12]"The Social Import of the Professions," pp. 3-4.

[13]"Christian Vocation: An Examination of the Political
Symbolism of Biblical Faith," lecture at Denison University, c. March 1955 (typewritten), p. 3.

[14]"Religion and the Ideologies," Confluence, IV, No. 1
(1955), p. 81.

efficacy reveals itself ultimately in the impersonal
institutional precipitate."[15]

The institutional aspects affect social policy and
not simply one's own form of organization. Adams agrees
with Troeltsch's observation that the types of social
philosophy emanating from the churches often reveal a
correlation with the individual church's own type of
ecclesiastical organization. The Roman Catholic Church
has shown a preference for a hierarchical type society
while aggressive Left Wing sects have been congregational,
pluralistic, and lay oriented. This complex theory of
structural analogy does not always yield the most desired results. For example, Adams sees the possible
roots of laissez-faire economic theory in the Left Wing,
since economic and ecclesiastical theorists within that
movement believed in a type of pre-established harmony.
Moreover, it is likely that the theory has worked in
reverse as well, that ecclesiastical theorists were influenced by social theory developed by an emerging small-
business leadership.[16] In our own day, Adams finds a
similar interpretation of ecclesiastical theory affecting
social understanding.

. . . The increasing demand for social control
of the economy or of the repercussions of in-
dustrialization must meet especially vigorous
resistance at the hands of people (church members or not) whose background is the tradition
of congregational polity. . . . At the same
time, the Churches of the Right Wing of the
Reformation as well as the Roman Catholic
Church have for long shown ready sympathy with
theories of the welfare state or of planning.[17]

_____

[15]"Religion and the Ideologies," Confluence, IV, No. 1,
(1955), p. 81. Adams sees a similar approach in Tillich:
"As we have indicated he [Tillich] believes that the actual
ultimate concerns of men -- and of churches -- are to be
discovered by penetrating their very embarrassments; if one
can discover what has caused the embarrassment one may discover what the ultimate concerns have been and also what
they should be." Paul Tillich's Philosophy of Culture,
Science, and Religion, p. 16.

[16]"Religion and the Ideologies," pp. 82-83.

[17]Ibid., p. 83.

58

The categories of sacred/secular penetrate structural analogy and pragmatic theory. There are nonreligious, pragmatic consequences eventuating from sacred or religious symbol systems and institutional structures. From Adams' sociological perspective, theological thinking influences and is influenced by the secular realm and has pragmatic implications. Such interaction has importance for any Christian ethics concerned with the relationship between belief and behavior. Symbols, meaning, sacred and secular are also important in Adams' understanding of revelation.

Revelation

For Adams, revelation, which he understands to be God's own self-affirmation, occurs in history. Revelation, moreover, is dynamic, that is, continuous, and has a secular context. His ethics, as we shall see, also focus on history, the dynamic, and the secular. In his view, revelation and ethics are interrelated and this interrelation also involves the sociological categories discussed in the first section of this chapter.

Some early insights into Adams' understanding of revelation can be traced back to a 1931 article in which he warns the minister of the inherent danger in seeing himself solely as a clergyman. Such a single role may well be encouraged by the congregation which wants its minister to be "pure and unspotted from the world," distant from politics or economics. Adams sees the sacred and the secular existing in a healthy dialectic.

> . . . A certain alternation between the otherworldly and this worldly, between the intellectual and the moral, between the sacred and the secular, is indispensable. Only in this way can pragmatic energy be given to the spiritual, and ideal glow to the practical. Not that there is a reconciling of opposites here, but rather that the abundant life emerges from the tension between these two poles of experience.[18]

In another context, he speaks of the differences "between a faith once delivered and a progressive revelation or a

---

[18]"The Minister with Two Occupations," _The Christian Register_, CX, No. 38 (1931), p. 713.

new opening, or the witness of the Holy Spirit. . . ."[19]
The liberal Christian, clergy and layperson alike, seeks
to respond positively to the Word of God conceived of as
God speaking to man in a personal way through Jesus, the
Gospel, other persons, mind, conscience, and nature.

"Because of the ambiguous elements in human awareness and because of the richness, the freedom, and the
hiddenness of the Word of God, it [liberal Christianity]
emphasizes the uses of diversity, self-criticism, and
openness."[20] Diversity is necessary since truth is known
only in a variety of situations. Such response to the
power of God, offering "new opportunity and demand in the
everchanging situations of the human condition,"[21] releases creativity and newness. God's living Word speaks
to the uniqueness of each situation and is likewise conditioned by the situation. This demands openness to hear
God's Word. God's Word is creative and redemptive, but
it must be contextualized to be relevant. Thus liberal
Christianity seeks to understand itself in history but
not to be bound to the situation in which it finds itself. Self-criticism is necessary for this process; and
the liberal must continually seek a transformation of concern since relevance is essential to such a form of
Christianity.[22]

Revelation is a theological category for Adams, and
he contrasts it with religious experience which is a
psychological-philosophical category.[23] Since religious

---

[19]"A Theory of Revelation for Liberals," Address at New
Testament Club, University of Chicago, c. 1937, p. 2.

[20]"The Ages of Liberalism," The Journal of Religious
Thought, XIV, No. 2 (1957), p. 101.

[21]Ibid., p. 102. Adams quotes Tillich as follows: "The
Word of God is any reality by means of which the eternal
breaks with unconditioned power into our contemporaneity."
(Paul Tillich's Philosophy, p. 9). Adams shares Tillich's
view that the Bible cannot be considered truly "the word
of God" if it is separated from the here and now.

[22]"The Ages of Liberalism," p. 101.

[23]"The Liberal Conception of Religious Experience and Revelation," Outline for Address at International Association

experience is effectively grounded, it lacks a self-authenticating cognitive element. Imaginative symbol is the means of interpreting, remembering, and communicating religious experience. Symbol criticizes the experience and provides a norm for experience in and through a community. Through this process, the meaning of revelation is ascertained. The dialectical strain in Adams is present here: religious experience/revelation, individual/community.[24] In his International Association for Liberal Christianity and Religious Freedom outline, Adams assigns five characteristics to revelation, each of which has implications for the development of his theology and ethics.

1. The verbal form of revelation is a myth which is a body of imaginative symbols. Myth, however, stands in tension with rational criticism, insights from other religious traditions, and new concerns arising in the religious experience of individual or community. This understanding of myth makes sense in view of Adams' first liberal principle, man's incompleteness.[25]

Symbol systems thus stand in tension with man's critical capacity. Effective symbols are powerful but power must be appropriately used. This is not an automatic process in human affairs. Irrationality, domination and greed may be present, rendering the symbol inappropriate. Rational criticism is an effective partner of symbol systems. Once again, we see that Adams' pragmatic orientation is highly qualified and critical.

> . . . The appropriateness of a religious symbol is to be determined, not by its practical effect alone, but also by its relation to knowledge of the speculative and intellectual order. And a symbol is not appropriate unless it provides the quintessence of what we can in some measure know, by means of the ordinary processes of knowing.[26]

---

for Liberal Christianity and Religious Freedom Congress, Bentveld, Holland, 1939, pp. 15-16 (typewritten). The outline is also contained in Year Book IARF 1939, p. 1 (Utrecht, Holland: Secretariat IARF, 1939).

[24] Ibid.

[25] See above, pp. 36-37, as well as "The Ages of Liberalism," p. 101.

[26] "A Theory of Revelation for Liberals." Address to New

2. Adams discusses the second characteristic of revelation:

> . . . Revelation is socially conditioned and incarnational, transmitted in a community from person to person. . . . Thus its kernel is special revelation which illumines general revelation coming from reason, nature, history and conscience. It is inextricably related to the Bible.[27]

For Adams, biblical faith fits within the wider theological perspective of revelation. In this context, one must ask what biblical faith means to him. Negatively, the Bible is not a receptacle for ethical ideals. For some within the Unitarian tradition, the principles of reason, tolerance, and freedom are self-sufficient in the formulation of a theology; the liberal in Adams' view relies on other resources.

Transcendent resources giving substance to a way of life and fellowship are at the heart of biblical faith. He judges " . . . that the Bible is most concerned with the resources upon which meaningful existence is ultimately dependent, with the resources that give rise to a community of viable justice and righteousness. . . ."[28] In the biblical view, human history is a struggle between forces which facilitate personal and social integrity and forces which impede them. The important point, however, is that the ultimate resource for this human development is not man, creative though he be.

> . . . Paradoxically, the integrating forces represent at the same time a divine gift and a divinely given task or vocation for men. . . . The image of divine liberation from bondage and the divine promise of newness of life is determinative.[29]

Testament Club, University of Chicago, c. 1936-37, pp. 13-14. The International Association for Liberal Christianity and Religious Freedom Address is a refinement of this one. See above, p. 60, footnote 23.

[27]"The Liberal Conception of Religious Experience and Revelation," p. 1.

[28]"Changing Frontiers: Vanishing and Emerging," p. 4.

[29]Ibid.

In the name of these divine powers, the prophets oppose all bondage imprisoning the human spirit. For the prophets, moreover, obedience to the divine power and inward fellowship with God are bound up with human fellowship. History is directional in the prophetic tradition and

> . . . they [the prophets] see men as responsible under God for the character and direction of their social existence. . . In Old Testament prophetism, man's relation to the final resource -- to the Lord of History -- is intimate and ultimate; and its active thrust is towards the corporate, for salvation is for time and history.[30]

No human accomplishment, however, is an end in itself. Adams returns, once more, to the object of faith and that alone is God, "the transforming power that creates justice and fellowship among men."[31] This power makes mercy, forgiveness, repentance and new beginnings possible. Thus, the question behind biblical criticism is "what is biblical faith to us?" It is the most difficult of frontiers because it is the most elemental: what is the meaning of life? The answer is revealed within the society of men, acting in fellowship.

3. "Revelation must be recognized and responded to by the recipient; thus it must elicit decision, conversion, commitment, in accordance with values and disciplines implied."[32] Although eighteenth and nineteenth century religious liberalism deemphasized these elements, Adams, in viewing revelation as process, reaffirmed them. Not to do so would be to neglect the deeper levels of human consciousness and of reality itself. He is critical of his own contemporaries still rooted in what he refers to as eighteenth century "non-tragic" tradition.[33] He finds fault with their adherence to a rationalistic liberalism, emphasizing reason over affection and seeing history as a "progressive movement toward harmony" rather than as an illogical process.[34]

---

[30]"Changing Frontiers: Vanishing and Emerging," p. 4.

[31]Ibid.

[32]"The Liberal Conception of Religious Experience and Revelation," p. 1.

[33]"The Changing Reputation of Human Nature," p. 22.

[34]Ibid., p. 24.

4. Revelation is ultimate, communal and intimate. Ultimate in the sense that it is God's self-affirmation, communal since it is mediated by a faith community, and intimate due to the necessity of conversion.[35] Conversion depends upon God's self-affirmation and communal mediation. How is this self-affirmation mediated by the community? Adams' understanding of the Left Wing of the Protestant Reformation helps to answer these questions.

The English Left Wing's search for a congregational polity was a political and ecclesiastical issue. This anti-hierarchicalism was defended by a doctrine of the freedom of the spirit. "Every child of God has his own individual conscience, for the Holy Spirit is available to every child of God."[36] In other words, man's self-understanding was not revealed once and for all through the Scriptures in a particular historical epoch. God's self-affirmation is manifold. The scriptural image, in this case the Holy Spirit, illuminated a new situation producing a new revelation. This ongoing nature of revelation is further reinforced within the Left Wing by not requiring uniformity of belief within the religious fellowship.

. . . A religious fellowship should rather be the place where the members, respecting each other in mutual confidence, will hear from each other (and will test) what the Holy Spirit prompts; thus the fellowship and also each member of the fellowship were to be enriched. . . . In this fellowship the so-called minority position was to be protected in the very name of the Holy Spirit. According to this view, God works in history where free consensus appears under the great Taskmaster's eye.[37]

---

[35]"The Liberal Conception of Religious Experience and Revelation," p. 1.

[36]"The Liberal Christian Looks at Himself," p. 3.

[37]Ibid., pp. 3-4.

5. There is, for Adams, another dialectical element
in the Christian understanding of revelation in terms of
finality and historical process. On the one hand "the
Christian 'way' will always be in the Spirit of Jesus and
involve love to God and love to man. . . ."[38] There is a
certain "finality" to this revelation. On the other hand,
"revelation is unsealed: it expands through new 'open-
ings' and new applications. . . The full revelation
can only occur in the eschaton."[39] If revelation is continuous, it takes place within history. Adams, as we
have seen,[40] sees human history as not moving necessarily
toward harmony. Thus, there is greater complexity in
human history than in nature. History is tragic, for here
the will to mutuality and to power conflict in a way not
possible in nature.

The social ethical implications of Adams' theory of
revelation begin to emerge once he enunciates his understanding of history. He sees the progressive harmony
view of earlier liberalism as reducing the tension between the Gospel and the world.[41] This reduction of tension is accomplished by disregarding the tragic elements
of history: the depth of perversity available to men;
the dissolution of values; the appearance of collective
demonries; the phenomenon of the mass man. If revelation is continuous, these facts of history must be faced.
Once they are faced there is an irreducible tension between Gospel and world.

However, Adams does not reduce religion to ethical
observance and historical process. There is the other
aspect of the dialectic, the "finality" of revelation.
If one views the parables of Jesus, for instance, from
a purely ethical viewpoint, their metaphysical nature is
neglected. These parables point "to the more-than-human
resources of human existence, to the Kingdom of God 'that
grows of itself' and not ultimately by any human devising."[42]
Adams roots revelation in a doctrine of grace, prayer, and
a theological interpretation of great social issues.[43]

---

[38]"The Liberal Conception of Religious Experience and
Revelation," p. 1.

[39]Ibid.

[40]See above, pp. 47-48.

[41]"The Liberal Christian Looks at Himself," p. 8.

[42]Ibid., p. 9.

[43]Ibid.

Authority

Adams' understanding of authority as exercised in
the ministry provides us with one perspective on his
interpretation of this doctrine. Adams' doctrine, however, has a wider base than that of authority within the
Unitarian tradition or church.

Adams' sense of community as the context for the
individual has implications for his understanding of
authority. Very often the individual minister bears
much of the burden for constructive ideas, having to
rely on his own accomplishments and personality for
credibility. In the Greenfield Papers, Adams points out
that the above isolation "weakens the awareness and the
authority of a tradition."[44] He proposes as remedy the
grouping together of ministers for solidarity.

> The visible presence of two or three men
> holding and expounding similar ideas will
> stimulate response and will restore to
> the church some of the authority that is its
> rightful heritage.[45]

The ministers, operating in the context of a liberal church, must seek to maintain and support the
tension

> between order and freedom . . . between
> tradition and experiment, between col-
> lectivism and individualism, between
> submission to the Church and loyalty to
> Christ, between a faith once delivered
> and a progressive revelation or a new
> "opening," or the witness of the Holy
> Spirit, between the consensus gentium
> and personal conviction.[46]

They must maintain these tensions while taking communally authoritative stands in relation to the Scriptures
and the church's ethics.

In these areas of tension, revelation, as Adams
understands it, is the source of authority. For Adams,
"effective revelation presents itself as authoritative,

---

[44]"Some Practical Applications," p. 46.

[45]Ibid., p. 47.

[46]"A Theory of Revelation for Liberals," p. 2.

66

as demanding commitment to the truth that lies behind
the symbolism and action in accordance with the hierarchy of values involved."[47] Revelation is "truth
reflected through personality effecting commitment in
terms of character and community."[48] Revelation as
source of authority manifests itself through Event and
demands or evokes commitment of new Event. The appeal
is to the affections and the will in such a way that
the authoritativeness of revelation speaks for itself;
it is not imposed, yet it occurs within a communal
context.

The minister, indeed the faithful at large, must
realize that this understanding of a communally-based
authority applies to the church's ethic as well as to
the Scriptures. Therefore, no temporal understanding
of this authority should become absolute and permanently
binding. It has a dynamic quality. "The best way in
which it can be apprehended is in the way of common
Christian prayer and discussion."[49]

In Adams' thought, the nature of authority is closely
associated with the liberal congregational church and
with democracy. He sees both liberalism and democracy as
closely allied, "for both make their final appeal to reason and a critical estimate of the evidence. This is
another way of saying that congregationalism recognizes
no specific authority as absolute."[50] Freedom is integral to such a conception of authority and is an acknowledgment that doctrines and symbols of the faith will
change, since they are "earthen vessels" subject to change
and criticism.

Adams' analysis of the relationship between authority and the society in which it is exercised utilizes his
pragmatic theory of meaning. A civilization can be understood by identifying its ultimate orientation and leadership pattern. "The forms of authority determine or express
distinguishing features of the ethos of the society."[51]

---

[47] "Theory of Revelation for Liberals," p. 20.

[48] Ibid., p. 24.

[49] Adams with E.E. Aubrey and others. "The Ethical Reality
and Function of the Church," memorandum by the Chicago
Ecumenical Discussion Group, 1940, p. 9 (mimeographed).
See above, pp. 61-63.

[50] "The Congregational Idea," p. 4.

[51] "The Social Import of the Professions," p. 3.

The prophet in ancient Israel typifies this understanding. The prophetic concept "presupposes the very source and meaning of the life of the individual and of the covenanted community."[52] The prophet embodies the paradox of God's judgment vis-à-vis his sanctification of Israel as incarnated in the priesthood. Israel's ability to carry out self-criticism is symbolized by the prophets, but the carrying out is not an automatic process.

In contrast to Israel's structure to which the prophet is integral is the society without a prophet: the "mass society" presupposing technology and an elaborate division of labor. "In this milieu a crypto-authoritarianism exercises its force largely through anonymous controls that play upon anonymous, multi-personal and multi-grouped creatures who imagine they are free."[53] Formation and control of public opinion especially through the mass media create an "ethos of obedience." Thus, "radical prophetic or rational criticism of the authoritarian ethos or the social structure is throttled by the compulsive demand for security."[54] Such a society is in sharp contrast to the social model in which authority resides in free consensus through discussion, where prophetic criticism and creative conflict are encouraged.

While affirming God's self-manifestation to man through the orders of creation, nature, and human nature, Adams holds that none of these orders can be completely identified with God, " . . . with what is worthy of absolute loyalty or of absolute authority. This would be to give the finite an absolute status."[55] Thus, the use of structural analogy will not permit the maintenance of absolute authority within a finite structure.

In Adams' view, then, no individual or group can be considered the manifestation of divine authority. Any individual or group so doing would be pragmatically stating

---

[52] "The Social Import of the Professions," p. 4.

[53] "Authority and Freedom in a Mass Society," Report of the Fourteenth Congress of the International Association for Liberal Christianity and Religious Freedom, Oxford, August 1952 (The Hague: IARF Headquarters, 1952), p. 23.

[54] Ibid., p. 24.

[55] "Crystallizing Unitarian Beliefs," Outlines of lectures given at Lake Geneva Unitarian Summer Conference, 1942, p. 1 (mimeographed).

a doctrine of God which said, in effect, that ultimate authority is both individual and social. A profound respect for the dignity of the individual flows from the _imago dei_ symbol, correlates of which are respect for individual conscience and the abjuring of coercion. However, liberalism also maintains that the unique individual is only properly realized through cooperation with others. "The Unitarian Way is the way of open socionomy -- reliance upon divinely given resources and openness to truth openly arrived at. It is the way of discussion."[56]

Ecclesiology

Definition of Church

Adams' prevailing concern with institution manifests itself in a particularly rich body of writings on the church. Locating it within society, defining it, spelling out its functions and characteristics, Adams demonstrates a power of insight which goes beyond Unitarianism. His methodology has much in common with that of Tillich.[57] Observing the concrete and very human questions which arise about the church, he sets about answering them and, in so doing, develops an ecclesiology.

Adams' operational definition of church seems best expressed in a sermon entitled "We Wrestle Against Principalities and Powers." The church is for him "a community that is alert to the struggle against the distorting demonries of social and personal existence."[58] The church is "the House of the Interpreter" for personal and social life. He would assert "that wherever mercy and understanding are brought to birth, there is

---

[56]"Crystallizing Unitarian Beliefs," Outlines of lectures given at Lake Geneva Unitarian Summer Conference, 1942, p. 1 (mimeographed). While coercion is abjured as a principle, it may be resorted to in extreme circumstances.

[57]It is important to note here Tillich's method of correlation, starting with the human situation and determining the Christian answer. For Adams and Tillich alike the human predicament is grounded in the ontological, but the latter is discerned in the former.

[58]"We Wrestle Against Principalities and Powers," Sermon preached at First Parish, Cambridge, Mass., June 7, 1964, p. 4 (mimeographed).

the church, whether Christians have anything to do with
it or not."[59] This is not the institutional Christian
church as we know it, but a radical concept of church
which fits Adams' dialectical approach to reality and
his understanding of revelation. Although concerned
with the institutional church, Adams refuses, as we
shall see further on, to let it become an absolute value.

Carl Braaten, in writing about Tillich, mentions
one of the latter's seminal ideas which might well have
had an impact on Adams' broad understanding of church.
Tillich integrates the Logos doctrine into his theological system in such a way that it becomes a universal
principle of the divine self-manifestation, present beyond the boundaries of the church, "making it possible for
men in all religions and cultures to have a partial grasp
of the truth, a love of beauty and a moral sensitivity."[60]

A Functional Understanding

Adams and Tillich share a deeply functional understanding of church. Adams' earliest writings reveal his
preoccupation with the role of the church. In a 1927
sermon, he states that "unless the church can inspire in its
members a growing sensitiveness to sin it is a failure.
. . ."[61] However, a lively social life and welfare work
can never be equal to the task of getting man to realize
his potentialities and shortcomings owing to selfishness.
The church's function is to bring man to God, effecting
conversion and commitment. Central to this function is
the proclamation

> . . . that there is a creative, divine power
> working in the world, a power waiting to ac-
> complish the miracle of renewal according as
> men will permit it to do so, a power working
> for righteousness and also a power working

---

[59]Untitled sermon notes, early 1930's, p. 6.

[60]Carl Braaten, "Paul Tillich and the Classical Christian
Tradition," in A History of Christian Thought, Paul Tillich,
ed. Carl Braaten (New York: Touchstone Books, 1972), p.
xix. Adams' understanding of the Spirit, his pneumatology,
is very close to Tillich's Logos doctrine.

[61]"In Praise of Shame," Salem Evening News, May 2, 1927, p. 4.

for catastrophe, but a power that tends
toward the creation of liberty and community.[62]

Opposed to despair, the church proclaims a creative and
redemptive process which

. . . cuts across all class and race and
national, and creedal lines and preserves
a basis of community as well as a basis
for theonomous criticism. The message
therefore is a part of a universal creative
process, and it is a protest against any
tendency toward self-sufficiency or self-
absolutization.[63]

Bringing man to God requires certain functions of
the church; the church must provide a social context
which will facilitate the emergence of "a generally
accepted and progressively growing conception of the
nature of Reality. . . ."[64] Concomitantly, the church
should also function to find and use the means "which
will help him [man] to appropriate the resources that
make for good in himself or in his surroundings."[65]
If the liberal church is to be effective in assisting
man, it must give him the disciplines whereby he can
achieve adjustment and growth. The religious man needs
the stimulation and help of a group and a tradition:
interstimulation and cooperation will facilitate the
growth of man's relationship to God. "But more than
this, there must be, as in the spheres of art and government, socially agreed upon conventions which will
aid in the development of the characteristic virtues
and attitudes of religion."[66] For Adams, then, one of

---

[62]"Crystallizing Unitarian Beliefs," lectures 5-6, p. 2.

[63]Ibid.

[64]"Some Practical Applications," p. 31. See above,
Adams' understanding of Reality, pp. 37-39; 47-48.

[65]"Some Practical Applications," p. 32.

[66]Ibid., p. 33.

71

the primary functions of the church is public worship and prayer as indispensable means of grace; they constitute the substance of religious life.[67]

Adams' emphasis on the need for prayer and worship in the church appears to be contradicted by his doctrine of the church identified in terms of mercy and understanding.[68] He indicates that the church could be found almost anywhere, say in a communist collective, as long as mercy and understanding are present. Then he says prayer and worship are intrinsic to the church. How can these two views be reconciled?

Adams, the pneumatologist, understands the Spirit and the revelatory process as universal, present in diverse cultures and religions. Response to Spirit and revelation takes many forms, some explicitly and others implicitly religious. Adams, of course, is culturally rooted and is involved in a particular experience of church as institution. On this institutional level, he perceives the need for agreed upon conventions which maintain and develop religious identity. Public worship and prayer foster this sense of identity. Why? From a pragmatic point of view, the church is known by its actions; but Adams has more than a pragmatic view of the church. The primary function of the church is to bring man to God.[69] Thus, the transcendent reference point, God, which specifies the nature of the church, cannot be collapsed into a merely functional theory of stimulating mercy and understanding among people.

The church is present where mercy and understanding are alive, since these are qualities of redemption or salvation. And the church by its nature signifies redemption. But does this type of church necessarily eventuate into a church explicitly recognizing God as transcendent referent? Adams is not interested in that type of theological issue. What he is concerned with, characteristically, is his own cultural context. While this

---

[67]"Some Practical Applications," p. 34.

[68]See above, pp. 69-70.

[69]See above, p. 70.

context involves the Unitarian church as the one Adams identifies with institutionally, what he says about the church has similar implications for other churches taking God as explicit referent. The substance of the religious life for the Unitarian church (and others) is public worship and prayer because this church explicitly affirms God; and this affirmation must be explicitly made within the church. Once again, Adams comes across to us as a qualified pragmatist. He demands mercy and understanding of the church, but he sees the church as more than action. God is at its source.[70]

Membership

Adams espouses a radically lay community. He champions the Protestant doctrines of the priesthood of all believers. Thus, each person has access to the "ultimate resources" of religion and is responsible for the development of an explicit faith. But Adams also speaks of "the prophethood of all believers," a term original to him and one which points up very clearly his social concern. "The prophetic liberal church is the church in which all members share the common responsibility to attempt to foresee the consequences of human behavior (both individual and institutional). . . ."[71] The ethical mandate is thus not very far from his ecclesiological concerns. If the search for truth is essential to the church,[72] then, says Adams, minister and layperson alike must be free to pursue and express the truth about social reality as they see it. The church, for instance, must encourage its minister "to avail himself of the liberty of the Christian man, to make himself a well-informed and courageous spokesman of the best thought of his time. . . ."[73] If it does this, it will get prophecy.

The prophetic community has a precedent in the community founded by Jesus. With Jesus, the Kingdom of God broke into history and was uniquely manifest in Him and by His relationship with His community. Jesus' followers formed continuing intimate groups,

> . . . a social organization in which the
> power of the spirit, the power of love,

---

[70]This understanding impacts upon his ethics as well. See below, "The Theonomous Nature of Adams' Ethics," pp. 89-92.

[71]"The Prophethood of All Believers," p. 25.

[72]"The Tyranny of a Free Minister," p. 451.

[73]Ibid., p. 469.

could find organizational embodiment.
Moreover, in the concept Body of Christ,
they found a new ontological basis for
the working of the divine power that was
in Jesus, namely, the koinonia, a group
living a common life with Jesus Christ as
its head and informing power.[74]

The members of the Body of Christ are not just individuals
but groups of committed individuals. "There cannot be
Christian commitment without decision in Christian fellowship."[75] The continuing Reformation is in the cell group,
which cannot become the salt of the earth "unless it can
find its way to the underprivileged, the downtrodden, and
bring them into the loving bond of fellowship."[76] The
divine power works in and through participation in a be-
lieving fellowship.

Discipline, says Adams, functions as essential to
the ecclesiola's sense of self-identification. It is
necessary for the koinonia's vitality.

In the primary group alone can the counter-
models against the models of the world be
defined and made effective. The function
of discipline, then, is to provide the conditions under which the judging, transforming
power of God may be released.[77]

The church-within-church, the ecclesiola in ecclesia,
this primary community, is the soil which will nurture
intentional disciplines or what he calls the "vitalities
of the sect." Specifically, these include

. . . "pneumatic" fellowship in word and
sacrament, explicit faith, the identification of the adversary, achievement of consensus, the protection of the freedom of
the spirit, the definition of models, . . .
the practice of self-criticism of the group,

---

[74]"Theological Bases for Social Action," Journal of Religious Thought, VIII, No. 1 (1950-51), 6-21, using
article as reprint in Taking Time Seriously, p. 56.

[75]"Cell Groups and Social Action," Conference on Cell
Groups, Oct. 23, 1948, p. 15 (mimeographed).

[76]Ibid., p. 18.

[77]"The Place of Discipline in Christian Ethics," Crane
Review, IX, No. 3 (1967), p. 147.

the disciplined application of norms to
the personal life, family, work, politics
and business -- in short, the joining of
the priesthood and prophethood of all believers.[78]

Disciplines, thus, should create "an intimate community of memory and hope," one which encourages prophetic criticism and creative conflict, "that provides
cultural, religious, and ethical values and responsibilities and that releases redemptive powers in individual and society. . . ."[79]

Maintenance of the Church's identity will depend
on "the practical means by which a Christian group maintains its character and resists accommodation."[80] Adams
is concerned with a sense of discipline as the means that
opens the way for "the process in community out of which
the gifts and fruits of the spirit are engendered."[81]
The creation and recreation of community occur through
discipline in Christian ethics, through the dialogue
between spirit and law. One notes here Adams' dialectical approach to theological thinking in his counter-
balancing of spirit and law vis-a-vis the church.
"Spirit is subjective, inward, personal; law is objective,
external, impersonal. Spirit is original, vividly present,
transcendent; law is derivative, a precipitate from the
past, conditioned form."[82] Only dialogue will give both
tangible character and power. Spirit gives depth and
concern and life; law gives tangibility, order and direction to church life.

---

[78]"The Place of Discipline in Christian Ethics," Crane Review, IX, No. 3 (1967), p. 148.

[79]Summary for sociological section of Congress dealing with
Authority and Freedom in a Mass Society, in Report of the
Fourteenth Congress of the International Association for
Liberal Christianity and Religious Freedom, p. 24.

[80]"The Place of Discipline in Christian Ethics," Crane
Review, p. 138.

[81]Ibid., p. 145.

[82]Ibid.

75

The Prophetic Church

Several constant factors are operating in Adams'
approach to the church: a method involving theological and sociological categories which focus his dialectical approach to ethical thinking. This approach
is seen in his demand that the church be subject to
revelation and yet be relevant to social structures.
The transforming power of the koinonia, operant in all
areas of lay and ministerial life, is indicative of
Adams' faith in a "radically lay apostolate." He does
not restrict church or the Spirit to religious things.
In speaking of a belief in the laity he says "only by
being such [a radical lay apostolate] can it [the church]
offer promise of casting out the demons of the mass culture or (even within the church) of subverting the iron
laws of oligarchy."[83] The koinonia depends upon tradition, a sacramental group life and upon the unexpected
working of the divine spirit.

> . . . Just because of the complexity and sub-
> tlety of the mysterious working of the power
> of God 'his wonders to perform' the agent of
> healing and renewal must be the koinonia
> which nourishes and protects and responds to
> the diversities of gifts that come from the
> hand of God.[84]

The very agents for resisting accommodation are the laity
who act from within the cultural system and are the
koinonia at work.

The Church as Focus for Kingdom of God

Adams' understanding of the church is ordered by
his doctrine of the kingdom of God. There will always
be a tension between the concrete reality which is the
church, and God, the transcendent reality which is the
source of the church. "Fulfillment of the will of God
cannot be achieved within the visible church; and in
this sense the kingdom of God is suprahistorical."[85]

---

[83]"Changing Role of Ministry of Today: Sociological Factors and Theological Implications," c. 1950, p. 11.
(Mimeographed.) Adams' approach to ethical issues is
Christian at its base, open to secular insights, and
concerned about the world. See below, pp. 89 ff.

[84]Ibid.

[85]"The Ethical Reality and Function of the Church," p. 3.

To the extent that love and righteousness are found within the church, the kingdom is found there. The kingdom of God will embrace all creation in an ultimate unity. "Because God is already the ultimate ruler, the kingdom of God is the basis of whatever validity our moral striving may possess, and gives to the church its hope and strength."[86] The church is only a means to and a part of, the redemption of the world. The kingdom of God, ruling the hearts of men, is found "wherever faith, purity, love and obedient service reign."[87] God's kingdom, then, is an invisible bond among men which the church must make more explicit. This kingdom is present in the visible church only where community is attained and grounded in the love of Christ (agape) and empowered by the Holy Spirit.

For Adams, there can be no doctrine of the church without a doctrine of the kingdom.[88] The kingdom, likewise, is central to Adams' social ethics, for he affirms that "political metaphor aims at preventing the reduction of the social-ethical sphere to the exclusive realm of the individual. . ."[89] The symbol of the kingdom of God has a high degree of pragmatic meaningfulness. A political symbol, it has implications for the social-institutional sphere. It highlights the societal demands placed upon man by the covenant. Adams seeks to avoid a reductionist interpretation which views the kingdom as merely interior. The interiority of the kingdom is a necessary part of the symbol but not the only one. He feels that "the kingdom of heaven is within you," is a false translation. The better one is Cadbury's "the kingdom of heaven is available to you (among you)." The ontological reality of the kingdom is central to Adams' ecclesiology.

---

[86]"The Ethical Reality and Function of the Church," p. 3.

[87]Ibid. When Adams speaks of the church being present "wherever mercy and understanding are brought to birth," he is, I conclude, speaking of the kingdom as described here. See above, pp. 70, 72-73.

[88]For an understanding of Tillich's views on the kingdom of God and how they influenced Adams, see "Tillich's Interpretation of History," The Theology of Paul Tillich, ed. Charles W. Kegley and Robert W. Bretall (New York: Macmillan, 1952), pp. 302, 307, 308. Adams' understanding of the kingdom is very close to that of Tillich.

[89]"Is Marx's Thought Relevant to the Christian? A Pro-

God

The Meaning of God

Adams' doctrine of God has marked trinitarian features, for he views the symbolism of the Trinity as a viable way of expressing the nature of God. Only when Father, Son, and Spirit are known and loved together does the Christian come into contact with God himself.[90] In his essay on "The Ages of Liberalism" Adams describes the periodization of history into the Ages of Father, Son and Spirit as a way "to give a compact statement of the ways in which Liberal Christianity has come to terms with the principal foci of Christian faith. . . . The trinitarian periodization proposed is obviously a heuristic device."[91]

Always conscious of time and history, Adams views the nature of God from the perspective of social structure, historical event, and the significance of symbol vis-a-vis the particular time period. Thus Adams' trinitarian periodization, related to liberal Christianity, begins with the Spirit and then goes on to the Father and Son.

The Age of Spirit

In developing his heuristic of trinitarian periodization, Adams assigns to each "age" of liberalism a dominant moment which serves to determine the characterization of the period. The winds of the Spirit constitute the first "moment" of modern liberal Christianity, a "moment" which was recognized by the Radical Reformation of the sixteenth and seventeenth centuries. In the Anabaptist periodization of history, the Age of the Spirit is identified with the birth of the Church, Church seen as basically democratic due to the presence of the Spirit within all believers. Spiritualist periodizations, although not placing the above emphasis on the Church, are characterized by a progressive theory of revelation, the Third Era of History (their own era) being the outpouring of the Spirit.

---

testant View," Marx and the Western World, ed. Nicholas Lobkowicz (Notre Dame: Notre Dame Press, c. 1967), p. 380.

[90]"The Ages of Liberalism" p. 117.

[91]Ibid., p. 103.

Adams observes that the above conceptualizations
gave birth to a new era of freedom but an era which
also set some sects at war with others. Emphasis on
the Spirit gave rise as well to a new way of doing
ethics, for doing ethics in this era resulted in the
growth of a society based on democratic principles.
"A religious fellowship should rather be the place
where the members, respecting each other in mutual confidence, will hear from each other (and will test) what
the Holy Spirit prompts. . . ."[92] It is the Spirit, as
we have seen,[93] who symbolizes the radicality of the
Left Wing's Reformation just as the Spirit is the symbol uniting the church at Pentecost.

The Spirit is guardian of unity in diversity.
The gifts of the Spirit, for instance, are always sub-
ordinate to love for one another and the building up
of the church. While the Spirit's authority resides
in the apostles and prophets, "the community is a pneuma-
tocracy in which the members test and acknowledge the
bearers and workings of the Spirit."[94] Such openness to
the Spirit also results in mystical tendencies and a
view which is trans-Christian in attitude, an understanding congenial to Adams.

The Age of the Spirit, in Adams' thought, brings in
its train the demand for radical laicism and the voluntary church. The Spirit is responsible for the dispersion of power and responsibility in the church. Pragmatic theory and structural analogy enter in here since
Adams sees symbol and practice as closely related. As
a case in point, Adams views the development of democracy, particularly in England, as having been aided by
this conception of the Spirit.[95]

He considers the effects of the Spirit to be: freedom of conscience, Congregational polity, democratic
political movements.

---

[92]"The Liberal Christian Looks at Himself," p. 3. This
understanding, as we shall see in Chapter Four, has a
strong influence on the way he does ethics.

[93]See above, pp. 64-65.

[94]"The Ages of Liberalism," p. 105.

[95]Ibid., p. 107-08. Adams here notes that this analogy
is not definitely proven.

. . . Indeed, a new conception of autonomous
Christian personality supported by "inner
light," the rejection of coercion in belief
and in the shaping of public policy, the
principle of the consent of the governed,
a pluralistic conception of the churches and
of society emerge, or are newly emphasized in,
the Age of the Spirit.[96]

Conversely, the Age of the Spirit produces unhealthy ex-
tremes and misinterpretations of the Spirit: fanaticism
and authoritarianism, unrestrained individualism, radical
congregationalism. All of these foreclose the possibility
of vital tension between individuals and their churches
and between local churches and other churches. The Holy
Spirit in Adams' interpretation is not understood in
dogmatic terms but rather from a historical, pragmatic
perspective embracing his principle of analogy. This
conceptualization has important implications for Christian
social ethics. One begins to see that criteria for knowing the nature of God are closely connected to an understanding of human behavior.

The Age of the Father

The Age of Reason, the Enlightenment, manifests for
Adams the characteristics of the Age of the Father. "Reason and common sense were now to be the guide."[97] In the
Age of the Father, "religious autonomy" evolved into
"inner light" as the guiding principle; man comes to seek
"truth and justice written into the structure of the uni-
verse and inherent in the mind and conscience. . . ."[98]

As with the Age of the Spirit, the understanding of
the Father produced its own extreme: man's freedom and
responsibility show that belief in original sin is ir-
rational. Jesus is simply an example of extraordinary
humanity. Fatherhood is equated with Godhead and the
tension within the Trinity is dissolved.

---

[96]"The Ages of Liberalism," p. 108.

[97]Ibid., p. 110.

[98]Ibid.

The Fatherhood of God and the doctrine of creation are powerful symbols understood in terms of their impact on and relation to a historical era and social structure. Doctrines of natural rights, social contract, historical consciousness, empiricism and technology develop in and are stimulated by the symbolism of the Father. Yet even these developments bear their own dehumanizing aspects. Thus, doctrines of God must remain in tension and under scrutiny. A litmus test for their validity is the consequences belief has for human interaction. Adams' theological understanding impels him to an ethical one which has important secular concerns.

> Paradox is evident also in the antimony that emerges between the highly creative movement of liberation from arbitrary restriction upon human freedom and the new impediments to human fulfillment that issues from the bourgeois use of "reason" for the manipulation of natural and human resources (in the name of automatic harmony).[99]

The structurally analogous implications of Adams' doctrine of the Father are spelled out in an essay on "The Love of God." Adams states that it might be difficult for an observer to discern differences between the old Lutheran and Quaker words about love of God, but that differences become clear if one studies the respective conceptions of family. On the one hand, Lutherans sanctioned the patriarchal family with an authoritarian father as vicar of God in a home where love of God among the children brought (supposedly) instant, unquestioning obedience. And quite distinctively, the Quaker group opted for a permissive, persuasive family atmosphere. "In general, then we may say that the meaning of a religious or ethical imperative becomes concrete when we see it in relation to the social context in which it operates."[100]

The Age of the Son

Adams, the dialectical theologian, finds the nineteenth and twentieth century emphasis on the Son an effective counterbalance to the abstract tendencies peculiar

---

[99]"The Ages of Liberalism," p. 111.

[100]"The Love of God," in The Meaning of Love, ed. Ashley Montagu (New York: Julian Press, 1953), p. 246.

to the Age of the Father. Jesus as mediator gives a highly specific Christian character to "the God of the Enlightenment," who, as Adams understands him, "came short of being the God of their [Christian] worship, the Father of Jesus Christ -- the redeemer God as well as the creator."[101]

Liberal Christianity's openness to Christology stems, in Adams' view, from a need for specificity within the Christian tradition,[102] but also from contemporary analyses of man. Criticisms from orthodoxy, Neo-orthodoxy, and secular sources such as Marx, Nietzsche, and Freud have forced the liberal to abandon his unrealistic approach to history. The Age of the Father, according to Adams "had made the primary point of contact between God and man the latter's natural goodness rather than his limitations."[103] A rebirth of interest in Luther and Calvin, along with the development of existentialism, stimulated an awareness of man's need for redemption.

> . . . It is through Jesus that God's reality, his power, his judgment, his love become uniquely available to the Christian. Indeed, through him and the cross man becomes sharply conscious of his separation from God and his need for grace.[104]

Adams pictures Jesus as seeking a higher form of grace for man than that available in the Law of Moses or of the Pharisees. Jesus permits "a more pervasive and creative kind of love" to flow into human society.[105] The Christian church is brought to birth by Jesus as a

---

[101]"The Ages of Liberalism," p. 113.

[102]Adams is critical of the early Tillich (pre-1945) because the latter allows the category of the unconditioned to replace any developed Christology. Cf. Paul Tillich's Philosophy of Culture, Science and Religion, p. 274.

[103]"The Ages of Liberalism," p. 115.

[104]Ibid., p. 115-116.

[105]"The Evil That Good Men Do," Sermon preached at the University of Chicago, May 17, 1942, p. 4. Also in Voices of Liberalism: 2 (Boston: Beacon Press, 1948).

new kind of human association. Thus, the symbol of Jesus has structural consequences and positive pragmatic effects. An understanding of Jesus is a concern of Christians because "they have seen in him the cosmos achieving strength and abundance of expression. . . ."[106]

Love for Adams, is "fullness of being, . . . the union of that which is separated,"[107] and Jesus expresses the fullness of being. Adams sees Jesus on the cross as the lover who unites that which is separated. Through his sacrifice, "the ultimate meaning and destiny of man is expressed."[108] Jesus represents the essence of unification through love, for he is "a highly individual person who formed a community of persons, bringing together that which was separated. . . ."[109] Moreover, he formed this community through "the free and independent expression of individuality reaching out to individuality, rising through self-sacrifice and self-giving, to that union with others which is fulness of being. . . ."[110]

Although there is a uniqueness in Jesus, Adams sees manifestations of being's fullness in other aspects of creation such as music and art.[111] Protestant confidence is placed in divine power which Adams equates with the Lord of History, yet this power manifests itself in various aspects of civilization, which civilization is not to become the object of our confidence. Again, the dialectical, tension-filled nature of Adams' understanding of reality and his consistent approach to secularity are manifest in his Christology.

---

[106] "God is Love," Sermon preached at Meadville Seminary, Nov. 7, 1947, p. 7 (typewritten).

[107] Ibid., p. 7.

[108] Ibid., p. 8. See also "Christian Vocation: An Examination of the Political Symbolism of Biblical Faith," Lecture at Denison University, c. 1955, p. 11 (typewritten).

[109] "God is Love," p. 8.

[110] Ibid.

[111] "Basic Causes of Progress and Decay in Civilization," Orientations in Religious Education, ed. P.H. Lotz (New York: Abingdon-Cokesbury, 1950), p. 34. Pagination used here is from the article as contained in Taking Time Seriously, p. 34.

83

Adams, in a later essay, "Changing Frontiers:
Vanishing and Emerging," views Christology from yet
another perspective. Why have Jesus' followers given
him a special place and function in the order of being?
Adams points to several reasons: his inwardness; love
of persons; audacious liberation from the bondage of
tradition; confidence in the Kingdom that grows of itself in reaction to human response; his faithfulness
to his unique mission; his forming of a new community;
his trust in God's mercy. Through all of these elements,
Jesus "has made and makes more readily known and available to us the powers that can release from self-worship
and give us constant renewal of life and love."[112]

Jesus for Adams is not simply the leader of men.
Christ as the "power of the New Being" mediates God's
grace in a unique way. It is the consequences of who
Jesus is and the nature of the community he formed that
stimulate this Christology. Adams gives high priority
to community and thus he cannot fail to give importance
to Jesus. This does not mean a simplistic return to
ancient categories. Adams sees the hermeneutic involved.
Categories and confessions are creatures of human thought.
They require translation for present-day relevance. And
in the case of the persons of the Trinity, understanding
who they are is dependent upon a knowledge of the types
of community men form.

Father, Son, and Spirit must then be reinterpreted
in each age, for penetrating and going beyond traditional
categories is integral to Adams' belief in the ongoing
nature of revelation. Moreover, it is important to realize
that from a dialectical viewpoint none of the Ages can be
separated because none of the persons of the Trinity can
be known in isolation. "Each of the Unitarianisms needs
the others. Only when taken together can they express
the dynamic tension in God himself, the Creator and the
Re-Creator."[113]

Adams expresses this tension in his doctrine of God,
while at the same time clearly delineating the monotheistic
nature of his belief, when he states:

I do not believe in the supernatural as the
latter is interpreted by most people. There

---

[112]"Changing Frontiers: Vanishing and Emerging," pp. 5
and 6.

[113]"The Ages of Liberalism," p. 117.

84

is no God existing somewhere as a Supreme
Being who created and rules the world in
accordance with the suppositions of those
who believe in what is (by way of attack
upon it) called side-by-side metaphysics.
. . . I think that ultimately you as well
as I have to choose between certain basic
possible interpretations of existence and
meaning. . . . Exclusive monotheism finds
the ultimate in a majestic power and purpose that are partially realized in everything that exists, but it does not identify
the ultimate with the existent or with any
section of reality. Thus its God is ever-
present but can be got into no one's pos-
session; nor is its God ever exhausted by
the actual -- there is always something
beyond; thus prophetic criticism "from
beyond" is indispensable. Monotheism combines the concreteness of polytheism (cf.
prophetic insistence on God's purpose as
taking place in time and history and community and as frustrated by injustice
which brings judgment) with the unity
striven for in pantheism (cf. the omni-
potence of God in monotheism which means
that no part of reality is completely without meaning or completely at odds with the
purpose of God, else it would not be able
to exist; the universality of natural and
moral law also illustrate this unity).
Its defect: a defect in human nature,
namely that as Hume says, man's natural
tendency is to be a polytheist. Its merit:
it recognizes life and possibility of
growth of meaning as gifts to be boldly
and humbly shared. It asserts that God is
never exhausted and especially that he is
never completely and finally manifest in
any particular section or moment of reality. It demands the prophetic criticism
that polytheism resists. It takes time
and history seriously. It envisages the
holiness and majesty of God as always
present but as never tangible in the sense
that they become "possessions"; and since
they can never be "possessions" of men,
human ethical norms as well as accomplishments must not be absolutized. . . . Thus

the divine is the support and the demand
for meaningful existence, offering the
concomitant threat that is merited by
all pretensions of grasping man who turns
away from the giver of good to "construct"[114]
lucrative devices of self-salvation.

The Relevance of Adams' Theological
Presuppositions for the Christian Ethicist

This chapter has dealt with Adams' theological beliefs that have a direct bearing on his ethics and on
Christian ethics as a field of endeavor.

1. Within Adams' theological framework his orientation to sociology provides direction for the ethicist
seeking relevance and meaning in the contemporary context. An openness to the secular and the sacred, understood to be in a dialectical relationship, overcomes a
need to choose between the two in developing a viable
Christian ethic. More specifically, the sacred/secular
motif, is exemplified in Adams' heuristic of pragmatic
theory and structural analogy. These conceptual tools
provide the ethicist with categories that relate theory
and practice in a close fashion. Theology, therefore,
does not evaporate into the abstract but provides a
concrete foundation for the doing of ethics.

2. In dealing with the theological category of
revelation, Adams portrays the ethicist as one who seeks
to know communally God's self-affirmation in all facets
of human experience. He thus provides several avenues
of approach for the Christian ethicist seeking to know
the will of God when ordering what the good is.

Authority, an important theological and ethical
category, flows from his theory of revelation. Authority wells up from the community through communal consensus and discernment under the dialectic of Scripture
and the present day situation. Although no group possesses absolute authority, Adams, as we saw earlier, is

---

[114]This is in the fragment of a letter which could be dated
around 1942-43. It bears strong resemblance to Adams'
notes on "Crystallizing Unitarian Belief." Adams' use of
trinitarian symbolism is an exception within the Unitarian
tradition. It is, however, indicative of his freedom from
the dogmatisms of liberal schools of thought as well as of
more traditional ones.

not naive about the necessity of using force in some situations. He presents the ethicist with a complex but meaningful understanding: history is ambiguous and overrun by demonic powers, yet the authority to deal with these powers flows from communal consenses and persuasion. The latter are not absolutes and may demand the use of force.

3. While the institutional church does not have an absolute value for Adams, he presents it as an integral part of the God-man relationship, effecting conversion and commitment. I would conclude that, for Adams, Christian ethics cannot be done without a sense of the church and the churches, all under the criterion of the kingdom. The ecclesiola in ecclesia seems especially important for developing an adequate ethic, for here prophetic criticism can flourish, nourished by communal support, consensus, and prayer.

4. Adams offers a trinitarian doctrine of God which has important ethical implications. Furthermore, God is both immanent and transcendent; neither pole of that dialectic can be tampered with without affecting the type of ethics one does. His understanding of the Trinity receives its clarity from the historical contextualizing that Adams brings to bear on the symbols of Father, Son, and Spirit. Criteria for understanding the persons of the Trinity are shaped by ethical demands. Here is a clear example of Adams' pragmatic theory joined to an ontologically founded belief in God. The Christian ethicist will find this a valuable principle of interpretation for ethics directed to God and man.

We now turn directly to the formulation of his Christian ethics, the groundwork for which has been laid in the first three chapters of this book.

87

CHAPTER IV

JAMES LUTHER ADAMS: CHARACTERISTICS OF HIS ETHICS

The Theonomous Nature of Adams' Ethics

Theological presuppositions have a direct bearing
on Adams' ethical thought. To deal with such presuppositions in a separate chapter without explaining
their relevance for Adams' ethics would be to misrep-
resent his approach. Adams insists on maintaining an
integral relation between ethics and theology. Ethics
"is faith seeking understanding in the realm of moral
action. . . . In its practical outcome, it is 'faith
active through love' . . . ."[1]   Adams' ethics are
more specifically, then, Christian theistic ethics.
They can, however, be characterized even more sharply.
I see his ethics as theonomous, theonomous in the sense
that Adams assigns to the word. When Adams uses the
word theonomous, he utilizes it as a theological category with no specific application to his own thought.
However, I see the word theonomous as an appropriate
description of Adams' ethics, with its reliance on the
best features of autonomous and heteronomous approaches.
Characterizing a theonomous approach to doing ethics are
the following "principles" of theonomy laid down by Adams
in his "Glossary":

1. Man is related to a given reality -- God;

2. Through the power and creativity of His being,[2]
God is the source and support of human existence;

3. God not only supports existence but calls for
conformity to certain conditions of existence.[3]

---

[1] "Ethics," A Handbook of Christian Theology, edited by
Marvin Halverson (New York: Meridian Books, 1958), p. 111.

[2] In a previously cited paper prepared with James Bissett
Pratt for a Congregational-Unitarian-Universalist meeting at
Yale in 1940, Adams speaks of the necessity of God's grace
for man. "The freedom that man derives from God cannot manifest itself with deepest meaning or in richest fulfillment unless it is integrally related to the creative power upon which
all existence depends. . . ." "The Congregational Idea," p. 5.

[3] Adams defines the term theonomy in "Crystallizing Unitarian
Beliefs," lectures he gave at a summer conference in 1942.

When Adams defines ethics, he incorporates into his
definition the above underlying characteristics of theonomy. Ethics become the arena in which discernment of
man's relation to God is clarified. Ethics, for Adams,
is reflection on human conduct and has the following
aims:

> . . . clarity and consistency with respect
> to the ground and goal, the motives and
> norms, the means and consequences of right
> action conceived of as the response to and
> the working of the grace of God.[4]

Adams' ethics affirms that right action is a response
to and a manifestation of God's grace, which grace is synonymous with God's power.[5]   God's grace and power are
synonymous; but these two categories must be related to
a third in Adams' thinking, namely, God's judgment. This
is so because God's power is the means whereby "man's
sinful alienation from Him" is overcome. Such power implies judgment concerning man's alienation. But this very
judgment is also the work of God, His grace calling the
person to the fulfillment of his "personal and social
salvation from the powers of evil."[6]   Thus judgment and
grace are two perspectives or elaborations of God's power
which cannot be separated.[7]

Adams leaves no doubt that he is most at home with this
term. The description given above is based on his lengthy
definition in the "Glossary of Terms" prepared for the conference. Adams' religious liberalism and theological beliefs clearly support his understanding of the term. See
as well, Adams' essay "Tillich's Concept of the Protestant
Era," esp. pp. 293 ff, where he deals at length with theonomy as used by Tillich.

[4] "Ethics," p. 111.

[5] Ibid., p. 111, 114.

[6] Ibid., p. 111.

[7] Adams incorporates the concept of authority, a concept
that is found in heteronomous ethics. But Adams rejects
any heteronomous ethics, the authoritarian type exemplified in fundamentalist acceptance of scriptural authority
and in some aspects of Roman Catholicism. See "Glossary
of Terms." However, the fact that God makes demands on man
underlines what Adams calls a "limited autonomy: man is

Flowing from his emphasis on social ethics and
social structural problems, Adams speaks of God's
power, manifested as grace which flows through the
sacraments and as judgment which is the end product of
prophecy. It is interesting to note how he speaks of
sacramental media as being where divine power is seen
as present in given social realities or patterns.[8]
The church or state would be examples. But divine power
is also present in prophetism "which sees the divine
power primarily in the demand for personal and social
decision in the name of the coming holy community."[9]
The two aspects of God's power thus manifest themselves
most clearly in the social realm where God supports our
social interrelatedness but where our actions in society
are eschatologically judged.

Another characteristic further underlines the
theonomous nature of Adams' ethics. He uses the word
socionomy as an important aspect of religion. He maintains:

> The Unitarian Way is the way of open socionomy --
> reliance upon divinely given resources and open-
> ness to truth openly arrived at. It is the way
> of discussion, and the discussion is never fin-
> ally closed. There the spirit of the Lord is,
> there is liberty and community.[10]

Adams' concern for ethics, especially the social dimensions of them, is closely connected with an understanding
of the social means whereby ethical decisions are reached.

Adams does ethics within a specifically Christian
context. This must be said while remembering his respect
for non-Christian, non-theistic, secular ethics,[11] a respect
which is due to his understanding of the Spirit and
revelation.[12] The Christian dimension in Adams is further

---

held to be free and responsible to make his own decisions."
"Glossary of Terms." The power of God's creativity depends
on man's response to that power.

[8]"Ethics," p. 112.

[9]Ibid.

[10]Outline for "The Source of Authority," lecture delivered
as part of "Crystallizing Unitarian Beliefs."

[11]See above, pp. 78-80.

[12]See above, pp. 59-66.

reinforced by the symbol of the kingdom, which likewise
manifests God's grace and calls for our response. The
kingdom has entered time through Jesus' proclamation
and grows of itself, but it demands repentance.[13]

The Qualified Pragmatism of Adams' Ethics

Pragmatism, understood as a concern for the behavioral consequences of belief, characterizes Adams' ethics.
But his pragmatism is qualified by a dialectical understanding. Just as God's call and man's response are related for Adams, pragmatism is aligned with strongly held
beliefs and ideas in his thought. Consequences are not
the sole determinant of action. Theology cannot be collapsed into ethical demands for Adams.

This reduction is illustrated by Braithwaite's
conception of the meaning of Christianity as
an agapeistic way of life. An analogous reduction is to be observed in the Marxist attempt to transform metaphysics into social
criticism. In this view, metaphysics is only
a hidden social theory; more precisely stated,
it is only ideology.[14]

Qualified pragmatism informs all of his ethical thought.
It is, thus, an epistemological characteristic best understood by seeing how it informs his ethics.

We have encountered Adams' pragmatism in his pragmatic theory of meaning,[15] by which he holds that the
meaning of any belief is to be ascertained by examining
the behavioral activity of those professing the belief.
Consequences ought not be the sole determinants of action,
but should be examined as reflections of peoples' belief
statements. Adams' pragmatic theory should not be con-
strued to mean he is simply an observer of consequences in

---

[13]See above, pp. 76-78. Rudolf Otto strongly influenced
Adams when the latter was in Germany. Otto's The Kingdom
of God and the Son of Man, in particular, is a factor in
shaping Adams' ethics. Tillich's ontological orientation
is also evident in Adams' discussion of the kingdom as a
reality in and of itself.

[14]"The Use of Symbols," p. 125.

[15]See above, pp. 55-59.

order to academically define beliefs. He brings criteria such as respect for mutuality and the enhancement
of community and human rights to his consideration of
consequences. His pragmatism is informed by values
which clarify the original meaning, the consequences of
which are observed. Furthermore, he understands that
"the consequences of religious belief will depend largely
upon the distribution of power. . . ."[16] This is an important qualification of pragmatism and presumes an evaluation of power structures. For example, because consequences depend on power "no one configuration of authority
and power can be trusted."[17] In a monolithic social system, for instance, the dominant religious belief will
have monolithic consequences.

Lastly, no one ethical idea is final. As a result,
Adams maintains that:

> . . . the consequences of religious belief
> under a sovereign God must always be a re-
> jection of idolatry before any one ethical
> idea and a promotion of "free trade" and
> tension among ideals. . . . We confront
> the obligation to pursue simultaneously
> the opposite virtues of freedom and order,
> freedom and equality, participation and
> privacy, justice and mercy.[18]

Not only is his pragmatism qualified by an understanding
of the power which produces consequences, it is qualified
as well by an injunction against the idolatry of one
ethical idea. This latter position is certainly not surprising in view of his strong dialectical sense.

The Personal and Social
Dimension of Adams' Ethics

Man is called to respond to the power of God. He
responds as an individual, and, as we have seen, within
a community.[19] Moreover, all aspects of existence are

---

[16]I will return to Adams' understanding of power in Chapter
Five.

[17]"The Use of Symbols," p. 136.

[18]Ibid., p. 137.

[19]See above, Adams' principles of religious liberalism, pp.
34-48.

involved. Why? God's power or grace is manifest in
reality consisting of two poles: the totality of man's
environment (theocentric pole) and man's response to
that environment (anthropocentric pole). There is no
part of life exempt from ethical concern or scrutiny because man's response occurs within the context of a
total environment. As a result his ethical method has
many dimensions: ontological assumptions, pragmatic
theory of meaning, historical analysis, sociological and
psychological theory, and theological understanding.

The Demand for Community

An ethic of individual responsibility within society arises from the human experience of and demand for
community.[20] Man comes to know God through experience
and response, both of which are shaped in this community.
Dipolar reality forms the basis for such a position.
Thus, for Adams "every personal problem is a social problem and every social problem is a personal problem."[21]
His ethics, therefore, are at one and the same time personal and social.

The ground of meaningful community is God's love
which he defines as "the divine initiative issuing a
call to freedom and obedience and fellowship."[22] God's
love, then, is his power and his grace. History receives its direction from man's effort to create community but it is God's power, or agape, which alone can
reconcile and reunite man.[23] The interaction of the
personal and social is placed squarely under the Christian paradigm of love.

The Need for Institutions

Community and responsibility are concretized in
institutions within society. "The meaning of the religious-ethical idea of agape becomes clear only when

---

[20]Adams defines responsibility as "response to that divine,
self-giving, sacrificial love which creates and continually
transforms a community of persons." "Our Responsibility
in Society," p. 45.

[21]Ibid., p. 46.

[22]Ibid.

[23]Ibid.

we determine the habits, personal and institutional, which follow from it."[24] Pragmatic theory, therefore, reinforces Adams' concern for the personal and social elements of ethics. Structural analogy and his under- standing of symbols impact upon this demand for com- munity in his ethics, since "differences between the conceptions of God become evident in the differing con- ceptions of society and of social responsibility."[25] Adams contends that the love of God becomes fully clear and relevant only "when we know what it means for in- stitutional behavior, when we know what kind of family or economic system, or political order it demands."[26] The social context makes the ethical imperative con- crete. For Adams, then, the context of ethical decision- making and the validity of personal ethics rests solely within a communal setting. While personal and social ethics must operate in tandem, it is the communal sense of these ethics that is crucial for him.

In drawing the above conclusion, I want to make it clear that Adams does not accept the Communist credo of institutional transformation as the cure to man's social and personal ills.[27] He denies the possibility of a utopia in which a classless, conflict-free society will obtain. Adams' religious liberalism informs his belief as to the dialectical nature of transformation: insti- tutional and personal renewal exist in relation to each other. Human nature, as Adams sees it, is incomplete, always demanding consensus, at times coercion, and de- cision-making. Communism envisions a future lacking in conflict. To Adams this would spell the end of freedom and diversity, concomitants of consensus and decision- making. Thus, Adams' concern for the social context of man's life is not based on a theological naivete about the limitless possibilities of man. "From a Christian perspective, pride of prestige, individual good before common good, will obtain regardless of the nature of social institutions."[28] Therefore, personal and social transformation go together.

---

[24]"Our Responsibility in Society," p. 48.

[25]Ibid., p. 50.

[26]"The Love of God," p. 246.

[27]"Liberal Christianity and Modern Social Problems," pp. 23-24.

[28]"Is Marx's Thought Relevant to a Christian?", p. 385.

The Personal Dimension

The Christian view is that God is Lord of History but also of personal life. There must be corporate and individual fear of God and respect for His Lordship over institutional and personal life. Adams, nevertheless, is wary of a Kierkegaardian spirituality which would overemphasize the personal element in ethics. The Kierkegaardian approach is pietistic "in the sense that it tries to find the meaning and vocation of life primarily in the existence of the individual and in the realm of its person-to-person relations."[29]

While not placing a major emphasis upon it, Adams is nevertheless concerned with personal identity, notably in the areas of greatest need: diffusion and rigidity of personality. Here, again, his dialectic is operative, a dialectic which is deeply involved in his consideration of personality growth. "The formed self requires structure, and if this structure is to grow and become relevant to changing situations, it must be a dynamic structure."[30] Hence the role of opportunity, choice and decision in shaping self-identity: each has a role in shaping the self, as does its development within the social context.

> The growth and improvement of sensitivity and of self-identity requires the sharing that is possible only in community, in a fellowship that provides the opportunity for participative enjoyment, for mutual correction, and for implementation in the life of the society at large.[31]

For Adams, it is the group that makes history. The depth of our sensitivity and commitment is closely associated with, in fact, determined by, the groups with which we associate. "It is through group participation that sensitivity and commitment to values are given institutional expression; it is through groups that social power is organized."[32] Adams' strong emphasis on the relation of

---

[29] "Changing Frontiers: Vanishing and Emerging," p. 9.

[30] "Centerstance: An Essay on the Purpose of a Liberal Arts Education," The Liberal Context, II (Winter 1962), p. 10.

[31] Ibid., p. 11.

[32] Ibid.

individual to group will be further clarified in a fifth chapter dealing with the voluntary association, a working example of Adams' ethics.

Adams' ethics cannot be understood without such a consideration of the social element, for he is strongly critical of any religion or system of ethics which stresses the personal over the social dimension of man. He criticizes the belief that individual regeneration within the immediate personal milieu is the one thing necessarily demanded by the Christian religion. "In short, the return to religion [in the 1950's] is primarily a middle-class phenomenon that does not call in question its own social presuppositions."[33]

If time, history, and community are central to biblical understanding, it stands to reason that the Christian cannot simply accept his or her social presuppositions or sanctify the status quo. Once again, the pragmatic social meaning of doctrine must be faced. Adams cautions, however, that the pragmatic social meaning, though essential to the vitality of Christianity, does not exhaust the meaning of the religious belief. "The individual is something more than a member of society. He stands directly before God and he has an inner life that relates him to God and to other men in a deeper sense than is articulated in tangible institutional patterns."[34] Again and again, the tension or dialectical elements of personal and social ethics appear in Adams' thought.

The Dialectic Between Personal and Social Ethics

Adams' sensitivity to rationalization and ideological barriers is seen in his attack on any doctrine of vocation that is narrowed to personal calling and responsibility.[35] A typical justification for such an attitude is found in the need to avoid "distractions" which would affect the quality of one's work.[36] Such sins of omissions committed

---

[33]"Taking Time Seriously: An Approach to the Theology of Political Responsibility," Address at Penn State, 1960, p. 4 (typewritten).

[34]Ibid., p. 15.

[35]Adams' understanding of the individual's relation to God brings this out. See his doctrine of God, esp. pp. 147 ff.

[36]"Our Responsibility in Society," p. 44.

by social eunuchs are sins for which "the Hitlers of any age or community are grateful."[37] In Adams' eyes, an emphasis on personal salvation carries with it an implicit assumption

> that the institutional patterns are essentially adequate and also the assumption that individual regeneration within the immediate personal milieu is one thing necessarily demanded by the Christian religion.[38]

Adams sees personal and social salvation as interactive, and this vision is strongly influenced by the social sciences. There is no doubt, however, that his theological presuppositions also influence this dialectical sense of ethics that he espouses.[39]

In order to conceptualize this personal/social dialectic[40] Adams not only relies on social scientific analysis but also on theological investigation. The latter affirms community as intrinsic to man's existence.[41]

---

[37]"Our Responsibility in Society," p. 45.

[38]"Taking Time Seriously: An Approach to the Theology of Political Responsibility," p. 4.

[39]Adams' understanding of revelation as an ongoing process relies upon an understanding of the interaction between the person and his social context. See above, pp. 64-65. I think this sense of person and society in Adams is evident in my discussion of Adams and Neo-orthodoxy on pp. 27-32. Furthermore, authority in Adams' thought depends upon the tension between individual and community. See above, pp. This same thrust is found in his ecclesiology which emphasizes the prophetic character of churchly participation. The individual is responsible for society. See above, pp.

[40]See his discussion of the individual and the group in "Freud, Mannheim and the Liberal Doctrine of Man." In this article, Adams sees Mannheim reinforcing his understanding of utopia. As with Adams, Mannheim rejects Marxist utopianism because it lacks any sense of self-correction and is naive about humankind's tendency to self-absolutization. Yet Adams affirms "the courageous dynamic of what Mannheim calls 'utopian' (i.e., progressive) action. Faith in the possibility of achieving human fulfillment and community must be maintained." "Freud, Mannheim, and the Liberal Doctrine of Man," p. 109. This utopianism correlates well with Adams' understanding of the kingdom. See above, pp. 76-77.

[41]See above, Adams' principle of community, pp. 39-46.

98

It [Liberal Christianity] holds that God is
the Lord of the personal life as well as the
Lord of History, that every personal problem
is a social problem and every social problem
a personal problem. The divine and the demonic struggle against each other in both of
these dimensions of existence which are
linked together.[42]

Adams is concerned that neither individual nor group
is emphasized to the neglect of the other.

For Adams "the decisive differences between conceptions of the love of God become most clear when we
determine the social-institutional implications of
these conceptions."[43] Personal piety and political
piety only exist dialectically. Thus,

. . . . if any individual's or group's religious belief does not have any positive
effect upon these dimensions [the social
organization of the community, the family,
business, church, state] of his life and
upon the life of the community, then in
these respects the individual or the group
do not take time and history and community
seriously.[44]

Adams cautions that the individual must be considered as far more than a member of society. After
all, Adams comments, the individual has a personal
inner life and is related to God in a way that trans-
cends institutional patterns.[45] This tension Adams
sees between individual consciousness and communal
solidarity is an important theme in contemporary religious and sociological literature, a theme Adams
is familiar with in both fields.[46] There is a state

---

[42] "Liberal Christianity and Modern Social Problems," p. 24.

[43] "The Love of God," p. 234.

[44] "Our Responsibility to Society," p. 15.

[45] Ibid.

[46] Ibid., p. 16. On this theme of individual and society,
see also "The Evolution of My Social Concern."

of tension between individual and social existence that Adams sees as integral to human life -- a true dialectic since both the individual and the community are necessary to the definitions of each other. Person and community are not simply functions of each other. "On the one hand, the individual shares alienation and guilt with the community in its defection from the covenant. On the other, the individual possesses an integrity that must be protected."[47]

Humans are, for Adams, associational. They are understood by the types of associations formed and by the relationship between the voluntary and involuntary associations to which they belong and in which they participate.[48] I think Adams' emphasis on the types of associations formed and their purposes gives body to his understanding of man's social nature. His pragmatic sense, qualified as it is, flows from his sense of community.[49] This pragmatism[50] which focuses on institutional consequences of behavior highlights the different associational aspects of each person's life. Family, civic, professional, religious associations, as well as issue-oriented ones, are necessary, but each has a special orientation. To say man is communal necessitates differentiation of associational activity. Adams' qualified pragmatic associationalism reinforces this differentiation and asks ethical questions about man's involvement in this type of activity.

---

[47]"Contributions of Occidental Religions to Cultural Understanding," Proceedings of the IXth International Congress for the History of Religions (Tokyo: Maruzen, 1960), p. 731.

[48]It was Otto von Gierke's Genossenschaftsrecht which was influential in rooting Adams' lifelong conviction about the necessity of seeing both personal and social aspects of life. See "The Evolution of My Social Concern," pp. 18-19. This entire address is valuable as a statement of Adams' understanding of personal/social ethics. On this, see also, "Human Nature and the Nature of History," transcript of speech at May Meeting of American Unitarian Association, 1961, especially pp. 14 ff.

[49]See above, pp. 39-46.

[50]See above, pp. 55 ff., 92 ff.

Nevertheless, the very differentiation in modern society which allows for pluralism in associational activity and behavior is, in Adams' mind, ambiguous in value since "it is precisely within this differentiated, pluralistic society that the individual can give devotion to one cluster of values [i.e., personal ones] to the neglect of other fundamental and more embracing values and responsibilities [i.e., social justice]."[51] However, Adams does not seek a return to pastoral communities. Rather, he insists upon a heightened awareness of tendencies inherent in the structure of modern society.

Political Symbolism:
The Context for Christian Ethics

Covenant and Social Concern

Adams associates with the political symbol of the covenant certain qualities he sees as essential to the doing of ethics. This symbol points to and interprets the existence of an entire people. "Political symbolism refers to a people who have some kind of structural relationship to each other. It refers to the institutional framework within which individual existence appears."[52]

Adams' ethics, though open to secular thought, are grounded in the Scriptures; he chooses a Scriptural symbol, the covenant, as central to his ethical system.[53] In the covenant, God and man-in-community are bound in a personal relationship. This image situates his ethics within the Judaeo-Christian tradition. Adams envisages God's People bound to Him through a covenant and on a journey through history, always on a frontier. Movement and a sense of God as Lord of History impregnate the picture Adams paints.

Political symbol, as in the covenant image, is highlighted by contrasting it with what Adams sees as the narrow individualistic symbolism of "justification by faith" as in the Lutheran tradition.[54] In Adams' view the

---

[51]"The Sociology of Freedom and Responsibility," Hibbert Lecture delivered at Manchester College, Oxford, February 26, 1963, p. 4 (typewritten).

[52]"The Liberal Ministry in a Changing Society," Address to Unitarian Universalist Ministers' Association, January 1964, p. 5 (mimeographed).

[53]"Changing Frontiers: Vanishing and Emerging," p. 1.

[54]"The Liberal Ministry in a Changing Society," p. 5.

Social Gospel, a modern interpretation of the covenant, is

> . . . a major illustration of the adoption,
> the readoption, the revival of political sym-
> bolism as over against mere pietistic or per-
> sonalistic symbolism that is concerned with
> the individual and individual relations with
> other individuals.[55]

The covenant symbol as a principle of Adams' ethics
serves, likewise, as a heuristic in criticizing individualistic trends in existentialism. He demands of exis-
tentialists such as Kierkegaard, Heidegger and Bultmann
that their critique of contemporary society be put in a
political context.[56] Freud also comes under attack since
he interprets the human situation in the light of individual relations. Freud's orientation is parallel to
the domestic imagery also found in the Scriptures (i.e.,
church as family, bride of Christ), an imagery Adams
acknowledges but does not emphasize.[57]

Covenant and the Demands of Reality

We have seen that in Adams' understanding of reality,
man is called to respond to his total environment. Moreover, the very nature of reality supports mutuality among
human beings; and that support is a key factor in the
response to the total environment. In the covenant, likewise, man's fidelity is seen through concern for his total
environment. God as man's covenant partner, the creator
of reality and Lord of History, supports man's response,
a response which is seen in terms of other people. Adams'
understanding of reality receives historical specifica-
tions in terms of covenant. He moves from the abstraction
of philosophical language to its concretization in the
symbolism of the Jewish and Christian tradition.

Adams goes so far as to say that "man is not man
until he has entered into the covenant."[58] Does this

_____

[55]"The Liberal Ministry in a Changing Society," p. 6.

[56]Ibid., pp. 7 ff. Adams also includes Sartre among
those thinkers but Sartre's openness to Marxist theory
and opposition to the Vietnamese war would show the development of social concern.

[57]Ibid., pp. 14-15.

[58]"The Theological Ground of Protestant Social Responsibility," Early version of a Hibbert lecture., c. 1963,
p. 21 (typewritten).

mean Adams is advocating the superiority of the Jewish or Christian tradition? As I have shown in my discussion of liberalism and Neo-orthodoxy,[59] I do not think so. The absolute, as we have seen, is relativized in the peculiarities of history. Covenant is a specification of the universal demand for mutuality. Adams also holds "that where community-forming, where covenant-making is taking place, God is working, i.e.,[60] that which is productive of meaning is taking place."[60] Adams' trinitarianism as well as his qualified pragmatism, makes his concern for covenant-making transcend the particularities of his own tradition. "God is working where there is community-forming taking place." Covenant concerns do not have to be expressed in covenant language peculiar to our tradition, and therefore they transcend the Judaeo-Christian tradition.

Covenant and Law

The political symbol of the covenant creates a specifically religious principle for Adams' approach to ethics. I think that the covenant principle, by way of structural analogy, stimulates Adams' concern for law and judicial review. This is not surprising in view of his interest, from a religious and sociological perspective, in the structure and institutions of society. Law and the courts, likewise, have this focus.

In commenting on separation of church and state and on state support for religious schools, Adams feels that a Congressman cannot be required to stand on conviction since the political pressure on him is so strong. Yet I am sure that Adams' strong prophetic strain would lead him to qualify this pragmatic statement. He would surely affirm that conviction must win out in particular situations. The courts, of all bodies in a democracy the least subject to political pressure, must play a significant role in dealing with social problems. "We should recognize," he says, "the difference between political functions and judicial functions, and see that the judicial has a special role and a recognized special privilege."[61]

---

[59] See above, pp. 27 ff.

[60] "The Theological Ground of Protestant Social Responsibility," p. 21.

[61] "Statement on Separation of Church and State," Judicial Review, March 10, 1966, p. 170.

He sees a need for stability within society, as well
as a built-in means for the preservation and increase of
social responsibility within a court system, thus preserving the legislature and executive "from carrying the brunt
of this kind of decision-making."[62] The courts provide a
means of overcoming the many conflicting pressures experienced in the political world. In a recent review of
Harold Berman's The Interaction of Law and Religion, Adams
observes that "if religion for its part ignores the legal
element and the attendant social responsibilities, it re-
duces itself to mere Innerlichkeit and privatization; it
makes the vain attempt to escape from history into relig-
iosity and sentimentality."[63]

The political aspect of Adams' ethics manifests itself in the centrality of covenant and a concern for law.[64]
This aspect provides the context for the personal/social
dimension of Adams' ethics. Moreover, it roots the theonomous nature of Adams' ethics within the concrete historical milieu of the Old Testament.

Ethics: Call and Response

Another characteristic of Adams' ethics is that he
sees God's call manifested through historical circumstances.
Man's response is equally conditioned by such circumstances.
Adams, therefore, situates his ethics within the historical
context, by delineating two sets of dialectically-related
types of ethics, namely sacramental/prophetic and conscience/

---

[62]"Statement on Separation of Church and State," Judicial
Review, March 10, 1966, p. 170.

[63]Manuscript of review, dated August 22, 1974, p. 2. Sub-
sequently appeared in Interpretation: A Journal of Bible
and Theology, XXX, 1 (1976), pp. 106-108.

[64]Adams has lamented for years the lack of knowledge Protestant theologians have about law. He always urged his
own students to take Law School courses particularly in
jurisprudence. He himself took pre-legal courses in college and audited a year's seminar on philosophy of law at
Harvard under Dean Roscoe Pound and William Ernest Hocking.
(Letter of August 22, 1974.) In the 1960's he conducted
an extracurricular seminar on theology and law with Professor Harold Berman at Harvard Law School.

consequences. While Adams deals with these four as ideal
types, he incorporates aspects of them into his own ethics.

Ethics which focus on "divine power present in given
social realities or patterns"[65] highlight "sacramental media."[66]
An example of this is the Chronicler's viewpoint in the Old
Testament, a viewpoint which stresses worship and conceives
of Israel as a kingdom of priests whose life is centered
in the Temple. Adams' own emphasis on the Church follows
the trend of this type of ethics.[67] But, while he appre-
ciates its merits, he cautions against the evils of in-
stitutionalization, of acceptance of the status quo without
question.

In contrast to "sacramental ethics" are the ethics
which point to an eschatological social reality -- the
coming kingdom of God. Adams calls these prophetic ethics.[68]
Divine power is manifest in the demand for decision in the
face of the kingdom and in opposition to the present social
reality. An example of this is found in the book of Amos
or the present-day civil rights movement. Adams himself
is at home with this approach in his concern for justice
and criticism of social structures. Yet he is no anar-
chist and, as we have seen, has respect for social structures, having participated with enthusiasm in the life of
the church, politics, and the university.

Adams also delineates an ethics of conscience where
the power and call of God is heard within the individual
and the proper disposition.[69] Both Old and New Testament
demand this personal sense of commitment and purity of
motives and Adams himself embraces such commitment and
purity of motives. But he warns against the degeneration
of this emphasis into an individualistic ethic focused
on personal salvation as in some forms of pietism.

---

[65]"Ethics," p. 112.

[66]Ibid.

[67]See "The Congregational Idea."

[68]Ibid. See also "The Axis is Longer Than You Think,"
and "The Geography and Organization of Social Responsibility."

[69]Ibid.

The opposite of this approach is found in an ethics where God's will is manifested in a concern for the effects of actions.[70] The uniqueness of a historical period determines the particular emphasis in ethics. A socially stable culture might well bring a keen sense of introspection and emphasis on purity of conscience, a situation which in fact occurred in the nineteenth century with the insights of the philosopher/theologian Kierkegaard. Disruption of the social milieu will often bring about an ethic stressing social or personal consequences as in the anti-war movement of the 1960's or in the current re-evaluation of sexual ethics. As with sacramental and prophetic ethics, the ethics of conscience and of consequences are not in opposition to each other, but exist, rather, in a dialectical relationship.

These two sets of dialectical and historically conditioned approaches manifest the reality of God's call. These are the time-filled motifs of Adams' ethics. The creative and redemptive power of God requires man's historically-conditioned response. However, there are always new forms of alienation blocking this interaction. One of these is the dark side of dipolar reality: man does not always respond to God's grace. Adams places heavy emphasis on the societal causes of alienation, forms of which "grow out of class,or ethnic, or nationalist and other societal attachments."[71] This is not to neglect personal causes of alienation, but Adams himself as a historically conditioned ethicist works within the perspective of social ethics.

The problem of contextualization is further compounded by the pace of modern dynamic societies. Adams' Christian ethics speaks to the societies, particularly in the West, from the vantage point of the Christian tradition. He holds this tradition in tension with the insights of the social sciences, particularly sociology, upon which Adams relies in order to contextualize the heritage of the tradition. I will shortly address this openness to the social sciences, itself a determinative characteristic of his ethics.

The call/response character of Adams' ethics results in his adoption of guidelines rather than rules. These guidelines emerge from the ethical perspective

---

[70]"Ethics," p. 112. See also "The Use of Symbols."

[71]"Ethics," p. 114.

best suited to a given historical situation: sacramental or prophetic ethics, ethics of conscience or of consequences. The ethical perspective, then, delineates certain guidelines, ones which are appropriate to the call of God within a given historical moment. In setting up guidelines in this manner, he sees the temptation, and urges others to see the same, of giving static answers to the dynamic questions of mankind in history. He is cautious as well of an ethics of "uniquity" or situationalism which he finds in Kierkegaardian existentialism. Adams views the ethical process in the following way:

> Every situation is unique, but it lends itself to rational discrimination in time of persisting social structure or malstructures. Every decision in order to be relevant must be unique, but in the societal situation it cannot be merely the unique decision growing out of social consensus regarding the definition of the situation and its possibilities. Under these circumstances a conflict of values (for example, between freedom and order) and also a compromise of values in face of the actual situation will be inevitable.[72]

Adams sees a problem in understanding how "the application of norms or of the Christian ethos, the response of faith to the living God, in the concrete situation,"[73] takes place. (Notice here the way he goes from norms to Christian ethos to response of faith, practically equating them with each other.) In this application to concrete situations, different methods have been used:

> On the one hand, "middle Axioms" are employed to mediate between more general norms and the unique structural situation; on the other, stress is placed on the ostensibly more complex and flexible response of a faith that is skeptical regarding the validity or adequacy of rationally articulated "principles" and that aims to remain sensitive in the ever-shifting contextual situation. (Both approaches today seek assistance from the social

---

[72]"Ethics," p. 116. On p. 56, footnote 11, I discussed the problem of Adams' explicit ethical theory. Use of the term "guidelines" highlights the difficulty I have had in coming to grips with certain aspects of his thought.

[73]"Ethics," p. 116.

sciences for the empirical analysis of the
actual situation.) . . . The issues are the
perennial issues of Christian faith under
the paradoxical imperatives of law and gospel. These dangers arise in the encounter
with ethical problems of the individual. . .
as well as with those of institutions. In
either sphere and under both law and gospel, the God of the Christian moves in a
mysterious way his wonders to perform; and
yet he is not a God of disorder.[74]

This analysis by Adams underlines the perspective
he himself brings to the doing of ethics. The use of
method in concrete situations is a perennial problem
for Adams. Yet Adams' stance is within the realm of
social ethics, and from such a perspective the question of context always arises. I think this gives a
solidity to Adams' ethics because when "doing the loving
thing" is the question, he does not see this as an issue for the isolated individual. Societal consequences
and values are involved. Moreover, he brings the complex tradition of ethical theory to bear on problems.

In 1967, Adams participated in a round-table discussion on "Religion and the New Morality." It is one
of the few instances I have come across where he addresses problems of sexual behavior. In discussing
premarital sex, he speaks of an authentic conception
of love as

. . . an abiding affection that carries with
it responsibility and respect for the other
person in the context of a community. . .
Out of this complex of values emerge guidelines, not neatly formulated rules. One
thing is clear: Sexual experience cannot
be properly separated from the rest of experience.[75]

Adams speaks of decisions in ethics "growing out
of social consensus regarding the definition of the
situation and its possibilities." Are ethics simply a
matter of consensus? Consensus does not mean adjustment

---

[74]"Ethics," p. 117.

[75]"Religion and the New Morality," _Playboy_ (June 1967),
p. 63.

to him. "What people do cannot be a basis for an ethical standard."[76] Consensus, for Adams, is a complex process involving sensitivity to principle, tradition, the secular sciences, the present situation, the redemptive power of God, the movement of the Spirit, the community at prayer and in discussion, minority positions. Consensus thus has this call/response character. It is this multi-faceted orientation of his ethics which I see as giving in continued value in our day.

Optimism and Realism

Adams' reformulation of religious liberalism[77] leads me to another characteristic of his ethical framework: optimism/realism. His optimism is rooted in the power of God, his realism in the tendency of man to set up his own God.

He regards humankind's incompleteness as source of its idolatrous tendencies, but looking upon the dignity given human beings, he is given hope. This sense of hope comes from the Creator, whose power is the source of man's dignity. It is this dignity (a source of renewed optimism for Adams) which gives rise to mankind's responsibility to create and to bring about growth in the world.[78] In order to achieve this goal, mankind must engage in communal endeavor as a corrective to self-centeredness.[79] The task is not an easy one, but its theological base is clear: mutuality in community is ontologically supported.[80]

A concrete example, Adams' evaluation of World War II, gives body to these elements of optimism and realism in his ethics. The grandeur of man finds expression, according to Adams, in his sense of responsibility, in his admission of guilt, "in the moments of honesty when he knows he should blush."[81] Yet despite

---

[76]"Religion and the New Morality," Playboy (June 1967), p. 66.

[77]See above, pp. 23 ff.

[78]See above, p. 38-39.

[79]See above, pp. 39.

[80]See above, pp. 47 ff., 27 ff.

[81]"Liberal Religion in a United World," The Christian Register, CXXIII, No. 2 (1944), p. 54.

this fact, many Americans deny their guilt regarding
the war. Adams criticizes self-proclaimed innocence
and isolation in the nation as well as other attitudes
adrift in the World War II era: pre-war isolationist
alibis; selling scrap iron to Japan; remaining neu-
tral in Spain. He finds fault as well with those who
live on war profit -- laissez-faire politicians and
capitalists.

        The liberal has a distinct role vis-a-vis this
world scene. His liberalism convinces him that the
old world is dying, that a new world is already in
the works, one in which want and special privilege
no longer exist. He gains courage in seeing the power
of the United States against Fascism and hopes that
"the world . . . make[s] a similar effort to fight
undernourishment, disease and unemployment."[82] The
liberal must realize that the American people might
have defeated Fascism but "they [the underprivileged
and oppressed] will not long maintain their obligation
to the 'democracies' if they do not receive the bene-
fits."[83] And if they do not, the peace will only be
a continuation of the struggle between democracy and
Fascism. "When peace rears her ugly head we shall
discover that during the war we have been in one of the
easier rooms in hell. . . . The outcome is by no means
settled by a kind Providence or by the 'dialectic of
history.'"[84] From my perspective today and fully thirty
years after the war, I find Adams' perception quite
accurate.

        Adams also observes that the war is actually a
continuation of the First World War; yet he balances
a realistic assessment with an optimistic vision. "Our
infirmities are taking a long time to come to their
crisis."[85] Adams speaks here also of the few rich and
the many poor nations, emphasizing, however, that this
is not the whole story of the modern period.

            It would be more accurate if we should say
            that the culmination of the last two cen-
            turies of Western history in two world wars

---

[82]"Liberal Religion in a United World," p. 54.

[83]Ibid.

[84]Ibid., p. 55.

[85]"Sources of Religious Insight," The Christian Register,
CXXIV, No. 2 (1945), p. 45.

is itself both a distortion and a consequence of an original impulse that was and
still is of great promise.[86]

This was the promise of a new order, a society of, for,
and by the people.

Adams' realism leads him to demand _planning_ for
freedom, since this is the only way a more stable and
just economic and political order can be established,
an order with both stability and elasticity. On the
one hand, he opts for co-ordinative planning rather
than comprehensive planning, calling for rules to govern
business, agriculture, even private investment. On the
other hand, he urges that "business and government . . .
be decentralized in order to allow for a wide democratic
participation,"[87] since decentralization protects
against the corruption of power.

In other words, we must plan our economy so
as to create enclaves of freedom in which
consumer and producer, laborer and farmer
may experience the deepest satisfactions
of democracy -- freedom of initiative and
a freedom from the suicidal anxiety of in-
security.[88]

For Adams social justice is the main issue of life.[89] By
means of such justice, his covenantal understanding is
affirmed and holds in tension his optimism and realism.

The Universality of Ethics and Natural Law

The ethical imperative is not the concern of the
Christian tradition alone. It is universal as a quality
of human self-understanding. Adams uses a category from
outside the Christian tradition, natural law, or law of
nature, to clarify this quality. (The category, of course,
has been used within the Christian tradition as well.)
Characteristically, he redefines the category in view of

---

[86]"Sources of Religious Insight," _The Christian Register_,
CXXIV, No. 2 (1945), p. 45.

[87]_Ibid_., p. 67.

[88]_Ibid_.

[89]_Ibid_., p. 48.

social scientific analysis but also in terms of his trinitarian theology. It is the trinitarian dimensions of Christianity[90] which lend "theological validity for justice or moral law as known apart from revelation through Christ."[91] The Father, as Creator, is the source of all that exists and the Spirit speaks through all men. It is the Spirit which guides "a theonomous pedagogy in and outside the church."[92] Trinitarianism becomes further justification for Adams' understanding of dipolar reality as man's response to the total environment. It further clarifies the Christian base yet secular outreach of his ethics.

Adams regards the law of nature as that which deals with "the problems of establishing and justifying ethical standards in their relation to the essential nature of man and of things."[93] Yet Adams brings many qualifications to his use of natural law. He affirms that interpretations of the meaning of natural law have for the most part been "in the direction of emphasizing the singleness of humanity and the universality of truly ethical standards."[94] He finds that any society which has passed the archaic stage is interested in distinguishing the ideal from the actual and right from might, unless of course that society has become victim of relativism or tyranny. Not only are relativism and tyranny problems, but the most difficult aspect of natural law is the wide variety of interpretations which stems from ambiguity surrounding the concepts of both nature and law.

With regard to nature as used in natural law, it can have the following meanings: "it may denote the nature of things or of the world, as well as the nature of man and society, and the denotations may aim to refer to both what is and what ought to be."[95] Nature may mean a structure immanent in the world, having a unifying power or it may refer to an immanent structure

---

[90]See above, pp. 78-86.

[91]"Ethics," p. 115.

[92]"Christianity and Humanism," address delivered at the University of Iowa, 1937, p. 6 (typewritten).

[93]"The Law of Nature: Some General Considerations," Journal of Religion, XXV, No. 2 (1945), p. 88.

[94]Ibid., p. 89.

[95]Ibid., p. 91.

in human nature. In either case there are still wide varieties of interpretation possible vis-a-vis both immanent structures. "It would seem that 'nature' may mean almost anything existent or nonexistent, actual or ideal."[96]

The concept of law, both descriptive and prescriptive, has a wide variety of meanings. Law has been described as having been written on men's hearts and obversely as something to be imposed. Adams concludes that the ambiguity over the terms is a reflection of human complexity. Thus "theories of natural law . . . are a product of the mind of man in search of meaning and not something directly 'given.'"[97] Since they are products of the mind, their meaning will vary, being employed for social change as well as maintenance of the status quo. "What natural law is at any particular time depends, then, upon who is using it and for what purpose. This is the ideological predicament of natural-law theory."[98]

While affirming most emphatically that natural law theory has had a checkered history, he holds that variety of interpretation is not a reason for repudiating the principle. It must be remembered that Adams says this at the end of World War II, a time which he feels is ripe for a renewed concern about universal principles of morality. Basically Adams sees the main purpose of the concept as being "to establish and justify a criterion of justice. . . ."[99] Yet even here he offers an essential qualification: "In face of complex human situations, no universal definition [of justice] will ever be adequate or wholly valid."[100]

Despite the immense number of qualifications and inherent problems Adams relates to the concept of natural law, he steadfastly maintains that "none of these difficulties can properly exempt men from concern with the problem of natural law."[101] It shares the same problems

---

[96] "The Law of Nature: Some General Considerations," _Journal of Religion_, XXV, No. 2 (1945), p. 92.

[97] _Ibid._

[98] _Ibid._, p. 94.

[99] _Ibid._, p. 95.

[100] _Ibid._, p. 96.

[101] _Ibid._

that complex concepts such as God, goodness, or holiness have always had: perversion; ideology; and desire for power on the part of humans. It is Adams' hope that our awareness of difficulties surrounding natural law discussions will lead to a seriousness about the topic and new attempts at synthesis. He does not develop a synthesis himself but rather affirms the importance of the category for it has brought about some ethical insight and provides a bridge for discussion with varieties of cultures.[102]

Focus of the Social Scientific
Influence on Adams: Ernst Troeltsch

In a previous chapter, I have noted the philosophical influence of Paul Tillich on Adams. I wish to focus here on the influence of the social sciences on Adams' ethics, an influence which I view as coming particularly from Ernst Troeltsch (1865-1923). The generic term, "analyst of religion," best describes Troeltsch since he is at once theologian, philosopher of history, and sociologist. A concern for vital religion coupled with political involvement in Germany in the first part of this century characterize Troeltsch's concern for the interaction of religion and society. Both Barth and Brunner consider him to be "a major misinterpreter of Christian faith and the Reformation."[103] Adams, in contrast, finds Troeltsch to be the most decisive influence in the development of his social ethics.[104] Adams' communal reading of Troeltsch's The Social Teachings of the Christian Church in the Unitarian ministers' group was a decisive influence on his subsequent thinking. Central to Adams' ethics is the Troeltschean doctrine of the reciprocal relation between individual and society.[105]

---

[102]The question of natural law is also dealt with by Adams in the following articles: "Contributions of Occidental Religion to Cultural Understanding," p. 733; "The Religious Problem," New Perspectives on Peace, ed. H.B. de Huszar (Chicago: University of Chicago Press, 1944), p. 250; "The Law of Nature in Greco-Roman Thought," Journal of Religion, XXV, No. 2 (1945), p. 108.

[103]"Ernst Troeltsch," Encyclopedia Brittanica, 14 ed., XXII, p. 489.

[104]Taped interview, February 10, 1973. Adams has consistently taught a Troeltsch seminar over the years and is presently translating a volume of Troeltsch's writings. See also Adams' article "Why the Troeltsch Revival," The Unitarian Universalist Christian, XXIX, 1-2 (1974), p. 4-15.

[105]Taped interview, March 6, 1972.

Historical Consciousness and Method

Historical consciousness "as the awareness of the contingent and singular character of the events of history,"[106] and the resulting historical method are central to Troeltsch's analysis of religion. Adams says that Troeltsch's underlying philosophical concern was "the problem of relating the living power of historical Christianity to the needs growing out of the cultural situation and the religious unrest of his time."[107] This historical consciousness and concern for relevance are seen in the characteristics of Adams' ethics.

A Normative Perspective

Adams characterizes Troeltsch as being concerned with "the tension between the claims of a categorical ideal and the demands, the possibilities, and the ambiguities of history."[108] In a posthumously published essay entitled "The Place of Christianity Among the World Religions," Troeltsch takes individuality and social conditioning very seriously but relates these factors to the truth question. He "retains the conviction that standards of truth and value in the various high religions are valid for them, and that the Christian standards are 'valid for us.'"[109]

Such a position is influential on Adams' understanding of ethics. He asserts that Troeltsch offers little solace to those seeking universality and certainty in religion; and in view of what we have seen of Adams, neither does he. Adams, with Troeltsch, believes that the absolute cannot be domesticated. It is only God who can make a final pronouncement. Yet both seek to overcome nominalism through the belief that truths about God must be formed in the unique moments that contribute to human history. At the same time, "truth for us does not cease thereby to be very truth and life."[110] Adams' assessment of Troeltsch's method

---

[106]Adams, "Introduction," The Absoluteness of Christianity and the History of Religion, by Ernst Troeltsch, translated by David Reid (Richmond: John Knox, 1971) p. 8.

[107]"Ernst Troeltsch," p. 489.

[108]"Ernst Troeltsch as Analyst of Religion," Journal for the Scientific Study of Religion, I, No. 1 (1961), p. 98.

[109]"Introduction," The Absoluteness of Christianity and the History of Religion, p. 17.

[110]Ibid.

could well be applied to the former's own approach to
ethical analysis: "The absolute must be discerned always in inextricable connection and in relentless ten-[111]
sion with the relative, and not in some abstraction."

A Sociological Perspective

Through the sociology of religion Troeltsch eval-
uates religion in relation to history. In The Social
Teachings of the Christian Churches, his interest is in
the reciprocal influences between ideas and institutions.
The same sociological concern is evident in Adams' understanding of symbols in relation to structural analogies. Troeltsch, like Adams, analyzes the ways in which
Christianity functions to change society; he emphasizes[112]
time and again the prophetic strain in Christianity.
More fundamentally, Troeltsch's typology of religious
associations provided a tool for Adams' social ethics.
The sect type, in particular, is influential in Adams'
view of the church.[113]

---

[111]"Introduction," The Absoluteness of Christianity and the
History of Religions, p. 14. This reaffirms the basic problem Adams sees in developing an adequate natural law theory.

[112]Adams describes Troeltsch's position as follows: "In general, then, a religious idea in its impact and in its exfol-
iation has to be understood by means of a sociological analysis of its influence upon the organizations and institutions
emanating from it, and of the influences of these institutions
upon it; these ideas and institutions in turn should be seen
in mutual relation to other social forces, institutions and
their value systems." "Ernst Troeltsch as Analyst of Religion,"
p. 104. Compare this to Adams' "The Pragmatic Theory of Meaning," Presidential Address, American Society of Christian Ethic
Washington, D. C., January 24, 1969 (typewritten).
Adams disagrees with Troeltsch's evaluation that the prophets of Israel were irrelevant in their criticisms of urban
life. Adams finds their criticism "perennially relevant."
"Stated in sociological language, the yearning of the prophets
for the rural ways of the idealized past was a yearning for a
society in which primary, affectional relations are dominant.
In an urban economy where division of labor is elaborate and
social inability is required, the total personality is not
brought into play in most social relations. . . . A certain
alienation reflected in the individual's feeling of isolation,
homelessness, and anxiety is the consequence." "Theological
Bases of Social Action," p. 54.

[113]See above, pp. 73-75. Adams describes how Troeltsch shows

Ethics in Action: A Case Study

I would like to demonstrate Adams' ethical analysis
by way of a significant essay he wrote in 1970: "Civil
Disobedience: Its Occasions and Limits." Its concern
is context: when and to what extent is civil disobedience
an ethical option? His method of approach involves many
of the emphases developed in this book. In particular, it
further concretizes the voluntary association theme and
shows the relevance of Adams' principles.

By 1970, Adams had been involved in debating ethical
questions for forty years. He knew the Depression, World
War II, the McCarthy era, all first hand. The vitality
of his thought is evident in his reflections on the domestic unrest caused by the Vietnam war.

In Adams' view, the movement of dissent as one valid
means of expressing power leading to resistance has deeply
historical roots. He traces it back not only to Gandhi,
Thoreau, Locke, and Jefferson but to figures within the
religious tradition, Knox, Lilburne, and Fox. He goes
back in history even further, stating that Christianity
from its origins "was an outlaw religion committed to
disobedience and to the 'world.'"[114] Here we see Adams
at work, interpreting Christianity in terms of structural
social understanding. He develops the wider ramifications of the question of civil disobedience. The act is
related to context, here in terms of the church's history.

Adams is quick to point out that civil disobedience
in the early church was very different from our modern
conception of it. His sense of the historical method is
operative here. Although today's movement must be understood in terms of historical nuance, one must start with
a definition of what civil disobedience means in the
modern era:

"that different types of religious association tend to
favor social philosophies analogous to the respective
types of organization; accordingly these types of association tend to interpret social-ethical doctrines. . . .
in corresponding fashion." "Ernst Troeltsch as Analyst of
Religion," p. 105. In Adams' definition of ethics, he
uses similar words in speaking of social philosophies:
"Varying types of church polity . . . tend to develop
characteristic social philosophies in which the general
structure of the polity serves as a model for social organization generally." "Ethics," p. 112.

[114]"Civil Disobedience: Its Occasions and Limits," p. 293.

117

Civil disobedience is (1) a nonviolent,
(2) public violation (3) of a specific
law or set of laws, or of a policy of
government having the effect of law (4)
which expresses a sense of justice in a
civil society of cooperation among equals
and (5) which is generally undertaken in
the course of a presumed higher authority
than the law in question (6) as a last
resort (7) for the purpose of changing
the law and (8) with the intention of
accepting the penalty which the prevailing law imposes.[115]

In contrast to this, early Christian civil disobedience, directed against the emperor worship required of
Christians as soldiers, was carried out in a much nar-
rower sense. The early Christians had no desire to im-
prove the law; an eschatological world-view dominated
their actions. Their interest was not in freedom of
religious association as such; they engaged in nonviolent protest even though they had no means available
to change the law.[116]

Implicit in Adams' discussion of civil disobedience
is his acceptance of the principle of constitutional democracy in the British and American tradition. This is the
"context" in which Adams has written. What he says about
disobedience, then, makes sense only in terms of Adams'
own acceptance of this social structure. This is evident in his declaration that

In a democratic society it [civil disobed-
ience] reflects the indisposition to wait
upon the slow procedures that bring about
change in the law; at the same time the
civil disobedient is willing to be subject
to legal police action and he respects just
court procedures. In general then, civil
disobedience presupposes a general acceptance of legal authority, due process, and
the legitimacy of the legal system as a whole.[117]

---

[115]"Civil Disobedience: Its Occasions and Limits," p. 294.

[116]Ibid., p. 295.

[117]Ibid.

118

Adams has a clear preference for the sociological
category of person-institution within society, but he
gives a high valuation himself to one particular type
of institution, constitutional democracy. This operates as a control factor in his evaluation of means
for effecting social change. Thus government and dissent interact dialectically in his thinking.

Adams supports the idea of constitutional democracy partly because it is the form of government in
which it is possible for the civilly disobedient to be
involved in shaping the law.

> The civil disobedient presupposes that his
> demand for justice possesses a universal
> validity and therefore holds it would be
> appropriate for other citizens or asso-
> ciations to undertake similar civil dis-
> obedience. . . . Civil disobedience pre-
> supposes the right to protest and the
> right to participate in the shaping of
> public policy.[118]

There is some difficulty in Adams' unqualified
statement concerning the universal validity of the demand
for justice. While demands for justice are universally
valid, not every means of protest to achieve justice has
the same universal validity. The protection of the civil
rights of blacks and whites is universally valid. But in
the Boston protest against busing, the criterion of universal validity (in terms of protecting black or white
civil rights) cannot be so easily translated into civil
disobedience. However, the chosen means of protest seems
absolute for many who are closer to the situation. This
example, however, highlights the difficulty surrounding
the point of universal validity since the value of busing
as a means is a debatable issue.

Adams admits that universal validity is not always
a concern for certain religious types, especially for
those whose values are incompatible with the ways of the
world. Withdrawing sects are willing to suffer for their
beliefs. They view the world as being under demonic control. Obviously Adams does not belong to this group. For
him, civil disobedience is not a purely personal issue involving purity of conscience, but the logical outcome of
historical-social analysis.

----

[118]"Civil Disobedience: Its Occasions and Limits," p. 296.

Adams demonstrates his sense of tradition in relation to contemporary thinking in his discussion of
civil disobedience in the face of both valid but unjust
and invalid and unjust laws. He traces the valid/in-
valid distinction back to Aquinas and sees, for instance,
the protest against invalid law operative in some contemporary resistance to war as in Vietnam.[119]

While Adams does not take a position on the question
of the validity or invalidity of the law in the case of
Vietnam, he affirms that civil disobedience does not wea-
ken the fabric of society. In fact, he points out, "the
danger is that the fabric of society at a given time may
actually be too tightly woven as a consequence of repres-
sion or the apathetic routinization of conscience."[120]
Utilizing civil disobedience as a means, vested interests
and narrow patriotism are overcome. Criticism of the
social structure is a given for Adams; he sees it as a
beginning point of ethics. While he does not espouse civil
disobedience as an ordinary solution for ethical problems,
he does not rule it out. Civil disobedience is an important ethical option for him, not only because of the
individual exercise of conscience and of power, but more
importantly because of the social issues involved. "In
the main . . . the issues at stake have been the values
of equality and nonviolence."[121]

Adams notes that both war and civil disobedience
are not normal procedures used in relations between the
individual and the state. Thus he sees the doctrine of
the just war (an important aspect of natural law tradition) as shedding some light on civil disobedience.[122]
He notes, however, that while the civilly disobedient
accept punishment by lawful agencies, the warring state
generally cannot be held accountable. In one sense,
civil disobedience is symbolic to Adams of deeper societal issues. He sees as axiomatic to modern society "the
presupposition that the individual is a legitimate 'authority' entitled to demand the consent of the governed. . . ."[123]

---

[119]"Civil Disobedience: Its Occasions and Limits," pp. 298-99.

[120]Ibid., p. 300.

[121]Ibid., p. 302.

[122]Ibid., p. 303.

[123]Ibid., p. 306.

For Adams, the integrity of society depends upon conflict of perspectives. Of course, this emphasis upon
the individual must be seen in relation to Adams' concern for and emphasis upon the legitimate authority of
government as well as on his understanding of the voluntary association, power[124] and civil disobedience.

Adams is critical of civil disobedience performed
in the name of conscience with no hope of change. Once
again, that sense of context and social ramifications
dominates his approach. In commenting on the maintenance of purity of conscience under all circumstances,
he had this to say.

> To be sure, this conception of integrity
> and of fidelity to conscience can become
> a form of irresponsibility, particularly
> if the civil disobedient in the name of
> conscience asserts that he is in no way
> concerned with consequences, whatever
> they may be. . . . The truly conscient-
> ious man should be willing to consider
> himself at least in part responsible for
> reasonably foreseeable, destructive con-
> sequences of his action.[125]

Responsibility for consequences which affect others
must always operate in relation to purity of motive
for Adams. He sees, it must be remembered, that civil
disobedience has for its aim a change of law or policy.
This is an effective use of power. "We have defined the
efficacy of civil disobedience as the capacity to raise
or reformulate the ethical issues in such a way as to
contribute to the process whereby public opinion re-
examines them with reference to a particular law or policy."[126]

Adams places much emphasis on the nonviolent character of civil disobedience,[127] yet he realizes that violence
may result when civil disobedience is a group action. At
no time, however, does perversion by civil disobedience
justify perversion in the form of police brutality by the

---

[124]The voluntary association and power will be considered
in Chapter Five.

[125]"Civil Disobedience," pp. 307-08.

[126]Ibid., p. 310.

[127]Ibid., pp. 305, 310, 311.

state. "One can say here that the ethical demands
ideally should guide the civil disobedient into the
mean between feckless timidity and reckless courage."[128]

All in all, while Adams reveals himself as deeply
concerned with justice within society, he emphasizes
preserving the fabric of society. He accepts as a
given that civil disobedience occurs within a state
where people believe in the integrity of the society.
What is sought is specific change in a law. "Complete
loss of confidence in the society . . . would seem to
call for 'systemic' disobedience from morally conscientious men; that is, would call for rebellion and not for
civil disobedience."[129] To indicate further Adams' approach to a question such as this, I want to note here
that his observations are by way of comment on Judge
Charles Wyzanski's criticism of almost all civil disobedience. Adams considers Christian tradition, natural
law theory, contemporary issues and judicial opinion in
discussing the issue. Implicit is his sociological sense
of institutions in society and the problems of change
within society.

In line with this consistent concern for the institutions of society, Adams goes to lengths to describe
the government's responsibility to protect the rights of
the disobedient. He does this because in our own country
"the agencies of government have permitted and promoted
the violation of civil liberties -- freedom of speech
and of association."[130] Public opinion and nongovern-
mental agencies or voluntary associations play a significant role in helping balance governmental power in
relation to individuals or groups. Adams' understanding
of civil disobedience involves a social complex: the
disobedient (individual or group), the state, nongovern-
mental groups, and public opinion. And it involves a
social problem: a questionable law or policy. The civil
disobedient, as Adams then sees him, "is not acting merely
for the sake of keeping his conscience clean, he intends
to act as a citizen, fulfilling the responsibilities of
conscientious citizenship."[131]

---

[128] "Civil Disobedience," p. 311.

[129] Ibid., p. 313.

[130] Ibid., p. 315.

[131] Ibid., p. 314.

Adams' concern for the broader issue of social context shows itself in the relationship he sees between civil disobedience and freedom of speech and association. Moreover, he assigns a position of importance to voluntary associations which depend on that type of freedom. He sees these issues surfacing in the Spock case which clearly points out the responsibilities of government to protect the rights of dissenters.[132]

Civil disobedience is, for Adams, causative of democracy as we know it. And voluntary associations played a central role in this development. "Indeed, it has been the voluntary organizations which have impressed upon the community and the state the demands for democratic rights."[133] And, as we shall see, behind the voluntary association is the issue of power.

The origins of democracy, civil disobedience and voluntary associations are historically linked. All are closely related for Adams, and at the conclusion of this article he develops at length his arguments in favor of the voluntary association and the normal procedure of governing in a democracy. Civil disobedience is an important and useful tool but "it cannot make broad, frontal constructive attacks. . . ."[134]

Adams' analysis of social context and social structures is clearly evident in this article. I join in his skepticism expressed elsewhere[135] about the viability of the voluntary association in working out the massive problem society faces today. That we must be concerned about the social context as a first step in valid ethical decisions is a key to understanding Adams. But that this concern must necessarily eventuate in championing the voluntary association, as we have known it, does not necessarily follow.

In this chapter I have focused on eight characteristics of Adams' ethics as well as on an example of how he does ethics. Adams' analysis of civil disobedience leads me to two aspects of his thought which deserve detailed analysis. Chapter Five will focus on these aspects: the voluntary association and power.

---

[132]"Civil Disobedience," pp. 317-323.

[133]Ibid., p. 330.

[134]Ibid.

[135]See below, pp. 145 ff.

123

CHAPTER V

THE VOLUNTARY ASSOCIATION AND POWER

Introduction

In this chapter I will examine the dialectic between the voluntary association and the use of power
in Adams' thought. In his understanding of ethics
Adams sees right action as "response to and the working of the grace of God."[1] Community and consensus
(socionomy), two of the leading categories in Adams'
religious liberalism, are essential to this attainment of right action.[2] Furthermore, God's power,
synonymous with His grace, is the source of this action.
It is this power which enables man to overcome alienation from God. "Where the Spirit of the Lord is, there
is liberty and community."[3] Thus the voluntary association, an important locus for the Spirit's revelation,
is a place where human nature, as understood by Adams,
can attain mutuality and community. In view of Adams'
belief that mutuality has an ontological foundation,[4]
the voluntary association is rooted in the way Adams
understands reality. Mutuality has an ontological
foundation and thus the declarative precedes the imperative. In this context, the voluntary association,
a concrete expression of mutuality, is a moral norm as
opposed to a descriptive category. Adams is not a
sociologist but a Christian ethicist.

Adams understands man as becoming fully human
within the context of community, with a dominant emphasis on consensus in that community.[5] He regards the

---

[1]See above, pp. 37-46.

[2]See above, pp. 89 ff.

[3]"Crystallizing Unitarian Beliefs."

[4]See above, pp.

[5]Voluntary associations such as churches and public interest
groups (Common Cause, American Civil Liberties Union, Independent Voters of Illinois). See the Appendix for some

mediating role of the voluntary association as having a
moral quality, mediating, that is, between the individual and collective structures in society, such as the
state. Adams' stress on freely formed groups enters
into his understanding of the church also. He stands in
the tradition of liberal democracy and the defenders of
the voluntary association within the tradition, "Bosanquet
and Follet, Lindsay and Barker, Hocking and MacIver. . . ."[6]

Religious Significance of the
Voluntary Association for Adams

Introduction

It has been evident that Adams places much emphasis
on man's will as a dominant factor in interpreting human
existence. I see the voluntary association model as a
derivative of this voluntaristic orientation. In the
voluntary association, freedom is effectively limited
by group structure and becomes meaningful. Power is thus
exercised by means of the voluntary association which
offers a practical solution to the abstraction of theory
through "training in the technique of social organization
and in the assumption of responsibility with respect to
value orientation and to specific practical tasks related
to social decisions."[7]

The voluntary association functions to overcome the
impersonalism of mass society and to break down the barriers of race and class. Such an understanding of the

---

indication of the voluntary associations to which Adams be-
longs. Pennock and Chapman point out that "voluntary associations" cover a broad spectrum of groups. "Any association by definition has at least an element of voluntari-
ness." "Preface," Voluntary Associations, ed. J. Roland
Pennock and John W. Chapman (New York: Atherton, 1969),
p. ix. Adams uses a more specific definition for voluntary
associations. "The voluntary association stands between the
individual and the state and provides the instrumentality
for achieving consensus either through political or through
non-political means." "By Their Groups Shall You Know Them:
A Protestant Theory of Vocation," Hibbert Lecture delivered
at Manchester College, Oxford, March 12, 1963, p. 10a
(typewritten).

[6] J. Roland Pennock and John Chapman, "Preface," Voluntary
Associations, p. viii.

[7] "The Political Responsibility of the Man of Culture," Comprendre, publication of La Societe Europeenne de Culture,

voluntary association is for Adams a confrontation with the ultimate issues of existence. The voluntary association is a means of striving for freedom in community and of handling power.

The fact that the voluntary association may operate within a totally secular context does not nullify its religious, in fact its prophetic, significance. For Adams,

. . . voluntary associations represent a point at which "the dearest freshness deep down things" can emerge into the social conscience and into social action. Ideally they can provide the kind of social situation and organization in which the spirit may blow where it listeth and where it may create community.[8]

Voluntaryism and Vocation

Adams utilizes the term "voluntaryism" to describe the voluntary principle which gives rise to associations. Voluntaryism emphasizes not only the freedom of the individual as found in the Bill of Rights but also the merits of persuasion over coercion. Adams, however, stresses the social connotations of the term. He objects to strictly individualistic interpretations of voluntaryism which "fail to take explicitly into account the institutional ingredient, namely, the freedom to form, or belong to, voluntary associations that can bring about innovation or criticism in the society."[9] Voluntaryism as Adams defines it receives moral impetus from his understanding of vocation as

. . . a response to the divine, self-giving, sacrificial love which creates and continually transforms a community of persons. This response by which community is formed and transformed is the process whereby men in

Venice, Italy, No. 16 (1956), pagination from brochure edition, p. 12.

[8]"The Political Responsibility of the Man of Culture," Comprendre, publication of La Societe Europeenne de Culture, Venice, Italy, No. 16 (1956), pagination from brochure edition, p. 12.

[9]"The Voluntary Principle in the Forming of American Religion," p. 218.

obedience, freedom, and fellowship come to
know God and to enjoy him. Responsibility
is response to a divinely given community-
forming power. . . .[10]

The true Protestant doctrine of vocation involves
responsibility for social policies within human associations. For Adams, this doctrine clarifies the covenant
concept. "All callings that serve the commonwealth or
the family, or the church, or economic wellbeing, are
lawful and of God."[11] This theory of vocation, developed
within the Puritan tradition especially, is a "mediating
concept for relating the covenant to man's participation
in history, to his bringing about a new order."[12]

There is a close relation between Adams' understanding
of voluntary association, and of vocation conceived of as
extending beyond one's work to both the church and the
community. Adams regards the voluntary association as the
way in which the church is involved in the world.[13] He
points to the Levellers in seventeenth century England and
their interpretation of the Calvinist understanding of vocation. For them, Christian vocation must be exercised in
the civil sphere and with appropriate means.[14] Adams

---

[10]"Our Responsibility in Society," p. 45. This understanding
is the theological equivalent of his political belief that
"socially effective freedom requires participation in associations that define or re-define freedom and that attempt
to articulate or implement that freedom in a specific social
milieu." "The Voluntary Principle in the Forming of American Religion," p. 219. See also "The Geography and Organization of Social Responsibility," p. 246.

[11]"By Their Groups Shall You Know Them: A Protestant Theory
of Vocation," p. 3.

[12]Ibid.

[13]"The Responsibility of the Christian is to participate in
the associations that define and re-define the actual situation, in the associations that give utterance and body to prophetic protest and to social change or to social stability, in
associations that provide the occasion for the Christian and
the non-Christian to enter into dialogue and even to achieve a
working consensus; in short, in the associations that contribute to the shaping of history." "The Evolution of My
Social Concern," p. 22.

[14]"By Their Groups Shall You Know Them," p. 4.

notes "the rationalized technique for crystallizing and
implementing latent, sympathetic public opinion,"[15]
whereby Lilburn, a prominent Leveller, sought to bring
about change: organized agitation, pamphleteering, and
discussion.

The Protestant doctrine of vocation provides theological underpinning for Adams' emphasis on the voluntary association. How effective is this model in face
of complex problems requiring social concern? Adams
assures me convincingly of the effectiveness of the
voluntary associations model, in the past, at least. He
assures me as well that it takes time for ideas which
such associations espouse to come to fruition. The Agreement of the People, a proposed Leveller covenant for the
English nation, is a case in point. It called for biennial parliaments, reapportionment of representatives,
equality before the law and extension of suffrage.

It was never accepted, but Adams says, "In the
Agreement of the People, we encounter what constitutes
an agenda for two or three centuries of discussion and
conflict."[16] This discussion and conflict has not been
over tea and cake but in battlefields, demonstrations,
protests, picketing, strikes, and wars. Adams accepts
the ambiguity which a voluntaristic understanding of
humankind involves, and along with it, violence and conflict as necessary concomitants of the struggle for
social justice.

The Ultimate Context for the Voluntary
Association: Covenant and Kingdom

Adams, together with Troeltsch, seeks a transcendent
referent for his interpretation of man, a referent which
is, nevertheless, related to man's concrete historical
situation. Adams answers the ethical question "to whom
or what are we responsible?" within the Judaeo-Christian
context. As an avowedly Christian ethicist, Adams employs
the covenant metaphors to give a transcendent stance to
the Christian search for a viable sense of social responsibility,[17] a search greatly aided by the voluntary

---

[15]"By Their Groups Shall You Know Them," pp. 4-5.

[16]Ibid., p. 6.

[17]See above, pp. 101 ff.

129

association. Entering into covenant with God, man achieves more than a simple act of obeisance, he truly fulfills himself as a person.

The call to fulfillment as a person within the covenant relationship is directed toward persons involved in a community. The covenant is formed among a people; the community is related to God. It is more than a legal agreement. "The essence is abiding affection."[18] The betrayal of affection and community is, then, all the more serious and personal when such betrayal is the denial by an individual or the people of God. Corporate responsibility within society is contextualized within this framework, the framework of political/domestic symbolism which is a controlling metaphor in Adams' understanding of the voluntary association. Covenant relations are structurally analogous to the voluntary association: they are both freely entered into and are both concerned with social well being.

The second metaphor of which Adams makes use is the likeness between the voluntary association and the kingdom of God made manifest in Jesus who is "a charismatic figure through whose word and deed the faithfulness of God becomes evident and newly available."[19] Jesus establishes a new covenant with an attendant sense of responsibility, initially directed by the New Testament communities toward an immediate <u>eschaton,</u> and later toward what Adams calls an "organizational revolution."[20] The result was, in his view, a separation between religion and culture and concurrently, between religion and politics. He regards the primitive church as a voluntary association which broke the rigidity of an ethnic religion, Judaism, and which clearly differentiated itself from Roman civic religion. The resulting religion, universal in appeal, affirmed that the community was broader than the state. "The differentiation," Adams states, "therefore, represented a separation of powers."[21]

---

[18] "The Theological Ground of Protestant Social Responsibility," p. 16.

[19] "The Organizational Revolution: The Protestant Contribution," Hibbert Lecture delivered at Manchester College, Oxford, March 5, 1963, p. 7 (typewritten). See above, Adams' treatment of church and kingdom, pp. 76-77.

[20] "The Organizational Revolution," p. 8.

[21] Ibid., p. 10.

Further structural changes accomplished under
the matrix of the new covenant were the socio-economic
mix of members and increased mobility for women.[22]
While this accounts for a new integration of members,
a new differentiation or dispersion of power and responsibility also took place. "The constituency of this
covenant-community had to learn the skills of preaching
and teaching administration, missionizing and dispensing
charity."[23] The pragmatic meaning of the covenant as it
was operative in primitive Christianity is seen by Adams
as a prelude to the full-blown development of the voluntary association in the modern period.

Power and the Voluntary Association

There is no guarantee that the voluntary principle
will bring about positive change in terms of justice
and the common good. Private, narrowly conceived groups
can associate to further their own interests. Such a
possibility is inherent in the freedom to associate.

The Theological Context of Adams'
Understanding of Power

Adams brings to this political reality and problem a
theological understanding of power which relies on a
sociological awareness of structures within society.

For Adams, "power is ability, capacity to get things
done, and as such is essential to any person or society
and also to God."[24] Power is both "an expression of
God's law and love and the exercise of man's freedom."[25]
Seen as God's law and love, power is Being. As man's
freedom it is "his response to the possibilities of being,
a response which is both individual and institutional."[26]

---

[22]As previously indicated on p. 76 ff, Adams underlines the
fact that the kingdom manifest in Jesus is never achieved
solely by human effort. It stands as judgment over all human
attempts to fulfill the covenant and as vision and hope in
an ultimate fulfillment.

[23]"The Organizational Revolution," p. 10.

[24]"Blessed are the Powerful," The Christian Century, LXXXVI,
No. 25 (1969), p. 839.

[25]"Theological Bases of Social Action," p. 42.

[26]Ibid.

For Adams, God's power contains a command "and at the same time the idea that men are free to respond or not to respond."[27] God's power "becomes manifest in a community which struggles for righteousness, for justice and mercy."[28] This power is "the standard for and criterion of all other powers."[29] Man's power is a gift from God. It is freedom. "The perfection of God's power is to be seen in his giving to man the power to turn against him; for communion with God is not possible if no alternative exists."[30]

Man, created in God's image, participates in the divine creativity, and, in so doing, exercises the highest form of vitality that existence permits.[31] Creative freedom gives rise to a will to mutuality, a drive to create community, as well as to a will to power, the impetus to destroy communal life. The former represents, in Adams' mind, the living out of a dipolar understanding of reality; the latter, what can only be viewed as a tragedy of history.

Adams sees a basic contradiction in human nature, a contradiction of cosmic dimensions. Within man we see the forces of love, power, mutuality, and self-assertion. Man, as voluntarist, reacting to the theocentric pole of a dipolar reality, cannot but experience these forces which often are contradictory, and which pervade his entire existence.

His freedom has to be achieved in the teeth of this basic metaphysical and psychological tension, it has to be achieved through an attempted integration and balancing of power and mutuality, of self-assertion and love.[32]

[27]"Blessed are the Powerful," p. 839.

[28]Ibid.

[29]Ibid.

[30]Ibid.

[31]"The Changing Reputation of Human Nature," p. 25.

[32]"Man in the Light of War," The Christian Century, LX, No. 9 (1943), p. 257.

Adams relates power to faith and thus to a pragmatic theory of meaning. The true object of faith is that which moves the individual to action, that which he or she is most deeply concerned about personally and socially. Dependence upon the creative, ultimate power of God will issue in a socially sensitive faith, since dipolar reality, the arena of God's power, calls forth mutuality. Man's sensitivity to power operating within humanity will lead him to seek consensus and not compulsion, open discussion and not blind obedience.[33] Adams regards compulsion as a last resort, to be utilized only when freedom is grossly misused, but justifiably if this is the case.

Power has a religious base for Adams, since power is at once

> . . . the basic category of being and the basic category of social action. The crucial question for both religion and social action is the question concerning the nature and interrelation of divine power and human powers. All social action is therefore explicitly or implicitly grounded in a theology, and theology implies a fundamental conception of social action.[34]

Adams' religious understanding of power is not naive. When power becomes an instrument for tyranny within society, man is called upon to exercise power to correct the tyranny. Adams concretizes this principle by referring to the pacifist of World War II, a person whom he criticizes, for "he vainly imagines that Christians should act as if all men are regenerate, that is, as if all men, collectively, as well as individually, can under all circumstances be successfully appealed to through persuasion alone."[35] The religious problem with the pacifist is that he sees Gospel commands as the basis for a political status quo. The Good News, according to Adams, seeks to create an ethos of love, whereas the pacifist sees the latter as a law of love. "It is our duty, he [the pacifist] says, to obey the law of love regardless of the consequences that submission or unsuccessful persuasion brings."[36] Adams

---

[33]"A Faith for Free Men," Together We Advanced, ed. S.H. Frichtman (Boston: Beacon, 1946). Pagination from mimeographed text of essay, p. 5. (Mimeographed essay is longer and more complete.)

[34]"Theological Bases for Social Action," p. 43.

[35]"Man in the Light of War," p. 258.

[36]Ibid.

is by no means rejoicing in the war but he sees it as
a necessary reaction to the evil uses of power.

The Organization of Power

The social context of power leads Adams to affirm
the importance and necessity of "the power of organization and the organization of power."[37]   A man's faith
must always assume form. "The commanding, transforming
reality is a shaping power, it shapes one's beliefs about
that reality, and when it works through men it shapes
the community of justice and love."[38]   Adams, reiterating
his pragmatic theory of meaning, thus sees man's faith
taking some form. Response to the power of God brings
about community based on justice and love. Once again
we witness an affirmation of Adams' understanding of
dipolar reality, although that reality is not equated
with God, and an affirmation of his fourth liberal principle that mutuality has an ontological foundation.
This transforming power of God calls forth beliefs and
forms.

> It [response] is a co-operative endeavor
> in which men surrender to the commanding,
> transforming reality. The only way in
> which men can reliably form and transform
> beliefs is through the sharing of tradition
> and new insights and through the co-opera-
> tive criticism and testing of tradition
> and insight.[39]

This is the sole means whereby freedom can result in
justice and truth.

Power and Institutions

Adams points to the Judaeo-Christian understanding
of man as made in God's image as a source for affirming
man's dignity and modern democracy. This conviction
about man must be protected by law and by legal institutions. The voluntary association is not sufficient for
this purpose. Adams sees the law as giving body to the
visions of the just society proclaimed by the prophets.
Again and again he comes back to the demand for institu-

---

[37]"A Faith for Free Men" (book edition), p. 152.

[38]Ibid.

[39]Ibid., p. 153.

134

tional manifestations of power.[40] Adams calls for a
structural social ethic, not simply an existential one.
Power in relation to the human community is operative
when man relieves pain within society, but it is most
effective when man conceives and enforces laws which
prevent pain.

> According to any conception of love that
> is fully responsible, not only does the
> Good Samaritan have the duty of personally
> assisting the victim of lawlessness; he
> also has the duty of bringing about the
> enforcement of the law that stops the
> thievery.[41]

The nature of Christianity demands that law and justice
share an equal footing with charity and meekness.

Adams criticizes Senator Joseph McCarthy's flaunting
of the law and democratic traditions during his senatorial
investigation of subversive individuals and organizations.[42]
He emphasizes the voluntary association's use of power to
which we turn.

Power and Voluntary Associations

Adams sees the voluntary association as playing a
role in the uses of power, man's response to the "possibilities of being." If voluntary associations are strong
within a society, power is dispersed and the society open.
And the voluntary association is the prime organization
between the individual and the state "that (without political control) provides the opportunity for the individual
to achieve freedom and consensus with his fellows on mat-
ters of common concern."[43] There is a pragmatic test for
the quality of one's sense of responsibility for Adams,
and that is the degree of participation in associations
"that are concerned with the controversial issues of public policy, and with the redefinition of these rights in
the face of the changing historical situation."[44]

---

[40]"Love and Law and 'the Good Old Cause,'" The Divinity School
News, XVII, 3 (1950), pp. 1-8.

[41]Ibid., p. 8.

[42]Ibid., p. 4.

[43]"The Social Import of the Professions," p. 8.

[44]Ibid., p. 18.

The proper use of power is facilitated by the presence of community or mutuality. Individuals, institutions, voluntary associations pervert power when they
are destructive of communal efforts. Adams, however,
has a particular interest in the voluntary association,
for it is this instrument that mediates between personal
and institutional transformation. But the voluntary association as mediator is not a guarantor of a predeter-
mined use of power. "To suppose that man can create
Utopia is to overlook the fact that the continued existence of freedom implies the continual possibility of its
perversion as well as of its meaningful realization."[45]
The voluntary association does not promise morality even
though it is a moral agent. It has this moral quality
because power operates in it. Community struggling for
righteousness, justice, and mercy is its goal. And
such mutuality alone, requires power: "the power of
being or the power of affirmation, the power to make,
revise, and enforce law. . . . Hence love and power are
not properly to be understood as mere opposites."[46] In
this framework, Adams sees God operating within the context and tension of love and power. "Power without love
is the equation for tyranny. Love without power, is ultimately a prescription for suicide or non-existence."[47]

    Adams is very sensitive to the tendency of asso-
ciations to have only a verbal impact upon political life.[48]
Such an impact becomes more likely when groups are organized on the basis of vocation or profession. He asks
the question, "Does not effective political action for
the sake of the general welfare require participation
in associations that transcend class and vocational
boundaries?"[49]

    Adams gave his answer to that question in the orien-
tation of the Greenfield Group and the Brothers of the
Way to diverse reading and involvement in both sacred
and secular causes. Participation in an association
strictly within class boundaries can easily become a
reinforcement of the status quo. Participation in associations that overcome provincialism flows necessarily

---

[45]Letter fragment, c. 1943.

[46]Ibid., p. 2.

[47]"Man in the Light of War," p. 257.

[48]See "The Political Responsibility of the Man of Culture."

[49]Review of The German Phoenix: Men and Movements in the
Church of Germany by H. Franklin Littell, in The Harvard
Divinity School Bulletin, XXV, No. 1 (1960), p. 25.

from his understanding of the nature of revelation and the vocation of the minister.[50]

The very nature of democratic society abhors provincialism and supports the diversity fostered by the voluntary association. The differentiation and dispersion possible through the freedoms of association, speech, assembly, and the freedom to become highly individualized in personality and specialized in work are part and parcel of the democratic way of life. People are able to select from among many values and life styles within this ethos, an ethos we identify with the urban society.

However, Adams is quick to point out that "it is precisely within this differentiated, pluralistic society that the individual can give devotion to one cluster of values to the neglect of other fundamental and more embracing values and responsibilities."[51] He calls differentiation an "ambiguous value." By itself it cannot create or maintain viable, integrating structures within a society.

In view of this understanding, Adams maintains that power is to be understood as a "creative innovative relationship between those who have the freedom to participate in making social decisions and those who do not have that freedom."[52] Adams is thinking here of those on the fringes of society: the poor, minorities, third world countries; and those discriminated against, such as women and children. When such groups are ignored by or remain invisible to association members, the potential clout of the voluntary association for the public interest is nullified.

Adams' sensitivity to potentially destructive voluntary associations is reinforced by his interpretation of the Depression and his denial of pre-established harmony theories.[53] Exposure to public opinion through

---

[50]See "The Minister with Two Occupations," and "The Liberal Conception of Religious Experience and Revelation."

[51]"The Sociology of Freedom and Responsibility," p. 4.

[52]"Blessed are the Powerful," p. 840.

[53]See "The Tyranny of a Free Minister"; also, "Need Well-Informed Public Opinion for Ending Mill Strike," The Salem Evening News, July 17, 1933, p. 1; "Why Liberal?" "Taking

137

countervailing associations can reduce the potential
destructiveness of special interest groups, nevertheless, the voluntary group is easily controlled by an
elite. This control is often aided by public apathy
and bureaucratic developments. Paul Harrison's Authority and Power in the Free Church Tradition[54] corrobor-
ates this from the perspective of organization within
the American Baptist Convention. Philip Selznick's
TVA and the Grass Roots: A Study in the Sociology of
Formal Organizations[55] makes the same point within
the perspective of government organization.

     "Pluralism of itself does not produce liberty and
justice, or liberty and union."[56] One remembers that
Adams' first three principles of religious liberalism
(humankind's incompleteness, the dignity of men and
the primacy of mutual consent, community) are supported
by the fourth principle, the ontological foundation of
mutuality.[57] He calls for an ontological reality that
places his understanding of the human person within a
"viable, integrating structure," which affirms "fundamental and more embracing values and responsibilities."
In other words, Adams looks for a sense of ultimacy
behind pluralism, differentiation, dispersion of power
and the voluntary association. For Adams, responsibility
for one's fellow human is always response to God. The
vital voluntary association deals with the ultimate
issues of life according to Adams.

Power and Controversy in
the Voluntary Association

     The voluntary association's exercise of power in the
public interest is bound to create controversy. Speaking in the mid-sixties, Adams dealt with the creative
use of controversy. Power was being exercised in new
forms in the civil rights movement, the war on poverty,
and the new nations of the world and controversy was

Time Seriously," On Being Human - The Liberal Way, "The
Ethical Reality and Function of the Church."

[54]Paul Harrison, Authority and Power in the Free Church
Tradition (Princeton: Princeton University Press, 1959).

[55]Philip Selznick. TVA and the Grass Roots: A Study in the
Sociology of Formal Organizations (Berkeley: University
of California Press, 1949).

[56]Ibid., p. 5.

[57]See above, Chapter Two, pp. 34 ff.

138

generated. Adams sees controversy as a creative force
in all spheres of human existence. "The positive power
that engenders high-temperatured conflict is the power
that challenges expansive or dominant social power."[58]
This positive power and creative conflict is seen by
Adams in the overturning of colonial powers in the 1960's.
This same type of power was seen in the Reformation, the
rise of the middle class, the extension of suffrage, the
civil rights movement. "It is the strength that has dispersed power and responsibility."[59]

Thus power enables one to participate in creative
controversy. Participation is a capacity to act and an
ability to listen to others and to respond creatively
to their needs. Power, creativity, and conflict are
characteristics of voluntary associations as Adams sees
them. There is an open-ended quality peculiar to these
characteristics which makes them incompatible with any
theory of pre-established harmony. The voluntary association challenges the individual to accept creative
conflict and criticism of the status quo. No detailed
analysis is necessary to point out the difficulty in
such a challenge. It is one of the reasons that laissez-
faire or pre-established harmony theories are accepted.

> There is probably no more deceptive enemy of
> creative controversy than the strategy of
> "harmony" . . . . The yearning for harmony
> forgets that freedom entails the freedom to
> differ. More than that, it overlooks the
> fact that at any given moment many people
> will be profoundly dissatisfied with their
> lot, profoundly deprived, and will not feel
> at all like talking about harmony.[60]

The vitality of the general welfare associations depends
upon a personal acceptance and commitment by the individual. This being the case, Adams looks to the actual
situation within the country to see if there is a real
vitality. He finds that the average college graduate is
peripherally involved in a special interest group in
which he lets the bureaucracy protect his interests. In

---

[58] "Hits Win Ball Games: The Creative Thrust of Conflict,"
Address to the General Assembly of the Unitarian Universalist Association, May 17, 1966, p. 4 (typewritten).

[59] Ibid., p. 5.

[60] Ibid., p. 9.

reviewing another study, Adams finds that even philan-
thropically oriented associations tend to reinforce
class and racial barriers. Referring to a study by
Mirra Kamarovsky, who found that on the average the
citizen of Manhattan does not belong to one association concerned with public policy, Adams regards many
people as "eunuchs in the world of public policy."[61]

Adams sees the sinfulness of man in his indifference to "the exercise of freedom of association for
the sake of the general welfare and for the sake of becoming a responsible self."[62] He cannot conceive of
the good man as one whose totality of virtue resides
in the subjective realm. In this conceptualization,
Adams relies heavily on Troeltsch's distinction between
objective and subjective virtues.

The good man of the subjective virtues, to
be sure, provides the personal integrity
of the individual. Without it the viable
society is not possible. But from the
point of view of the institutional commonwealth, the merely good individual is good
for nothing. Moreover, the narrow range
of responsibility of the man who confines
attention merely to his family and his job
serves to dehumanize him.[63]

Subjective virtues are congenial with theories of
harmony since the problem of social structures is not an
issue. However, Adams does see that some harmony or
consensus must exist among those in conflict. Otherwise
violent conflict and revolution will ensue. But this
harmony is balanced, in his mind, by an understanding of
the growth of democracy and being dependent upon "the
extension of power, that is, of the freedom to participate
in making social decisions."[64] Democracy is dependent upon
"outsiders" being let in, for they inject vitality and
viability into the society. "The authenticity of democracy rests upon its protection of differentiation and
upon its allowing everyone an effective voice for the
sake of justice."[65]

---

[61]"The Indispensable Discipline of Social Responsibility,"
Journal of the Liberal Ministry, VI, No. 2 (1966), p. 86.

[62]Ibid.

[63]Ibid.

[64]"Hits Win Ball Games," p. 10.

[65]Ibid.

140

The freedom to participate in social decisions
is an aim of public interest voluntary associations.
This type of association is central to the democratic
tradition. Adams points to Boston and the lack of
power blacks have in the school system. It is not difficult for him to see that disenchantment with civil
rights legislation will lead to something "more positive and aggressive."[66] Pluralism, the lifeblood of
democracy, thrives on "the inclusion of the marginal
man in the systems of power. . . Society can be constantly enriched and enlivened by the marginal man
with his highly creative potential."[67]

Adams is not surprised that blacks will use power
and organize through the voluntary association in their
drive for inclusion within American society. Under the
slogan Black Power, "the main thrust of their [the
blacks'] appeal is a call to recognize that blacks must
be allowed to develop sufficient power to achieve self-
determination."[68] In effect, this movement calls for a
new type of American pluralism, one that mandates voluntary segregation by blacks to achieve self-sufficiency.
Adams makes no negative judgment on this and in fact
finds justification for this type of pluralism in an
Office of Economic Opportunity workbook which states:
"One of the major problems of the poor is that they are
not in a position to influence the policies and procedures of the organization responsible for their welfare."[69]

Adams' earlier condemnations of racial prejudice[70]
do not show this awareness of black identity. In this,
he is no different from many other thinkers who did not
see the black as having an identity similar to the ethnic identity of other groups in the country. A change
in the direction of realizing the overwhelming nature of
Western white racism is seen in Adams' 1964 sermon, "We
Wrestle Against Principalities and Powers." His essay,
"The Shock of Recognition," shows the further evolution
of his thought.

---

[66]"Hits Win Ball Games," p. 13. A good insight since the
year was 1966.

[67]"Blessed Are the Powerful," p. 841.

[68]"The Shock of Recognition: The Black Revolution and
Greek Tragedy," p. 8.

[69]Ibid.

[70]See "The Axis is Longer Than You Think--The Anti-Negro,

Thinking back to my attitude toward black separatism as it developed in the late 1960's and early 1970's, I see an evolution in my own thinking, one which has an impact upon my evaluation of Adams' views on Black Power. As this separatist movement began, I experienced resentment toward blacks. However, my own awareness of the sense of ethnicity in the country and my developing sensitivity to ideology, resulting from reading and research for this book, led me to see this movement differently. The blacks are seeking a more explicit identity, just as other national groups have done. As Adams says, such identity is an important source of power and is part of the mainstream of the American political system.

Thus, at first I found it strange that Adams makes no comment on this black separatism other than the observation that it is a main thrust within the black movement. As my own thinking and awareness have developed, I no longer find it so strange. Rather, I see Adams as viewing the black community developing an "ethnic" sense of itself in the same way that other communities are doing. In any case, Black Power should not deflect us from seeing the voluntary association principle at work among blacks as a means of bringing about change for the general welfare of the black community. "The only way in which blacks can achieve self-determination is through gaining economic control over their own homes, businesses and banks."[71] In this way whites will have to deal with effective power.

Adams' deepest concern is that the end products of power be examined before it is exercised in a given instance. "The authenticity of power is determined by the ends it serves and the means it uses."[72] The fulfillment of power requires "power with" not just "power over." Love must inform the exercise of power; otherwise, the end product might well be one in which the oppressed become the new oppressors. Adams brings a religious vision, inspired by the kingdom and the ultimate context of power, to an issue that involves the sociological problems of alienation and struggle between classes within society.

Anti-Semitic, Anti-Progressive Axis"; as well as "Sources of Religious Insight," The Christian Register, CXXIV, No. 2 (1945), pp. 45-48.

[71]"The Shock of Recognition: The Black Revolution and Greek Tragedy," p. 8.

[72]"Blessed Are the Powerful," p. 841.

142

Adams' Evaluation of
the Voluntary Association

In face of the demands for revolutionary change in
the 1960's, Adams views the voluntary association as "a
means for the institutionalizing of gradual revolution,"[73]
although as we shall see, he has second thoughts about
such revolution in the 1970's. Thus, for Adams, the
voluntary association is a moral agent in the civil rights
campaign and movements of economic protest. Through community organization, a long-standing means of bringing
about social change, gradual revolution will take place.

The history of freedom is equated by him with the
history of free associations. This is the way in which
power is exercised.[74] But he also points out that associations must act in relation to each other; as such,
they represent the "group ecology of the community."
"An ecology of associations is a flexible grouping of
associations in interplay with each other, affecting and
being affected by each other, together maintaining a
dynamic stability in continuity and change."[75] As with
the person, so with the individual group. There are always relationships and contexts. No individual or group
acts alone. Furthermore, new associations are always
springing up to express new concerns. This understanding is consonant with a view of reality that is dynamic
or dipolar, in which man is in constant interaction with
the total environment. Novelty and creativity are integral to such a view, one in which groups relate to
one another, giving rise to new groups and taking cog-
nizance of relevant causes.

The voluntary association underlines Adams' ethical
concerns especially in its role as locus for power and
facilitator of justice. His point of view is further
clarified by an analysis of the voluntary association
seen in relation to the state and to private interest
groups.

Adams declares the state to be one association
among many that exist for the common good. Far from

---

[73]"Blessed Are the Powerful," p. 83.

[74]"The Liberal Church and Community Organization," Address
at the Unitarian Universalist Seminar on the Liberal Church
and the City, Washington, D.C., March 25, 1968, p. 4.
(Abbreviated and revised; mimeographed.)

[75]Ibid., p. 8.

being an invisible or completely independent entity, the state is subject to citizen influence through elections and lobbying as well as through voluntary associations.

> As Althusius suggested, these voluntary associations exist in their own right as expressions of the larger community. They exist without requiring the concession of the state. It is precisely this intrinsic right of association which all totalitarian theory from Hobbes to Hitler has rejected.[76]

The state is only one association among many and certainly not the creator of community. Rather is it the other way around. "The community is therefore the source of a plurality of covenants or social contracts; the state is accountable to the community as are other associations."[77]

All associations have their own "sphere," as it were, existing in their own right, and "they may legitimately criticize the state and under certain circumstances may engage in organized dissent."[78] Adams' multi-group understanding of society, a community of associations, is commensurate with an acceptance of the secular world, in its pluralism and secularity, as part of the total environment or theocentric pole of reality. In other words, he views the structure of contemporary society as part of the reality wherein God reveals himself to man, and thus he supports an openness to the contemporary situation as the way to God.

Relations between general welfare voluntary associations and the state are complicated in Adams' view by forces within the private sector of the economy. Major national and multinational corporations influence government through the maintenance of pressure groups which work in concert with each other. They are in effect "private economic governments" with, in Adams'

---

[76]"By Their Groups Shall You Know Them: A Protestant Theory of Vocation," p. 10a.

[77]"The Geography and Organization of Social Responsibility," p. 252.

[78]Ibid.

144

mind, inordinate power. Adams regards the restoration of confidence in government as related to the accountability of the private to the public sector. "The absence of this accountability is a major cause of the current, widespread skepticism that obtains regarding the effectiveness of citizen participation in politics."[79] Public government must make the private governments accountable and both forms of government require monitoring by coalitions of voluntary associations which are more effective than individual voluntary groups."[80]

The problem of accountability, especially in this decade, had led to a shift of viewpoint on Adams' part. He has doubts about the feasibility of gradual change brought about by government or voluntary associations. He shows a continued critical assessment of his own beliefs inasmuch as he speaks of the limits of liberal theory and liberal pluralism. They are not the final answer to problems. True to his theory, he applies the pragmatic test and comes to some pessimistic conclusions. He accepts Troeltsch's view that "political democracy can remain viable only if it assumes responsibility for economic realities."[81]

Adams concludes that this responsibility has not been fully assumed. The middle class and ethnic minorities have developed and prospered through the use of the voluntary association principle. "But millions are still left out, and the cruelty and disease and deprivation are appalling, as are the bombings, kidnappings, and shootings. The spaces available to the deprived are simply too cramped."[82] In view of this statement, I think Adams' understanding of the possibilities of voluntary associations has been affected by the changing times.

In the past Adams put great emphasis on the gradual transformation that has come about through the democratic American system and voluntary asso-

---

[79]"The Geography and Organization of Social Responsibility," p. 257.

[80]Adams points to the collaboration of The American Friends Service Committee, the Unitarian Universalist Service Committee, the League of Women Voters and the American Civil Liberties Union in promoting "court watching" for more justice in legal processes. Ibid., p. 258.

[81]Ibid., p. 258.

[82]Ibid.

ciational activity.[83] He found the starkness of Tillich's dialectical approach to historical forces
strongly influenced by the chaotic situation in Germany after World War I. There appeared in Tillich's
thought at that time a certain inevitability about the
collapse of the present capitalist order and the rise
of a social one. Adams felt twenty years ago that
an evolutionary transformationist option to such inevitability has been present within the British and
American systems. He points to the voluntary association "as having made for gradual rather than for dialectical transformation."[84]

A recent essay by Adams is not as optimistic about
the transformation possible through gradual change.

> It may be that it is unrealistic to expect
> that a top-heavy civilization such as ours
> can solve its problems through deliberate
> thought and action. It may be that a wide
> measure of social and economic justice can
> come only after the advent of national or
> international crises of mammoth proportions.[85]

What intervened in the nineteen years to make Adams'
thinking similar to Tillich's dialectical approach? For
in Tillich's view,

> . . . as a social Gestalt moves forward into
> new situations, contradictions become in-
> creasingly evident and new possibilities
> emerge. Again and again an eruption is nec-
> essary to give room for new elements.[86]

How has Adams' view changed? It is not his evalu-
ation of the voluntary association that has been altered.
As a result of his German experiences in the mid-thirties,
Adams became convinced, as he later expressed it, that

---

[83]"Tillich's Dialectical Method in Social-Structural Analysis," Address to American Theological Society, Midwest
Division, 1955, p. 18 (typewritten).

[84]Ibid.

[85]"The Geography and Organization of Social Responsibility,"
p. 258. This was written in 1974.

[86]"Tillich's Dialectical Method in Social-Structural
Analysis," p. 11.

"a decisive institution of the viable democratic society is the voluntary association as a medium for the assumption of civic responsibility."[87] But he was quick to note that association is no guarantee of civic responsibility. It is but an opportunity for the implementation of consensus. Much depends on "the goals, the constituency, the internal organization of the association."[88] He finds no guarantees for success in human institutions; the human will is ambiguous and no guarantor of goodness.[89] Adams points out, as an example of this problem, "that participation in associations concerned with public policy is a middle-class phenomenon, and even then in special interest groups."[90]

However, twenty-five years after his German experiences, he has doubts about the viability of the voluntary association when confronted by the structures of contemporary capitalist industrial society. Structural problems are further compounded by the evolution of the American business corporation and the mass media. Adams sees these structures as "the principalities and the powers,"[91] the demonic forces that seek to bear mankind away. The task of Christian ethics, with the assistance of the behavioral sciences, is to confront these principalities and powers. But even here Adams cautions that ideology will develop. He has no delusions about the problems facing man. His enthusiasm for voluntary associations, always tempered by a realistic assessment of human fallibility, is further dampened by endemic tendencies in contemporary society. I began to sense that structural problems within contemporary society are exerting great pressure on Adams' thought patterns. There is no about face, but caution is stressed.

---

[87] "The Evolution of My Social Concern," p. 16.

[88] Ibid., p. 18. Adams' estimate of the ambiguity of human freedom has always stood over against any straightforward march toward utopia. See the treatment of the characteristics of his religious liberalism, pp. 34 ff.

[89] See this same theme in "Is Marx's Thought Relevant to the Christian? A Protestant View," pp. 384-85.

[90] "The Evolution of My Social Concern," p. 23. Adams notes one study which shows that professional and business people do not break through class and racial barriers by involvement in philanthropic and service organizations. Rather, they entrench themselves more deeply in their own perspective. Ibid.

[91] "The Evolution of My Social Concern," p. 24.

147

Adams' opinion of common law and the parliamentary tradition also reflects an earlier belief in gradualism. In his view, neither of these aspects of the democratic society guarantee automatic results, but he writes two decades ago that "one can claim that the operation of these agencies has given an evolutionary rather than a dialectical character to social change."[92] I see this statement as a reflection of the relative stability in American society at that time. Adams' views in the ensuing years are, in my interpretation, likewise reflections of the society. It is not surprising that he becomes much more skeptical about gradualism. Indications of this caution are present in the address discussed above.[93] Moreover, the assassinations, the war, the subtle undermining of the civil rights drive and the war on poverty, the growth of multinational corporations, as well as the Watergate revelations which point to the widespread imperialism of American domestic and foreign policy, are no doubt responsible for his less optimistic approach to social change today. I see[94] Adams influenced by the milieu of America in the 1960's and 1970's as Tillich was influenced by the milieu of Germany in the 1920's. Their positions are, as a result,

---

[92]Tillich's "Dialectical Method in Social-Structural Analysis," p. 20 (1955).

[93]See p. 147, footnote 90.

[94]See "Hits Win Ball Games: The Creative Thrust of Conflict." Adams notes that racial riots in Watts have quickened the pace of change in American society. Ibid., pp. 14-15. This seems to be in line with his growing belief that gradualism is being supplanted by more radical means of social change. Elsewhere, Adams evidences this same understanding of change in American society. "If we Americans recognize that ours is the only industrial democracy where one may count upon having riots every summer, we may be willing to admit that we, too, have an unconquered past." "Our Unconquered Past," The Unitarian Christian, Vol. XXVI, 3 (1967), p. 4. His sensitivity to the dynamics of social change and the seriousness of problems facing America in the last decade are also seen in "Liberty and Law," speech given at Loyola University, Montreal, July 1968. (Typewritten.) This same understanding is evident in "Blessed are the Powerful," pp. 838-41.

closer to one another. Adams' awareness of the severe
problem facing America at the end of the last decade
is graphically illustrated in an article he wrote at
the time. He states:

> We need not spell out here the current size
> and statistics of the grotesque powers that
> express Man the Destroyer today. The in-
> creasing disparity between the haves and
> the have-nots; the disparity in the national
> budget between the dollar-billions (and the
> men!) allotted to weaponry and those assigned
> to antipoverty. . . .[95]

This influence of milieu is evident in his views on
the civil rights movement. He saw the "old gradualism"
being replaced by the "walk-in, sit-in, boycott, mass
demonstration."[96] He declared:

> The demonic possession that is upon us all
> at the hands of racism is manifest much
> closer to home than Africa, in the custom-
> ary attitude of the White toward the Col-
> ored man in our midst. It is manifest in
> the fact that over a century after our
> Emancipation Proclamation our Senate is
> only now attempting to give full meaning
> to the Fourteenth Amendment. . . A new
> humanity for the Negro will require
> struggle for a long time to come.[97]

He characterizes the movement as a struggle but one that
appears to be ongoing within history. While Adams has
always seen history as ongoing, there is a tragic element
in contemporary American history, tragedy understood in
the classical Greek sense as issuing from betrayal of
"family, friendship, or nation." The tragedy we experience is that "the people who have been the victims of
white supremacy are bound together with us as our fellow
citizens and many of them as our fellow churchmen."[98]

---

[95]"The Grotesque and Our Future," _Unitarian Universalist
Association Now_, L, No. 14 (1969), p. 11.

[96]"America: A Land of Hope. The Churches and the Negro,"
p. 8a. English manuscript of "Amerika--ein Land der Hoff-
nung/Die Kirchen und die Neger," _Evangelische Verantwortuung_,
XI, 7 (1963), pp. 8-15.

[97]"We Wrestle Against Principalities and Powers," p. 6.

[98]"The Shock of Recognition: The Black Revolution and
Greek Tragedy," p. 7.

In describing attitudes of students and blacks toward Vietnam and racism, Adams evidenced the impact they have had on him in the following statement:

In a day when an increasing number of people, especially students and blacks, are speaking of the present "transition from dissent to resistance" as the advent of the second American Revolution, there could scarcely be a more timely subject for discussion than civil disobedience.[99]

In view of the year in which he writes, it is not surprising that Adams speaks of civil disobedience and, further on, of revolution[100] as an even more drastic alternative to the "normal political procedures" embodied in such institutions as voluntary associations, common law, and parliament. Thus, Adams' statement about "top-heavy civilizations and crises of mammoth proportions"[101] is understandable in view of changes that have taken place in American society. He also sees mass media: journalism; television; cinema; advertising as critical and dangerous developments in the American culture of the 1960's.[102] Adams' assessment of possibilities has thus become more cautious if not pessimistic. Does this present a change in his thinking? There is no change in his way of approaching problems and the interpretation of events, for he has always sought to be sensitive to the historical situation. There is, however, a change in his opinion about American society. Optimism and realism have always gone together in Adams' thought. In no way has his ultimate optimism about God's kingdom been diminished. However, his realism has become more stark, predominating more markedly over his optimism. This starkness or pessimism is not the same as apocalypticism. Adams is not waiting for God to accomplish the work of man, for "with the appearance of apocalypticism . . . the work of God is emphasized to the detriment of human responsibility."[103]

---

[99] "Civil Disobedience: Its Occasions and Limits," p. 293.

[100] Ibid., p. 331.

[101] "The Geography and Organization of Social Responsibility," p. 258.

[102] "Broken Cisterns and Earthen Vessels," Lecture delivered at Vassar College Chapel, February 28, 1965, pp. 4-7.

[103] "Is Marx's Thought Relevant to the Christian? A Protestant View," p. 380.

While Adams remains a staunch believer in voluntary associations, he finds potential for change radically affected by the social context in which they operate. The democratic traditions, the developing middle class, and the economic growth of America are integrally related to the viability of these associations. But millions are left out and thus the pragmatic test raises some sharp issues with regard to the voluntary association.

When we remember the fundamental relationship between power and the voluntary association, we realize that this associational principle is one means whereby power is expressed. Thus, we must face the future resolutely, willing to evaluate the voluntary association principle but even more importantly, to evaluate the use of power in a society apparently grown more complex. I say "apparently" because in any assessment of liberalism, or for that matter in any interpretation of reality, one must continually come back to the question of the accuracy of interpretation. Is our society more "complex" than in the past or could it not be that liberalism, even as Adams has redefined it, has been too gullible about the accountability of private and public sectors in society? Is our society more complex or could it be, as Beverly Harrison puts it, that Adams' liberal analysis "was never hard-nosed enough about power and class realities in spite of verbal commitments to 'realism' and that it is time to assess far more honestly the class location of liberalism?"[104]

These are important questions but I do see Adams' analysis of power assisting us in developing a more analytic understanding of contemporary problems and thus aiding us in answering these questions. Perhaps Adams has been too closely associated with voluntary associations by many of his students and readers, blocking any real linkage which Adams makes between these associations and the power issue. This discussion brings me to a final evaluation of Adams.

---

[104]Personal correspondence with the author.

CHAPTER VI

JAMES LUTHER ADAMS: A CONTEMPORARY ETHICIST

James Luther Adams' career spans over forty years
and he is still doing research, writing, teaching, lecturing, translating, editing, and joining and chairing
associations. He is uniquely important as a Christian
ethicist. His comprehensively social orientation and
the dialectical tension-filled nature of Adams' thought
lead him to a stance of constant interaction with his
environment. And in this light, historical-social analysis is the methodological tool he finds adequate to
accomplish cognitively what he encourages experientially of himself and others.

Today the critical task facing every theologian
is the evaluation and interpretation of historically
conditioned belief. I regard the particular way in
which Adams faces this challenge as important for those
theologians involved in Christian ethics. Concern for
this tradition, openness to the social sciences, and
active involvement in religious and secular associations lead Adams to an emphasis on the clear understanding of context and social structure as the necessary
presupposition which must be comprehended along with
ethical norms. That he uses norms is obvious but only
in relation to contextualization.

Because of this approach to the reinterpretation of
the tradition, I think Adams is significant within the
theological tradition. The complexity of the problems
we face, the interrelatedness of the disciplines involved in solving problems, the inherent pragmatism of
the American spirit, all of these characteristics of
our time and place find a relevant resource in James
Luther Adams.

Thus the dialectical orientation in Adams is concretized in this relationship between theological and
historical-social analysis. I see Adams clearly point-
ing to the contextual nature of ethics. Man, called to
decision making, must do so within a historical community. The validity of his decisions depends upon
acknowledgment of their time-bound quality. Since they
are temporal, decisions are not absolute. Even more

153

importantly, they are not absolute because of our difficulty in fully grasping the intricacies of our historical
moment. Such an understanding, I feel, leads Adams to
emphasize consensus as a way of grasping as fully as
possible the complexities of a situation.

Adams brings the theological tradition to bear on
this historical method. He is no relativist but he
constantly argues with the theological tradition and
history, striving to keep them both honest partners in
an ongoing conversation. God is God. This is an ontological fact for Adams. Justice and love likewise
transcend any particular historical manifestation and
understanding of them. These realities, however, obtain
historical character and are fleshed out in successive
communities. How this process occurs is described by
means of the historical method. Adams holds that the
essence of liberalism is relevance and the essence of
relevance is ontological reality: God, love, justice.
Far from being abstract ideas, these realities dwell
on the continents of earth and in the temporality of
history.

For Adams, historical method is wedded to social
analysis. Adams is not only concerned with the contextual understanding and demands of ethical relevancy;
he views history primarily from the perspective of
community and institutions. In a word, he is concerned
with the structures of society. As we have seen, this
theme has been consistently played out in his liberalism, theology, and ethics.

Stackhouse points to Adams' focus "on the social
and theoretical (theological and philosophical) pre-
conditions for meaningful existence in community."[1]
Adams does not accept automatically the context in which
decisions are made. Once again, we see his concern
with reality in relation to ideas. Theory and practice
go hand in hand. One must come to grips with the reality in which decisions are made if the decisions are to
be effective. "The primary job of Social Ethics," in
the Adamsean perspective, "is less the guidance of specific decision making in a casuistic fashion. . . than
the clarification of the social, ideational, and dis-
positional circumstances under which human life can become most significant and least destructive. . . ."[2]

---

[1]Stackhouse, "Editor's Introduction," On Being Human
Religiously, p. xxi.

[2]Ibid.

154

Adams' emphasis upon the church and his distinctive use of the term "prophethood of all believers" has a special attraction for me. As a Roman Catholic I think my church has much to learn from Adams' emphasis on community and consensus. Authority is too tightly in the hands of the hierarchical members. The latter do not act as if they really believe that the Spirit speaks through the church including the local congregation. Their rejection of women as priests and the maintenance of the status of celibacy are evidence that they maintain a constricted understanding of the church, one in which the Spirit addresses the laity only through those in authority.

Ironically, the Roman Catholic hierarchy in the United States has made important statements on social ethics in terms of nuclear disarmament, peace, world hunger, just wages, and human rights. Yet the popular image of the bishops in the mind of countless Catholics as well as Protestants is that the Catholic church is obsessed with sex in terms of prohibitions on birth control and abortion and in equating priesthood with maleness and celibacy.

Much of this distortion I blame on the press but there is more to it than that. The church's position on social issues does not reach the ears of the laity. The bishops tend to write isolated from the laity, but unless the local congregation is involved, their statements are useless. A renewed understanding of the congregation is in order, one which elicits active participation not passive reception from all members. The typical parish must be transformed from the "gas station" image where the faithful are "refueled" to one which upholds, as does Adams, the radical nature of participation in the church through the priesthood of all believers, but also through the prophethood of all believers.[3]

> The prophetic liberal church is the church in which men think and work together to interpret the signs of the times in the light of their faith, to make explicit through

---

[3] I have no doubts that other denominations have similar problems. It is not one peculiar to Catholics. Adams certainly was not directing his thoughts toward Catholics!

discussion the epochal thinking which the
times demand. The prophetic liberal church
is the church in which all members share
the common responsibility to attempt to
foresee the consequences of human behavior
(both individual and institutional), with
the intention of making history in place
of merely being pushed around by it. Only
through the prophetism of all believers
can we together foresee doom and mend our
common ways.[4]

Adams' doctrine of church has a sharp ethical edge.
Its members are "forthtellers," proclaiming God's action
in history interpreting the meaning of history.[5] This
is the transcendent dimension of prophethood. But this
dimension is complemented by an immanent one, that of
foretelling or social criticism. However, the church
as foreteller orients its membership to the secular arena.

While forthtelling and foretelling take place in the
ecclesiastical sphere, it is within the secular realm,
especially in the voluntary association, that I see where
foretelling has its most dramatic role. I find Adams'
emphasis on secular foretelling or social criticism
through voluntary associations important because it provides a means of solidarity with those who are committed
to social ethical concerns but who are not necessarily
Christian. Such solidarity is important in a pluralistic
society faced with complex social problems. Thus, consciousness of and concern for social issues are not the
monopoly of Christians nor is involvement in voluntary
associations. Through the latter, social criticism can
be effectively arrived at and enunciated. Furthermore,
such societal organization fosters not only criticism
but pressure for change. There is thus a theoretical
and practical side to such association.

Adams' ability to reevaluate the voluntary association is a facet of his thinking that I appreciate very
much. He has seen this type of association as an important element in Western civilization, especially in
the liberal democratic tradition. However, he is not

---

[4]"The Prophethood of All Believers," p. 25.

[5]Ibid., p. 21.

married to the concept. Adams is able to contextualize the voluntary association and criticize it vis-a-vis the effective use of power under changed circumstances. Along with him, I respect the role of such association as a moral agent and locus for mediating personal and institutional transformation, but I do not see Adams equating mutuality, community, or the achievement of justice solely with the voluntary association. The discriminate use of power underlies mutuality, community and justice, and the voluntary association is one means to achieve these goals.

On a more personal note, it is Adams' profound concern for and involvement in voluntary associations that was one of the initial reasons why I became interested in him. I believe, as he does, that they are vital to liberal democracy. Yet I am confronted by the apathy which has weakened the membership base of many types of voluntary associations. At the same time, I do not see the solution to this problem as a process of consciousness raising with regard to voluntary associations and their importance. The roots of the problem are in the changes taking place in American society. Rising levels of affluence coupled with increasing poverty seem to anesthetize Americans to the demands of a political process which affects them personally. Disillusionment with government and a lack of credibility in government leaders reinforce the frustration which the average person experiences with anonymous bureaucratic structures. The very pluralism and complexity of the American society and government, one of our strengths as a nation, contributes to this lack of concern about the political process, the loss of credibility in government, and the evolution of bureaucracy. Thus, while I remain convinced of the importance of the voluntary association, I realize that the contextual understanding of American society challenges the validity of this model. I have pointed to Adams' awareness of this as well.

As a result of this assessment of voluntary associations, I ask myself whether there is not a more substantial reason as to why the voluntary association is not as effective as it should be. The reason which recurs in my mind relates to the weaker power base supporting such associations. The voluntary association has been neglected as a mechanism for acquiring and channeling power by a rising middle class. Having acquired wealth and a knowledge of power in American society, many no longer need the

157

voluntary association. Despite their ambitions, for
the vast majority of people, the great American pie
provides a large enough slice. Voluntary associations
atrophy when the public interest of the powerful is
satisfied by affluence. For the poor, who do not share
in the pie and who have no power base, voluntary associations are meaningless. Adams' analysis of power,
especially as it relates to the voluntary association,
has enabled me to come to this view.[6]

There are three ideas in Adams that I find of special interest. They are his emphasis on theory and practice, the social nature of the individual, and the interaction of personal and social ethics. Sensitivity to
social ethics is greatly assisted by an awareness of
socialization and testing of the consequences of belief
in practice. Practice will always have its social consequences and thus become the material for analysis in
social ethics. At the same time, affirmation of the
self and personal ethics do not allow for the collapse
of the individual into the group.

In my understanding of Adams, the sense of life as
a dialectical process goes to the heart of his character. He stands in the voluntarist tradition emphasizing
creativity and man's will, the dynamic aspects of existence. Yet the intellect is also important for him. In
an early essay[7] Adams contrasts Dionysian and Apollonian
views of human nature. The Dionysian stresses will and
the Apollonian, reason. In many ways, I see Adams incorporating both views into his dialectical approach to
existence. On the one hand, Adams might well be called
Dionysian. In this view, will is given primacy over intellect and has a vitality that "imbues every form but
that also eludes and bursts the bounds of every structure."[8]
On the other hand, reason and a concern for structure,
Apollonian qualities, are also evident in his approach to
issues. A truly dialectical thinker, Adams incorporates
both qualities.

---

[6]See above, pp. 131 ff. I realize in saying this that many
Americans do use the voluntary association for the public
interest: ecology groups; the American Civil Liberties
Union; the National Organization for Women.

[7]"The Changing Reputation of Human Nature," pp. 64 ff. Adams
does not apply these characteristics to himself. I am applying them to him as a means of highlighting the dialectical
nature of his thinking.

[8]Ibid., p. 65.

Adams' dialectical bent makes itself most powerfully felt in the creative tension he keeps alive between the historical tradition of the Christian faith and the concerns of the present day. It is most decidedly here that Adams' greatest skill and unique contribution are to be found. Placing Christianity and contemporaneity in continual interaction, Adams' goal is to find a creative relationship between the two, utilizing theological as well as historical-social analysis to do so. This goal is supported by the breadth of his interests which range from politics to philosophy. The creative syntheses between Christianity and contemporality which he develops are evidence of his dynamic approach to religious thinking. Among Adams' students, the word has gone around that he is a "truly Renaissance man who believes in salvation by bibliography."

In retrospect, what can be said of the goals Adams' ethics concern? He places the achievement of mutuality as a central aspect of human existence. His theological presuppositions and ethical characteristics support this priority. Response to the power of God bringing about community based on justice and love clearly expresses this goal as an ethical norm. Response to the power of God is, for Adams, an effective use of power, for power is not only the ability to influence but also to be influenced.[9] Thus, response is an exercise of power. At the same time this response means activity. Theory and practice always go together for Adams, thus response necessitates efforts toward the production of community. The attainment of community can be ascertained by using the norm of justice and love. If they are present, community is attained and response to God has been effected.

While love and justice are both important for Adams, I see justice as having a special place in his thought. I say this in view of his commitment to social structural issues in which the production of justice is a critical norm. Moreover, Adams speaks to a pluralistic audience for whom justice has a clearer meaning than does love.

In various sections of this book I have noted difficulties with or expressed criticism of Adams' thought and I wish to review these in this concluding chapter. Adams does not develop any explicit ethical theory or principles.

---

[9]"Blessed are the Powerful," p. 839.

This is a result of his consistent focus on particular issues. I consider this a virtue in him that he does not feel impelled to work through a stated set of principles to issues. He certainly makes use of the ethical and theological traditions but as resources to analyze a problem. While I see this as a virtue in Adams, I also find it a "vice." His lack of an explicit set of principles has made the writing of this work difficult and is assuredly one reason why Adams' achievements are not as widely appreciated as they should be.

I have pointed to Adams' discussion of civil disobedience and the universal validity of demands for justice.[10] Adams seems to equate the universal validity of justice with the means to attain justice. I have noted the distinction, and I see it as related to the problem of natural law.[11] Adams emphasizes the difficulty in using natural law theory. I think he manifests this difficulty in the above-noted discussion of universal validity and means. I favor Adams' concern for natural law, but I also see, as he does, the great difficulty in working out the use of natural law theory.

With Beverly Harrison, I find myself frequently asking whether Adams is hard-nosed enough about power structures in American society. However, I cannot cast the first stone of criticism in this regard. I wonder whether he and I are aware enough of the class structure in which we operate and propose our social criticisms? This is perhaps the most difficult task of any theologian and especially of an ethicist: awareness that one's own theory is a moment in praxis and subject to the machinations of conflict and ideology. An inability to realize this might well be the cause of naivete in liberalism. Adams is no naive liberal, but he does operate out of a middle-class, academic framework. Though he is an ardent activist, he lacks a realism at times with regard to corporate power and lower-class powerlessness. He is, I must say, not alone in this fault. It is mine as well, and I am sure many readers of this work will also say mea culpa.

In conclusion, I hope this analysis has caught the spirit of James Luther Adams and that his spirit has been

---

[10]See above, p. 119.

[11]See above, pp. 111 ff.

communicated to my readers. Adams is well known and respected within academic, religious, and political circles in this country and abroad. As Max Stackhouse states:

> Surely no major theologian has preached in more local churches, attended more meetings where strategies for personal growth or social change were worked out, been president of so many academic societies, nor carried out a wider correspondence with leaders in many fields around the world. In fact, it is likely that no twentieth century theologian has been mentioned in the "acknowledgments" of other people's books more frequently than this man.[12]

Thus, Adams has achieved a unique place in American Christian ethics. However, he has characteristically focused on the thought of others (i.e., Tillich, Troeltsch) and he has not self-consciously developed a systematic approach to ethics. I hope this work will clarify his thinking in this regard.

One of the most important aspects in the writing of this book has been the personal contact I have had with Adams. He is a wonderful man whose ability to stimulate and edify are unusual. My life has been changed not only as a result of reading his writings but more especially because I have known him personally. I cannot thank him enough for this contact and for all the assistance he has given me by way of conversation, manuscripts, and insight.

I think Adams ranks among the top American theologians of his generation. Adams' use of the social sciences has given him an accurate sense of the context in which he has done his thinking. His fidelity to the Christian tradition has grounded his ethical concern in a transcendent framework. His understanding of power and the communitarian nature of humankind has given him a sense of realism and idealism. And, finally, his passion for social justice makes him a man sorely needed in our times.

---

[12]Stackhouse, "Editor's Introduction," <u>On Being Human - Religiously</u>, p. xxix.

BIBLIOGRAPHY

1. Articles and Books by Adams

Adams, James Luther. "Aberglaube." ["Superstition."]
Welkirchen Lexikon. Stuttgart: Kreuz Verlag,
1960, p. 8.

_____. "Academic Nudism at the University of
California." The Pittsburgh Courier, September 30,
October 11, 1950.

_____. "Affirmative Liberalism. 'Oyster-Shell'
and 'Jelly-Fish' Nihilism." The Christian Register,
CXXVII, No. 6 (1948), 22-25.

_____. "After Liberalism." No date. Inter-
nal evidence would indicate a date around 1940 (typewritten).

_____. "The Ages of Liberalism." The Journal
of Religious Thought, XIV, No. 2 (1957), 101-17.

_____. "Aging: A Theological Interpretation."
The Unitarian Universalist Christian, XXVIII, Nos.
2-3 (1973), 4-15.

_____. "American Churchman Sees Parish Aided
by Nazis." The Hour. New York: American Council
Against Nazi Propaganda, June 30, 1939, p. 1.

_____. "The American Religion." Transcript
of sermon at Berea College, Berea, Kentucky,
February 19, 1961.

_____. "Amerika--Land der Hoffnung: Die Kir-
chen und die Neger." ["America--Land of Hope: The
Churches and the Blacks."] Evangelische Verant-
wortung, XI, No. 7 (1963), 8-12. (English text used.)

_____. "Archibald Thompson Davison. In Mem-
oriam." Sermon delivered in Andover Chapel, Harvard Divinity School, February 16, 1961 (typewritten).

_____. "Are You With Us?" Speech at Victory
Meeting, June 1, 1942 (typewritten).

Adams, James Luther. "Arminius and the Structure of Society." Man's Faith and Freedom: The Theological Influence of Jacobus Arminius. Edited by G. O. McCulloh. New York: Abingdon Press, 1962, pp. 88-112.

_____. "The Arts and Society." Paper prepared for the Theological Discussion Group, Washington, D. C., 1955 (mimeographed).

_____. "Assailing the Liberal's Defense: Its Symptoms But Not Its Essence." The Christian Register, CXII, No. 12 (1933), 181, 194.

_____. "Authority and Freedom in a Mass Society." Report of the Fourteenth Congress of the International Association for Liberal Christianity and Religious Freedom. Oxford, August 1952. The Hague: International Association for Liberal Christianity and Religious Freedom Headquarters, 1952, pp. 23-24.

_____. "The Axis is Longer Than You Think-- The Anti-Negro, Anti-Semitic, Anti-Labor, Anti-Progressive Axis." The Protestant, IV, No. 5 (1942), 23-28.

_____. "Basic Causes of Progress and Decay in Civilization." Orientation in Religious Education. Edited by P.H. Lotz. New York: Abingdon-Cokesbury, 1950, pp. 61-74. Also in Taking Time Seriously. Glencoe, Ill.: The Free Press, 1957, pp. 26-41.

_____. "Baron Friedrich von Huegel." The Christian Register, CXIII, No. 37 (1934), 603-06.

_____. "Blessed Are the Powerful." The Christian Century, LXXXVI, No. 25 (1969), 838-41.

_____. "The Body and Soul of Learning." Commencement address, Meadville/Lombard Theological School, Chicago, June 13, 1976 (typewritten).

_____. "Bright Shoots of Everlastingness." Andover Newton Quarterly, X, No. 1 (1969), 12-18.

164

Adams, James Luther. "Broken Cisterns and Earthen Vessels." Sermon preached in Vassar College Chapel, Poughkeepsie, New York, February 28, 1965 (mimeographed).

_____. "Bruderschaften, geistliche. II. Amerika." ["Spiritual Brotherhoods in America."] Weltkirchen Lexicon. Stuttgart: Kreuz Verlag, 1960, pp. 184-85.

_____. "By Their Fruits." The Christian Register, CXIII, No. 18 (1934), 296.

_____. "By Their Groups Shall Ye Know Them: The Voluntary Association as a Distinctive Institution of Democracy." Lecture delivered at the University of Bonn on the occasion of the tenth anniversary of the Fulbright Program, November 1962 (typewritten).

_____. "By Their Groups Shall You Know Them. A Protestant Theory of Vocation." Hibbert Lecture delivered at Manchester College, Oxford, March 12, 1963 (typewritten).

_____. "The Catholic Crusade." Journal of Liberal Religion, V, No. 2 (1943), 101-10.

_____. "Centerstance: An Essay on the Purposes of a Liberal Arts Education." The Liberal Context, II (Winter 1962), 9-11.

_____. "Cell Groups and Social Action." Transcript of remarks at the 1948 Conference on the Cell Group, University of Michigan, Ann Arbor, October 23, 1948 (mimeographed).

_____. "The Challenge of the World's Today." Radio address over WGN. No location, no date. Internal evidence points to a date in the late 1930's.

_____. "Changing Frontiers: Vanishing and Emerging." Supplement to The Unitarian Christian, October 1957. Also in The Unitarian Register, CXXXVI, No. 6 (1957), 10-12, 45.

_____. "The Changing Reputation of Human Nature." Journal of Liberal Religion, IV, Nos. 2-3 (1942-43), 59-72, 137-60. Reprinted as a brochure.

Adams, James Luther. "Changing Roles of the Ministry Today. Sociological Factors and Theological Interpretations." c. 1950 (mimeographed).

_____. "The Chief End of Man." Harvard Divinity School Bulletin, XIX (1954), 39-47.

_____. "The Christian-Marxist Dialogue: An Introduction." The Unitarian Universalist Christian, XXVI, Nos. 3-4 (1971), 3-7.

_____. "Christian Socialism" Encyclopedia Brittanica, 14th ed., Vol. V, pp. 701-03.

_____. "Christian Vocation: An Examination of the Political Symbolism of Biblical Faith." Lecture at Denison University. Tentative dating: March 1955 (typewritten).

_____. "Christianity and Humanism." Address delivered at the University of Iowa, 1937 (typewritten).

_____. "Church and State." Report of James Luther Adams on behalf of the Committee on Church and State in "Annual Reports of Standing Committees." Civil Liberties in the Bay State, Summer 1970. Published by the Civil Liberties Union of Massachusetts.

_____. "The Churches and Social Reform: By Their Groups Shall Ye Know Them." J.M. Dawson Lecture on Church and State delivered at Baylor University, Waco, Texas, May 7, 1970 (typewritten).

_____. "Church-State Committee Chairman Adams Represents CLUM at Capitol Hearing." Report by Adams in Civil Liberties in the Bay State, Summer 1966. Published by the Civil Liberties Union of Massachusetts, p. 5.

_____. "Civil Disobedience: Its Occasions and Limits." Political and Legal Obligations: Nomos XII. Edited by J. Roland Pennock and John W. Chapman. New York: Atherton Press, 1970, pp. 293-331.

_____. "Civilization versus Pacifism." No copy is extant. An extended summary by Llewellyn Jones appeared under the title "Are We Christians? Ought We To Be?" The Christian Register, CXVIII, No. 35 (1939), 570-72.

166

Adams, James Luther. "Comparison of the Old Rationalism
and the New Rationalism; Comparison of the New
Rationalism and the Instrumentalism of Dewey, With
Particular Reference to Their Notions of Truth and
Ways of Attaining It." No date. (Typewritten.)

_____. "Contributions of Occidental Religion
to Cultural Understanding." Proceedings of the
IXth International Congress for the History of Religions. Tokyo: Maruzen, 1960, pp. 730-35.

_____. "A Council Observer Tells of Warmth,
Splendor." Boston Globe. November 22, 1962, p. 71.

_____. "Crystallizing Unitarian Beliefs."
Outlines of lectures given at Lake Geneva Unitarian
Summer Conference, 1942. (Mimeographed.)

_____. "Culture." A Handbook of Christian
Theology. Edited by Marvin Halverson. New York:
Meridian Books, 1958, pp. 67-70.

_____. "Danger Points in American Democracy
Today." Address, 1945 (typewritten).

_____. "A Day and a Place Set Apart." The
Christian Register, CXIII, No. 5 (1934), 70.

_____. "The Declarative Mood." Unpublished
essay. No date. (Typewritten.)

_____. "Der Gebrauch der Analogie in der
Sozialphilosophie." ["The Use of Analogy in Social
Philosophy."] Jahrbuch der Schweizerischen Gesell-
schaft, XXIII (1963), 1-17.

_____. "Dr. Adams' Letter to a Responsible
Official of the National Conference of Christians
and Jews." Protestant Digest, I, No. 8 (1939), 1-7.

_____. "Emancipation Proclamation--1941."
Protestant Digest, III, No. 12 (1941), 14-20.

_____. "Encounter with the Demonic: From the
Psyche to the Society. An Introduction to Christoph
Blumhardt's Letter to His Friends." Metanoia, III,
No. 3 (1971), 2-4.

Adams, James Luther. "Enlarging Horizons." Harvard Business School Bulletin, XLI, No. 2 (1965), 12-14.

_____. "Ernst Troeltsch." Encyclopedia Brittanica, 14th ed., Vol. XXII, p. 489.

_____. "Ernst Troeltsch as Analyst of Religion." Journal for the Scientific Study of Religion, I, No. 1 (1961), 98-109.

_____. "Established on the Floods: An Enduring Heritage." Sermon delivered at the 100th Anniversary of the Unitarian Society of Wellesley Hill, Massachusetts. March 1971 (typewritten).

_____. "Ethics." A Handbook of Christian Theology. Edited by Marvin Halverson. New York: Meridian Books, 1958, pp. 110-17.

_____. "The Evil That Good Men Do." Sermon preached at the University of Chicago, May 17, 1942. Also in Voices of Liberalism: 2. Boston: Beacon Press, 1948, pp. 53-64.

_____. "The Evolution of My Social Concern." Address at the annual meeting of the American Association for Teachers of Christian Social Ethics. Louisville, Kentucky, 1961 (typewritten).

_____. "Exiles, Trapped in the Welfare State." The Unitarian Christian, XXII, No. 4 (1967), 3-9.

_____. "The Existentialist Thesis in Current Christian Thought." Unpublished essay. No date. (Typewritten.)

_____. "A Faith for Free Men." Together We Advance. Edited by S.H. Frichtman. Boston: Beacon Press, 1946, pp. 45-65. In this book a mimeographed edition of the original was used. A summary appears in The Epic of Unitarianism. Edited by David B. Parke. Boston: Starr King Press, 1957, pp. 149-54.

_____. "A Faith for Liberals to Live By." Syllabus for course held under auspices of the Unitarian Religious Education Institute, Lake Geneva, Wisconsin, June 18-29, 1939 (mimeographed).

Adams, James Luther. "Foreword." The Age of the Person: Society in the 20th Century. Dietrich von Oppen. Philadelphia: Fortress Press, 1969, pp. vii-xi.

_____. "Foreword." Pastoral Care in the Liberal Churches. Edited by James L. Adams and Seward Hiltner. Nashville: Abingdon, 1970, pp. 10-13.

_____. "Foreword." The Real Meaning of Communism. Ellis H. Dana. Brochure. Madison, Wisconsin, 1962. No page numbers.

_____. "Francis Greenwood Peabody." The Harvard Divinity School: Its Place in Harvard University and in American Culture. Edited by George H. Williams. Boston: Beacon Press, 1954, pp. 180-82.

_____. "Free Church Movement Shows Limited Upsurge in Germany." Christian Science Monitor, XLII, No. 270 (1950), 11.

_____. "Fresh Air Into the Church?" Challenge, I, No. 3 (1963), 8-9.

_____. "Freud, Mannheim, and the Liberal Doctrine of Man." Journal of Liberal Religion, II, No. 3 (1941), 107-11.

_____. "From Cage to Cage: An Intellectual Agenda in a Period of Centralized, Bureaucratic Power." Kairos, I, No. 2 (1976), 6.

_____. "From the Essenes to the Kibbutzim." Land Reborn, VIII, No. 11 (1957), 13-16.

_____. "From Psyche to Society." Perkins Journal, XXVI, No. 1 (1972), 17-24.

_____. Frontiers of Freedom. Pamphlet reprint of NBC Blue Network Radio Broadcast, October 26, 1941. Reprinted in Congressional Record, XXCI, No. 191 (1941), A4887-A4889.

_____. "The Fundamentalist Far Right Rides Again: Congress Attacks 'Secular Humanism.'" The Humanist, XXXVI, No. 5 (1976), 8-9.

169

Adams, James Luther. "The Geography and Organization of Social Responsibility." Union Seminary Quarterly Review, XXIX, No. 3-4 (1974), 245-60.

_____. "Glossary of Terms," contained in "Crystallizing Unitarian Beliefs." 1942.

_____. "God and Economics." Excerpts from annual lecture on "God and the Modern World" at the General Assembly of the Unitarian Universalist Association. Unitarian Universalist World, VII, No. 11 (1976), 4.

_____. "God is Love." Sermon preached at Meadville Theological Seminary, November 7, 1947. (Typewritten.) According to James D. Hunt, Adams has acknowledged that the sermon was largely based on notes of Tillich's lectures at Union Theological Seminary. "James Luther Adams and His Demand for an Effective Religious Liberalism." Unpublished Ph.D. dissertation, Syracuse University, 1965, p. 207.

_____. "The Grace of Staying Together: Comments on the Ecumenical Movement." Faith and Freedom, VIII, No. 3 (1955), 131-34.

_____. "The Grotesque and our Future." Unitarian Universalist Association Now, I, No. 14 (1969), 10-11.

_____. "A Handbook on Postwar Reconstruction, Summary and Discussion with Bibliography." Journal of Liberal Religion, VI, No. 1 (1944), 47-55.

_____. "Hidden Dangers of Anti-Israelism." The Christian Register, CXXXIII, No. 9 (1954), 16-18. Reprinted in The Jewish Advocate (Boston, Mass.), CXVI, No. 1 (1955), 1, 11.

_____. "Historical Perspective on the Pluralistic Society." Address to conference on "The Voluntary Organization/ Church in a Pluralistic Society--A Look Back and a Look Forward." Loyola University, Chicago, June 7, 1974 (typewritten).

Adams, James Luther. "Hits Win Ball Games: The Crea-
tive Thrust of Conflict." Address to The General
Assembly of the Unitarian Universalist Association,
Hollywood, Florida, May 17, 1966. (Typewritten.)
This address appears in abbreviated form in The
Register-Leader (Boston), CIIL, No. 7 (1966), 3-5.

_____. "How Modern Sociology Looks at Man in
Community: And Some Problems to Take to the Bible."
Remarks at meeting of study group on The Biblical
Doctrine of Man in Society, Seabury Western Semin-
ary, c. 1954 (mimeographed minutes).

_____. "Human Nature and the Nature of His-
tory." Lecture at Colloquium on Man, American
Unitarian Association, May Meetings. May 1961
(tape transcript, incomplete).

_____. "In Memory of Paul Tillich." Prospect,
V, No. 7 (1965), 11-14.

_____. "In Praise of Shame." Sermon reported
in The Salem Evening News, May 2, 1927.

_____. "The Indispensable Discipline of Social
Responsibility." Journal of the Liberal Ministry,
VI, No. 2 (1966), 80-86.

_____. "Initiative and Response." The Uni-
tarian Christian, XV, 1 (1959), pp. 3-5, 17.

_____. "Inquisitions Old and New." The Chi-
cago Jewish Forum, IX (Summer 1951), 220-235.
With a few changes, this article is the same as
"Love and Law and 'The Good Old Cause.'" The
Divinity School News [Chicago], XVII, No. 3
(1950), 1-8.

_____. "The Institutional Consequences of
Religious Beliefs." Abstract of Presidential
Address, Society for the Scientific Study of Religion, April 11, 1959. Bulletin of the Society
for the Scientific Study of Religion.

_____. "Interrogation of Paul Tillich."
Philosophical Interrogations. Edited by Sydney
Rome and Beatrice Rome. New York: Holt, Rine-
hart & Winston, 1965, pp. 404-06.

Adams, James Luther. Interviews taped at Gould Farm,
Monterey, Massachusetts. Interviewers: D. B.
Robertson and James D. Hunt. July-August 1964
(transcribed).

_____. Interview taped at Winchester, Massa-
chusetts. Interviewers: George Williams, Max L.
Stackhouse, James L. Hunt. April 30, 1968.

_____. Interviews taped at Cambridge, Massa-
chusetts. Interviewer: John R. Wilcox, March 6-9,
1972 (transcribed).

_____. Interview taped at Meadville Seminary,
Chicago. Interviewer: John R. Wilcox. April
1973 (transcribed).

_____. "Introduction." The Absoluteness of
Christianity and the History of Religions. Ernst
Troeltsch. Translated by David Reid. Richmond:
John Knox Press, 1971, pp. 7-20.

_____. "Introduction." Outlines of Church
History. Rudolph Sohm. Boston: Beacon Press,
1958, pp. ix-xiv.

_____. "Introduction." Political Expecta-
tion. Paul Tillich. New York: Harper & Row,
1971, pp. VI-XX.

_____. "Introduction." What Is Religion?
Paul Tillich. Edited by James Luther Adams. New
York: Harper & Row, 1969, pp. 9-24.

_____. "Is Marx's Thought Relevant to the
Christian? A Protestant View." Marx and the
Western World. Edited by Nicholas Lobkowicz.
South Bend: Notre Dame Press, 1967, pp. 370-88.

_____. "Israel in the Near-East Context."
Land Reborn, V, No. 2 (1954), 14.

_____. "Kirche und Gruppe: Aspects of a
Christian Doctrine of Vocation." Address in German at the Free University of Berlin, May 1963
(typewritten).

_____. "Kurt Leese and German Liberalism."
The Christian Register, CXVI, No. 28 (1937), 463-65.

172

Adams, James Luther. "The Law of Nature in Graeco-Roman Thought." Journal of Religion, XXV, No. 2 (1945), 97-118.

_____. "The Law of Nature: Some General Considerations." Journal of Religion, XXV, No. 2 (1945), 88-96.

_____. Letter to the Editor. The Christian Register, CXX, No. 16 (1941), 409-10. A letter on Barthians and Niebuhrians signed by Adams and others.

_____. Letter to the Editor. Comprendre, No. 12 (1954), p. 55. Letter dealing with East-West relations.

_____. Letter to the Editor. Comprendre, No. 12 (1954), pp. 169-70. Letter regarding the establishment of the new article "Presence de la Culture," in Comprendre, publication of La Societe Europeenne ae la Culture.

_____. Letter to the Editor. Comprendre, No. 25 (1962), pp. 226-27. Letter regarding proposed congress on relations between East and West.

_____. Letters to the Editor. Comprendre, No. 29-30 (1966), pp. 320-21. Letters regarding possible collaboration between La Societe Europeenne de la Culture and The American Academy of Arts and Sciences.

_____. Letter fragment, c. 1942-43 (typewritten).

_____. Letter to Ira Blalock, Jr. November 26, 1962 (typewritten).

_____. "The Liberal Christian Looks at Himself." Foundations of Liberal Christianity Lectures. All Souls' Unitarian Church, Washington, D. C., 1955 (mimeographed).

_____. "Liberal Christianity and the Predicament of Man." Based on a lecture given at Oberlin College, January 6, 1949 (typewritten).

_____. "Liberal Christianity and Modern Social Problems." The IARF: Its Vision and Its Work. The Hague: The International Association for Liberal Christianity and Religious Freedom, 1955, pp. 22-24.

Adams, James Luther. "The Liberal Church and Community
Organization." Address at the Unitarian Universalist Seminar on the Liberal Church and the City,
Washington, D. C., March 25, 1968. Abbreviated
and revised, mimeographed.

_____. "The Liberal Conception of Religious
Experience and Revelation." Outline for address
at International Association for Liberal Christianity and Religious Freedom Congress, Bentveld, Holland, 1938. (Typewritten.) The outline is also
contained in Year Book IARF 1939. Utrecht, Holland:
Secretariat IARF, 1939, pp. 15-16. Referred to in
The Christian Register, CXVII, No. 32 (1938), 486.

_____. "The Liberal Ministry in a Changing
Society." Address to Mid-Winter Institute, New
England Unitarian Universalist Ministers' Association. North Andover, Massachusetts. January
28, 1964 (mimeographed).

_____. "Liberal Religion in a United World."
The Christian Register, CXXIII, No. 2 (1944), 54-55.

_____. "Liberalism in Europe." Address to
Unitarian Ministers' Institute, September 9, 1936.
(Typewritten.) A report of the meeting is to be
found in The Christian Register, CXVI, No. 34
September 24, 1936), 567.

_____. "The Liberalism that is Dead." Jour-
nal of Liberal Religion, I, No. 3 (1940), 38-42.

_____. "Liberals and Religion." The Christian
Register, CXII, No. 8 (1933), 118.

_____. "Liberty and Law." Address at Loyola
University, Montreal. July 1968 (typewritten).

_____. "The Liturgical Year." Sermon at
Andover-Newton Chapel. March 25, 1969 (typewritten).

_____. "The Liverpool Controversy." The
Christian Register, CXIII, No. 30 (1934), 496-97.

_____. "Love, Law and 'the Good Old Cause.'"
The Divinity School News, Chicago, XVII, No. 3
(1950), 1-8.

Adams, James Luther. "The Love of God." The Meaning of
    Love. Edited by Ashley Montagu. New York: Julian
    Press, 1953, pp. 233-48.

_____. "The Lure of Persuasion: Some Themes
    from Whitehead." The Unitarian Universalist Christ-
    ian, XXX, No. 4 (1975-76), 5-22.

_____. "Man in the Light of the War." The
    Christian Century, LX, No. 9 (1943), 257-59.

_____. "Memorandum." Consultation on a Pro-
    posed Center for Ethics and Society. Cambridge,
    Massachusetts. May 19-20, 1972.

_____. "Military Training in Our Colleges."
    The Christian Register, CXIII, No. 46 (1934), 760.

_____. "The Minister with Two Occupations."
    The Christian Register, CX, No. 38 (1931), 713-14.

_____. "The Ministry of the Clergy and the
    Laity." Teamwork, December 1957. Journal of the
    Universalist Ministers Association. Avon, Illi-
    nois, 2 pp. (no pagination).

_____. "Monthly Message." Faith at Work, I,
    No. 6 (1946), 4. Monthly publication of the Re-
    ligious Associates of the National Political Action
    Committee (CIO). (Congress of Industrial Organiz-
    ations.)

_____. "Mr. Coughlin and 'Americanism.'"
    Radio address over WHIP, Chicago. March 26, 1939
    (mimeographed).

_____. "Music as a Means of Grace." Crane
    Review, X, No. 1 (1967), 42-45.

_____. "Natural Religion and the 'Myth' of
    the Eighteenth Century." Harvard Divinity School
    Bulletin, XVI (1951), 17-32.

_____. "Need Well-Informed Public Opinion
    for Ending Mill Strike." The Salem Evening News.
    July 17, 1933. Account of sermon by James Luther
    Adams, pp. 1, 4.

_____. "Notes on the Study of Gould Farm."
    Cooperative Living, VII, No. 1 (1955-56), 8-10.

Adams, James Luther. "Nuclear Energy and Christian
    Perspectives." The Church and the Use of Nuclear
    Energy for Peaceful Purposes. Consultation spon-
    sored by Department of the Church and Economic
    Life, National Council of the Churches of Christ.
    Arden House, Harriman, New York. January 1959
    (mimeographed).

_____. On Being Human - The Liberal Way.
    Tract 359. Boston: American Unitarian Associa-
    tion, 1940.

_____. On Being Human - Religiously. Edited
    by Max L. Stackhouse. Boston: Beacon Press, 1976.

_____. "On Reading the Bible." Sermon notes,
    1935. (Typewritten.)

"The Order of the Devoted Life." Documents on The Bro-
    thers of the Way, a group of Unitarian Ministers of
    which James Luther Adams was a member (mimeographed).

_____. "Ordination Prayer." The Unitarian
    Christian, XIV, No. 1 (1958), 15.

_____. "The Organizational Revolution: The
    Protestant Contribution." Hibbert Lecture de-
    livered at Manchester College, Oxford, March 5,
    1963 (typewritten).

_____. "Orthodox Church and Soviet State."
    The Protestant, VI, No. 2 (1945), 13-17.

_____. "Our Responsibility in Society."
    Authority and Freedom. Liverpool: W. Gaade,
    1953, pp. 43-63. Also in Faith and Freedom, VI,
    Part 2, No. 17 (1953). Also in Taking Time Ser-
    iously. Glencoe, Ill.: The Free Press, 1957,
    pp. 59-72.

_____. "Our Unconquered Past." The Uni-
    tarian Christian, XXIII, No. 3 (1967), 3-5.

_____. "Paul Tillich on Luther." Interpre-
    ters of Luther. Edited by Jaroslav Pelikan.
    Philadelphia: Fortress, 1968, pp. 304-34.

_____. Paul Tillich's Philosophy of Culture,
    Science and Religion. New York: Harper & Row, 1965.

Adams, James Luther. "Peoples' Congress of Applied Religion." The Protestant, VI, No. 1 (1945), 30-32.

_____. "Phenomenology of Fragmentation and the Ecology of Dreams." The Phenomenology of Dreams, pp. 9-13. Publication of the Annual Congress of Fellows of the Society for the Arts, Religion and Contemporary Culture. Whitney Museum, New York City, February 26, 1972.

_____. "The Place of Discipline in Christian Ethics." Crane Review, IX, No. 3 (1967), 138-48.

_____. "The Political Responsibility of the Man of Culture." Comprendre, No. 16 (1956), 11-25.

_____. "The Pragmatic Theory of Meaning." Presidential Address, American Society of Christian Ethics, Washington, D. C., January 24, 1969 (typewritten).

_____. "Preface." Dimensions of Faith. Edited by William Kimmel and Geoffrey Clive. New York: Twayne, 1960, pp. 7-11.

_____. "Preface." The Directive in History, by Henry Nelson Wieman. Boston and Glencoe: Beacon and The Free Press, 1949, pp. v-xi.

_____. "Presence de la culture." Comprendre, No. 13-14 (1955), 203-05. Correspondence on Dr. Harold C. Urey.

_____. "Presence de la culture." Comprendre, No. 15 (1955), 146-47. Correspondence dealing with the atomic bomb and the scientist in relation to the state.

_____. "Presence de la culture." Comprendre, No. 16 (1956), 114-15. Correspondence on Malcolm P. Sharp.

_____. "Presence de la Culture." Comprendre, No. 21-22 (1960), 334-36. Correspondence on Erik Erikson and James McBride Dabbs.

_____. "Presence de la Culture." Comprendre, No. 25 (1963), 155-58. Correspondence on Leo Szilard.

_____. "The Progress of Unitarianism--For the Future." c. 1938 (typewritten notes).

Adams, James Luther. "The Prophethood of All Believers."
The Christian Register, CXXVI, No. 3 (1947), 95-96.
Also in *Taking Time Seriously*. Glencoe, Ill.: The
Free Press, 1957, pp. 21-25.

_____. "'The Protestant Ethic' with Fewer
Tears." *In the Name of Life--Essays in Honor of
Erich Fromm*. Edited by Bernard Landis and Edward
S. Tauber. New York: Holt, Rinehart & Winston,
1971, pp. 174-90.

_____. "Protestant Priests of Mammon: Spiri-
tual Mobilization, Incorporated." *The Protestant*,
V, No. 12 (1944), 14-18.

_____. "Public-Supported Higher Education:
A Unitarian View." *Religion in the State University*. Edited by Henry E. Allen, pp. 68-75.
Minneapolis: University of Minnesota, 1950. Appears under the title "Religion in the State University." *Perspectives* II, No. 1 (1966), 28-38.
(Published by Harvard Divinity School.)

_____. "The Purpose of a Liberal Arts Edu-
cation." *Journal of the American Ministry*, IX,
No. 2 (1969), 3-8.

_____. "Putting on the Whole Armour." *The
Jaybird Listens*. Lake Geneva, Wisconsin: Conference Point, Summer 1943.

_____. *Religion and Freedom*. Remarks in
Seminar sponsored by the Fund for the Republic,
New York City, May 5-9, 1958. New York: Fund
for the Republic. (Privately printed.)

_____. "Religion and the Civil Life." Lec-
ture, April 11, 1942 (typewritten).

_____. "Religion and the Ideologies." *Con-
fluence*, IV, No. 1 (1955), 72-84.

_____. "Religion, Politics, Economics, and
Social Issues." Subsection report of Commission
II: The Religious Approach to the Modern World.
XXth Congress of the International Association for
Liberal Christianity and Religious Freedom, Boston,
1969 (mimeographed). Summary contained in "The

Religious Approach to the Modern World." News Digest of
the International Association for Liberal Christianity and Religious Freedom, No. 66 (1969),
p. 22-24.

Adams, James Luther. "Religious Ethics: Don Quixote
and the Reality Test." Keynote address delivered
at the Inaugural Symposium for The Journal of Religious Ethics, The University of Tennessee. October 17, 1973 (typewritten).

_____. "The Religious Problem." New Perspect-
ives on Peace. Edited by G. B. de Huzar. Chicago:
University of Chicago, 1944, pp. 227-54.

_____. "Remarks." Participant in Conference
of Social Scientists on Religion. Sponsored by
the Union of American Hebrew Congregations, Committee on Worship Research, March 15-16, 1959 (mimeographed).

_____. "Reminiscences on Shailer Mathews."
Interview at Chautauqua, New York, July 25, 1975
(transcribed).

_____. "Report from the Vatican Council."
The Unitarian Christian, XVIII, No. 2 (1962), 13-14.

_____. "Review-Essay: Paul Tillich: His
Life and Thought. Vol. I: Life," by Wilhelm
Pauck and Marian Pauck. Union Seminary Quarterly
Review, XXXII, No. 1 (1976), pp. 36 ff.

_____. "Rudolph Sohm's Theology of Law and
the Spirit." Religion and Culture: Essays in
Honor of Paul Tillich. Edited by W. Leibrecht.
New York: Harper & Brothers, 1959, pp. 219-35.

_____. "Samuel Charles Spalding, 1878-1962."
Great Barrington, Massachusetts: Gould Farm, 1962.
Privately published, 3 pp.

_____. "Sermon Notes on Holy Week." No date
(typewritten).

_____. "Service of God First Task of Reli-
gious Man." The Salem Evening News, February 28,
1927. Report of sermon by James Luther Adams, p. 3.

Adams, James Luther. "The Shock of Recognition: The Black Revolution and Greek Tragedy." The Unitarian Christian, XXIV, No. 4 (1969), 4-9.

_____. "Sic et Non." The Christian Register, CXII, No. 19 (1933), 298.

_____. "Sin and Salvation." Paper read at the Chicago Philosophy of Religion Association, 1948 (mimeographed).

_____. "Small Groups in the European Churches." c. 1938-39 (typewritten).

_____. "Social Ethics and Pastoral Care. Pastoral Care in Liberal Churches. Edited by James Luther Adams and Seward Hiltner. Nashville: Abingdon, 1970, pp. 174-220.

_____. "The Social Import of the Professions." Bulletin of the American Association of Theological Schools, No. 23 (June 1958), pp. 152-68. Reprinted as brochure. Pagination from brochure used. Found, in part, in Selected Readings on the Legal Profession. Edited by a committee of the Association of American Law Schools. St. Paul: West Publishing, 1962.

_____. "Social Morality and Medical Care." Boston: American Unitarian Association, Department of Adult Education and Social Relations, 1950 (mimeographed).

_____. "Social Responsibility." Sermon delivered at Bond Chapel, University of Chicago, February 10, 1948 (typewritten).

_____. "The Sociology of Discipline and Spontaneity in Religious Groups." Essay outline. No date, but before 1956 (typewritten).

_____. "The Sociology of Freedom and Responsibility." Hibbert Lecture delivered at Manchester College, Oxford, February 26, 1963 (typewritten).

_____. "Some Practical Applications." Adams' contribution to the discussion of "The Religious Content of Liberalism" (also called Greenfield Papers). Presented at the Unitarian Ministers' Institute, Greenfield, Mass., September 11, 1934 (mimeographed).

180

Adams, James Luther. "Some Unsettled Accounts." The
Christian Register, CXIV, No. 17 (1935), 277.

_____. "Some Uses of Analogy in Christian
Social Ethics." Notes from informal address at
Yale Divinity School, c. 1960.

_____. "Some Uses of Analogy in Religious
Social Thought," Tokyo: Maruzen, 1960, pp. 469-74.

_____. "Sources of Religious Insight." The
Christian Register, CXXIV, No. 2 (1945), 45-48.

_____. Speech on presenting Paul Tillich
with Festschrift. 1959 (transcribed).

_____. "State Aid to Parochial Schools."
Journal of the Liberal Ministry, XI, No. 2
(1971), 12-15.

_____. "Statement on Separation of Church and
State." Judicial Review, March 10, 1966, pp. 163-178.

_____. "Statement on Watergate." 1973 (type-
written).

_____. "The Study of Christian Social Ethics
at the Divinity School." Harvard Divinity School
Bulletin, XXVI, No. 3 (1962), 11-21.

_____. Taking Time Seriously. Glencoe, Ill.:
The Free Press, 1957. Volume of essays by James
Luther Adams, collected and published at the time
of his appointment to Harvard.

_____. "Taking Time Seriously: An Approach
to the Theology of Political Responsibility." Address at Penn State University, 1960 (typewritten).

_____. "Thanksgiving Sermon." Delivered at
Andover Chapel, November 23, 1966 (typewritten).

_____. "Theocracy, Individualism and Associa-
tions: A Critique of Max Weber." Address at annual meeting of Society for the Scientific Study
of Religion, October 29, 1965 (typewritten). In
expanded form this address was published in Zeit-
schrift fur Evangelische Ethik, XII, Nos. 4/5 (1968),
247-267. With some changes, the article appears as
"'The Protestant Ethic' with Fewer Tears." In the
Name of Life--Essays in Honor of Erich Fromm.

181

Adams, James Luther. "Theological Bases for Social Action." *Journal of Religious Thought*, VIII, No. 1 (1950-51), 6-21. Appears in *Taking Time Seriously*. Glencoe, Ill.: The Free Press, 1957, pp. 42-58.

_____. "Theological Education." *Unitarians Face a New Age*. Report of Commission of Appraisal of the American Unitarian Association. Boston: American Unitarian Association, 1936, pp. 99-110.

_____. "The Theological Ground of Protestant Social Responsibility." Adams indicates this is an early version of a Hibbert lecture. c. 1963 (typewritten).

_____. "Theology, the Arts, and the Sciences: A Paradigm of Vocations." Address at Denison University, March 1955 (typewritten).

_____. "A Theory of Revelation for Liberals," Address at New Testament Club, University of Chicago, c. 1937 (typewritten).

_____. "Thou Shalt Not Commit Adultery." Unpublished sermon, c. 1965 (typewritten).

_____. "The Threat to Reason." *Biosophical Review*, IX, No. 4 (1951), no pagination. Adams' contribution to Symposium entitled "Why Another Fantastic Dogma in the Twentieth Century?" (On the dogma of the Assumption of the Virgin Mary.)

_____. "Tillich's Concept of the Protestant Era." Concluding essay in *The Protestant Era*, by Paul Tillich. Chicago: The University of Chicago Press, 1948, pp. 273-316.

_____. "Tillich's Dialectical Method in Social-Structural Analysis." Paper read at the American Theological Society, Midwest Division, April 22, 1955 (typewritten).

_____. "Tillich's Interpretation of History." *The Theology of Paul Tillich*. Edited by Charles W. Kegley and Robert W. Bretall. New York: Macmillan, 1952, pp. 294-309.

Adams, James Luther. "To Ask or Not to Ask." The Christian Register, CXIV, No. 33 (1935), 541.

_____. "Treasures New and Old." The Christian Register, CXVIII, No. 40 (1939), 653-55.

_____. "Tribute to William J. Barnes, M.D." Annual Report for 1963 of The William Gould Associates, Inc. Privately printed.

_____. "Two Approaches: Anglo-Saxon and Teutonic Methods in Theology." Address to International Association for Religious Freedom, Leiden, Holland, 1938 (typewritten). Summary in The Christian Register, CXVII, No. 32 (1938), 522-523.

_____. "The Tyranny of a Free Minister." The Christian Register, CXI, Nos. 29-30, 31-32 (1932), 451-52, 469-70.

_____. "Unitarian Philosophies of History." Journal of Liberal Religion, VII, No. 2 (1945), 90-107.

_____. "Unity and Freedom in the New Federated Faculty at Chicago." The Christian Register, CXXIII, No. 1 (1944), 29. Also in The Christian Leader, CXXVI, No. 4 (1944), 110-11.

_____. "The Unity of Mankind in Our Divided World." News Digest of the International Association for Liberal Christianity and Religious Freedom, No. 46 (1961), pp. 8-10.

_____. "Untitled sermons or essays." Topics: "Christ," "God," "Holy Week," "On the Comfort and Cross of Christ." No dates (typewritten).

_____. "The Use of Symbols." On Being Human - Religiously. Edited by Max Stackhouse. Boston: Beacon Press, 1976, pp. 120-38.

_____. "The Uses of Diversity." Harvard Divinity School Bulletin, XXIII, No. 7 (1958), 47-64. This convocation address, delivered September 25, 1957, was reprinted as a brochure.

_____. "Vatican II." Sermon preached at Syracuse, New York, May 10, 1964 (typewritten).

183

Adams, James Luther. "Vatican Council II: Pro and Contra." New Digest of the International Association for Liberal Christianity and Religious Freedom, No. 51 (1963), pp. 8-12.

_____. "The Voluntary Association as an Indispensable Institution of the Democratic Society." Lecture at the University of Padua, 1963 (typewritten).

_____. "Voluntary Associations in Search of Identity." Journal [of Current Social Issues], IX, No. 6 (1971), 15-22.

_____. "The Voluntary Principle in the Forming of American Religion." The Religion of the Republic. Edited by Elwyn Smith. Philadelphia: Fortress Press, 1971, pp. 217-46.

_____. "Voters' Protest." Christian Science Monitor. XLII, No. 253 (1950), 16.

_____. "We Cannot Rest on Reputation: Our Department of Social Responsibility." Unitarian Universalist Register-Leader, CXLVI, No. 10 (1964), 6-7.

_____. "We Wrestle Against Principalities and Powers." Sermon preached at First Parish, Cambridge, Massachusetts, June 7, 1964 (mimeographed).

_____. "What Kind of Religion Has a Place in Higher Education?" Journal of Bible and Religion, XIII, No. 4 (1945), 184-92.

_____. "Why Liberal?" Journal of Liberal Religion, I, No. 2 (1938), 3-8.

_____. "Why the Troeltsch Revival?" The Unitarian Universalist Christian, XXIX, Nos. 1-2 (1974), 4-15.

2. Works Coauthored by Adams and Others*

Adams, James Luther, and Allin, J. Bryan. "Memoir of Irving Babbitt." _Irving Babbitt: Man and Teacher_. Edited by F. Manchester and Odell Shepard. New York: G.P. Putnam's Sons, 1941, pp. 271-80.

_____; Aubrey, E. E.; and others. "The Ethical Reality and Function of the Church." Memorandum by the Chicago Ecumenical Discussion Group, 1940 (mimeographed).

_____; Aubrey, E. E.; and others. "Preaching as an Expression of the Ethical Reality of the Church." Memorandum by the Chicago Ecumenical Discussion Group, 1945 (mimeographed).

_____; Banning, Andrew; and Pomeroy, Vivian T. "The Religious Content of Liberalism." The Greenfield Papers, 1934 (typewritten).

_____; Beaver, Pierce; Bundage, Percival; Eby, Kermit; Morgan, Arthur. "Human Values and Economic Forces." _Proceedings of the International Association for Liberal Christianity and Religious Freedom_. 16th Congress, August 1958. Chicago. The Hague: IARF Headquarters 1958, pp. 71-72, 74.

_____; Discussion among James Luther Adams, Leon Bloy, Leslie Dewart and others. "Initiative in History: A Christian-Marxist Exchange." An occasional paper published by The Church Society for College Work. Cambridge, Mass., 1967.

_____; Clark, H. Stewart; and Goudoever, J. van. "World Religions and the World of Tomorrow." _News Digest of the International Association for Liberal Christianity and Religious Freedom_, No. 53 (March 1964), pp. 13-15.

_____; and Clark, Thaddeus B. "The Impact of Modern Thought on Unitarianism." _The Christian Register_, CXXVII, No. 5 (1948), 21-23.

_____; Cox, Harvey; Lynn, Robert W.; and others. "The Playboy Panel: Religion and the New Morality. Leading Liberals of the Clergy Debate the Church's Role in Today's Sexual Revolution." _Playboy_, Vol. 14, June 1967, pp. 55 ff.

---

*Arranged alphabetically by first coauthor's surname.

Adams, James Luther; Dreier, Alex; and Morgenthau, Hans J. Policies for Germany. University of Chicago Radio Round Table, No. 305 (January 23, 1944).

_____; Eby, Kermit; Helstein, Ralph; Johnson, Philip; and Turner, Douglass. Who Has Faith in Man? University of Chicago Round Table, No. 829, February 28, 1954.

_____; Erikson, Erik; Kaufman, Gordon; Wilder, Amos N. "Paul Johannes Tillich, 1885-1965." Harvard University Gazette. LXI, No. 37 (1966).

_____. Symposium with the Reverend Billy Graham: Professors Richard R. Niebuhr, Harold J. Ockenga, and James Luther Adams. "Evangelism and the Intellectual, Part 1." Decision, III, No. 10 (1962), 8-9.

_____, and Lehman, Paul. "Willard Uphaus Sentence Protested; New Hampshire's Interpretation of State's Bill of Rights Queried." Letter to the Editor. The New York Times, December 20, 1959, p. 6E.

_____. Letter to the Editor. The New York Times, August 3, 1955, p. 22. Adams' name does not appear in the letter as printed in The New York Times.

_____. Letter to the President. August 27, 1945. The letter deals with the atomic bomb and the postwar period. Signed by James Luther Adams, Charles Hartshorne, Reginald Stephenson, John A. Wilson and other members of the University of Chicago. Personal collection of James Luther Adams (typewritten).

_____. Festschrift tape. Presentation of the Festschrift, Voluntary Associations to James Luther Adams. Introduction by Samuel Miller. Addresses by John C. Bennett, George H. Williams, D. B. Robertson, James Luther Adams. Harvard Divinity School, November 12, 1966.

_____, and others. "The Family and its Future." A Ciba Foundation Symposium. Edited by Katherine Elliott. London: J. A. Churchill, 1970.

Adams, James Luther, and Pauck, Wilhelm. "The Responsibility of the Church for the International Order." Memorandum to Chicago Ecumenical Discussion Group. Late 1930's (?). (Typewritten.)

_____, and Pratt, James Bissett. "The Congregational Idea." Essay prepared for conference of Congregationalist and Unitarian representatives, 1932 or 1933 (mimeographed).

_____. Unitarians Unite! Report of the Commission on Planning and Review. Boston: American Unitarian Association, 1947. Adams is cited as co-author in "Writings of James Luther Adams," Voluntary Associations, 379. This source does not indicate the other authors. The report itself does not identify the authors.

3. Reviews by Adams

Albright, R. W. *Focus on Infinity. A Life of Phillips Brooks.* The American German Review, XXVIII (December 1961-January 1962), 36.

Babbitt, Irving. *On Being Creative: and Other Essays.* Hound and Horn, VI, No. 1 (1932), 173-196.

Bainton, Roland. *Early and Medieval Christianity.* Journal of the Liberal Ministry, II, No. 3 (1962), 151-53.

Barry, F. R. *Christianity and the New World.* The Christian Register, CXI, Nos. 27-28 (1932), 441.

Barth, Karl. *The Only Way;* Jaspers, Karl, *The Question of German Guilt;* Picard, Max, *Hitler in Ourselves.* Commentary, IV (December 1948), 588-90.

Beard, C. A. *The Discussion of Human Affairs.* Unity, CXIX, No. 4 (1937), 80-82.

Benz, Ernst. *Westlicher and Oestlicher Nihilismus.* Jaspers, Karl. *The European Spirit.* Theology Today, VII (1951), 540-42.

Berman, Harold J. *The Interaction of Law and Religion.* Interpretation: A Journal of Bible and Theology, XXX, No. 1 (1976), 106-08.

Bertocci, Peter A. *The Empirical Argument for God in Late British Thought.* Christendom, IV, No. 4 (1939), 601-04.

Bier, William. *Conscience: Its Freedom and Limitations.* Journal of Church and State, XV, No. 3 (1973), 465-69.

Bixler, J. S. *Religion for Free Minds.* The Christian Century, LVII, No. 18 (1940), 578.

Boas, George. *Philosophy and Poetry.* The Christian Register, CXII, No. 28 (1933), 475.

Brennan, Bernard P. *The Ethics of William James.* The Unitarian Register and the Universalist Leader, CXLI, No. 6 (1962), 23.

189

Brown, Stuart G., ed. We Hold These Truths; Documents of American Democracy. Chicago Theological Seminary Register, XXXIX, No. 1 (1949), 38.

Bryson, Lyman, et al. Approaches to National Unity. The Fifth Symposium of the Conference on Science, Philosophy and Religion. The Christian Century, LXII (November 14, 1945), 1257-58.

Bryson, Lyman, and others. Aspects of Human Equality. The Fifteenth Symposium of the Conference on Science, Philosophy and Religion. Harvard Divinity School Bulletin, XXIII, No. 7 (1957-58), 182-83.

Bultmann, Rudolf. Existence and Faith. Perkins Journal, XV (Fall 1961), 53-54. Also in Journal of the Liberal Ministry, II, No. 1 (1962), 45-46.

Buri, Fritz. Christlicher Glaube in Dieser Zeit. The Christian Register, CXXIII, No. 9 (1954), 3-4.

Burtt, Edwin A. Types of Religious Philosophy. Christendom, IV, No. 2 (1939), 282-85.

Cadbury, Henry J. Jesus, What Manner of Man? The Chicago Sun, December 3, 1947, 14A.

Clare, Lawrence. Prayer: Its Method and Justification. The Christian Register, CXII, No. 33 (1933), 556.

Conger, George P. The Ideologies of Religion. Christendom, VI, No. 3 (1941), 443-46.

Cross Currents. A Quarterly Review. Vols. VI (1956) and VII (1957), Harvard Divinity School Bulletin, XXIII, No. 7 (1957-58), 167.

Dobree, Bonamy. John Wesley. The Christian Register, CXIII, No. 11 (1934), 179.

Eckhardt, A. Roy. Christianity and the Children of Israel. Chicago Theological Seminary Register, XL, No. 1 (1950), 32-34.

Fenn, W. W. The Theological Method of Jesus. Unity, CXXII, No. 1o (1939), 158-59.

Fitch, Robert E. A Certain Blind Man, and Other Essays
on the American Mood. Journal of Religion, XXV,
No. 1 (1945), 152-53.

Haroutunian, J. Lust for Power. Chicago Theological
Seminary Register, XL, No. 1 (1950), 33-34.

Hasting, Hester. William Ellery Channing and L'Academie
des sciences morales et politiques 1870: L'Etude
sur Channing and the "Lost" Prize Essay. The
Unitarian Register and Universalist Leader, CXLI,
No. 5 (1962), 20.

Haubold, Wilhelm. Die Bedeutung der Religiongeschichte
fur die Theologie Rudolf Ottos. Journal of Religion,
XXI, No. 1 (1941), 69-70.

Hay, Malcolm. The Foot of Pride. Land Reborn, XII,
No. 6 (1951), 12.

Heard, Gerald. Morals Since 1900. Chicago Theological
Seminary Register, XLI, No. 4 (1951), 31-32.

Heard, Gerald. The Source of Civilization and The Third
Morality. Christendom, III, No. 4 (1937), 645-50.

Herman, Stewart W., Jr. It's Your Souls We Want; Temple,
William, Christianity and the Social Order; Tima-
sheff, N. S., Religion in Soviet Russia. Free
World, VI, No. 2 (1943), 185-186.

Hocking, W. E. Thoughts on Death and Life. Unity,
CXX, No. 8 (1937), 130-32.

Hordern, William. Christianity, Communism and History.
Bulletin of Crozer Theological Seminary, XLVII,
No. 3 (1955), 11.

Hough, Lynn H. The Christian Criticism of Life and
Patterns of the Mind. Review of Religion, VII,
No. 2 (1943), 193-96.

Hutchins, Robert M. and Adler, Mortimer J., eds. The
Great Ideas Today. Harvard Divinity School Bulletin, XXVI, No. 2 (1962), 23-25.

Hymns of the Spirit. The Christian Register, CXVI,
No. 38 (1937), 628-30.

Kee, Howard C. Making Ethical Decisions. Harvard
    Divinity School Bulletin, XXIII, No. 7 (1957-
    58), 184-85.

Kernan, William C. The Ghost of Royal Oak. Journal
    of Religion, XXI, No. 1 (1941), 106.

Kirk, K. E., ed. The Study of Theology. The Christian
    Century, LVII, No. 6 (1940), 183.

Landis, Benson V., compiler. A Rauschenbusch Reader.
    Harvard Divinity School Bulletin, XXIII, No. 7
    (1957-58), 166-67.

Langer, Susanne K. Philosophy in a New Key. The
    Christian Register, CXXI, No. 11 (1942), 415.

Lewis, H. D. Morals and the New Theology. Journal of
    Religion, XXIX (1949), 305-07. Also in Chicago
    Theological Seminary Register, XL, No. 1 (1950), 33.

Littell, Franklin H. The German Phoenix. Men and
    Movements in the Church of Germany. Harvard
    Divinity School Bulletin, XXV, No. 1 (1960),
    24-25. Also in The Unitarian Register, CXL,
    No. 3 (1961), 14.

Lovejoy, Arthur. Essays in the History of Ideas.
    Review manuscript. No indication of publication.
    Date: after 1948.

Macintosh, D. C. The Problem of Religious Knowledge.
    The Christian Century, LVIII, No. 45 (1941), 1373-74.

MacIver, R. M., ed. Dilemmas of Youth in America
    Today. Harvard Divinity School Bulletin, XXVI,
    No. 3 (1962), 25-26.

Malraux, Andre. Man's Fate. The Christian Register,
    CXIV, No. 43 (1935), 713.

Maritain, Jacques. Christianity and Democracy. Journal
    of Religion, XXV, No. 3 (1945), 217-18.

_____. Some Reflections on Culture and Lib-
    erty. The Christian Register, CXIII, No. 19
    (1934), 315.

_____. Three Reformers. Hound and Horn,
    III, No. 1 (1929), 114-20.

Maynard, Theodore. The Story of American Catholicism.
    New England Quarterly, XV, No. 3 (1942), 534-36.
    Also in The Protestant, IV, No. 8 (1942), 65-67.

Nichols, James H. Democracy and the Churches. The
    University of Chicago Magazine, XLIV, No. 5
    (1952), 4.

Niebuhr, Reinhold. The Nature and Destiny of Man,
    Vol. I. Christendom, VI, No. 4 (1941), 576-80.

Northcott, Cecil. Religious Liberty. Chicago Theo-
    logical Seminary Register, XXXIX, 4 (1949), 37.
    Also in The Christian Register, CXIX, No. 1
    (1950), 2.

Otto, Rudolf. The Kingdom of God and the Son of Man.
    The Alumni Review, Presbyterian Theological
    Seminary, Chicago. XIII, No. 4 (1938), 236-37.

Picard, Max. Hitler in Ourselves. Journal of Religion,
    XXVIII, No. 2 (1948), 298-99.

Pope, Liston, ed. Labor's Relation to Church and Com-
    munity: A Series of Addresses. New York: Har-
    per & Bros., 1947. Unpublished review.

"Recent Books on Democracy and Religion: A Survey."
    Journal of Liberal Religion, II, No. 2 (1940),
    93-100.

Roberts, William H. The Problem of Choice. Ethics,
    LII, No. 2 (1942), 243-45.

Rommen, H. A. The Natural Law. Church History, XVII,
    No. 4 (1948), 344-46.

Rosenstock-Huessy, E. The Driving Power of Western
    Civilization. Journal of Religion, XXXI, No. 2
    (1951), 150.

Ross, J. Elliott. John Henry Newman. The Christian
    Register, CXIII, No. 3 (1934), 43.

Scheler, Max. Ressentiment. Harvard Divinity School
    Bulletin, XXV, Nos. 3-4 (1961), 21-22.

The Second Symposium of the Conference on Science, Philo-
    sophy and Religion. Journal of Religion, XXIII,
    No. 4 (1943), 292-93.

Services of Religion for Special Occasions. The Christian Register, CXVIII, No. 40 (1939), 653-55.

Sharpe, G. Coverdale. Liberty at the Crossroads. The
Christian Register, CXIII, No. 40 (1934), 662.

Siegfried, Theodor. Das protestantische prinzip im
Kirche und Welt. Journal of Religion, XX (1940),
192-95.

Smith, Wilson. Professors and Public Ethics: Studies
of Northern Moral Philosophers Before the Civil
War. Proceedings of the Unitarian Historical
Society, XII, Part 1 (1960), 104-05.

Sonen, Robert W. A Unitarian States His Case. The
Christian Register, CXIX, No. 10 (1950), 3.
Also in The Chicago Theological Seminary Regis-
ter, XL, 4 (1950), 40-41.

Spencer, S. The Meaning and Value of Religion. The
Christian Register, CXII, No. 46 (1933), 765.

Sperry, Willard L. Wordsworth's Anti-Climax. The
Christian Register, CXIV, No. 35 (1935), 576.

Straight, Michael. Make This the Last War. The
Christian Century, LX (September 1, 1943), 989.

"Ten Books for Lenten Reading." The Christian Register, CXXII, No. 3 (1943), 84.

Troeltsch, Ernst. The Social Teaching of the Christian
Churches. 2 vols. The Christian Register,
CXXVII, No. 5 (1948), 11-12.

Vaughan, G. Temples and Towers. A Survey of the
World's Moral Outlook. American Bar Association
Journal, XXVIII (November 1942), 770.

Vigile, Quatre Cahiers, 1930. Volume I. Hound and
Horn, V, No. 4 (1932), 694-701.

Walker, Brooks R. The Christian Fright Peddlers.
Harvard Divinity School Bulletin, XXIX, No. 4
(1965), 118-23.

Webb, Clement C. J. A Study of Religious Thought in England from 1850. The Christian Register, CXIV, No. 11 (1935), 178.

Weinstein, Jacob. The Place of Understanding. Hyde Park Herald, Chicago, August 26, 1959. Also in Jewish Frontier, XXVI, No. 10 (1959), 23-25.

Wood, H. G. Frederick Denison Maurice. Chicago Theological Seminary Register, XLI, No. 1 (1951), 33-34.

Wright, C. Conrad, editor. A Stream of Light. Unitarian Universalist World, VI, No. 6 (1975), 12.

4. Edited Works by Adams

The Angel's Revolt. Coedited by James Luther Adams. Student Magazine. Minneapolis: University of Minnesota, 1923-24 (mimeographed).

"Bibliographical Focus: Ernst Troeltsch." Journal for the Scientific Study of Religion, I, Nos. 1-2 (1961), 114-24, 220-25. Papers from Adams' Seminar on Troeltsch, edited by James Luther Adams.

"Contemporary Thought Around the World." Symposium edited by James Luther Adams. The Christian Register, CXII-CXIII, 1933-34.

Dohrman, H. T. California Cult. Vol. II of Sociology of Politics and Religion. Edited by James Luther Adams. Boston: Beacon Press, 1958.

Hartshorne, Charles. Reality as Social Process. Edited by James Luther Adams. The Phoenix Series. Boston and Glencoe: Beacon and The Free Press, 1953.

Pauck, Wilhelm. The Heritage of the Reformation. Edited by James Luther Adams. The Phoenix Series. Boston and Glencoe: Beacon and The Free Press, 1950. Revised and enlarged edition, The Free Press, 1960.

_____. The Phoenix Series. Series under the general editorship of James Luther Adams. Boston and Glencoe: Beacon and The Free Press.

The Politics of Johannes Althusius. Translated by Frederick S. Carney. Volume IV of Sociology of Politics and Religion. Edited by James Luther Adams. Boston: Beacon Press, 1964.

The Saint-Simonian Doctrine. Translated by Georg Iggers. Vol. I of Sociology of Politics and Religion. Edited by James Luther Adams. Boston: Beacon Press, 1958.

Sociology of Politics and Religion. Series under the general editorship of James Luther Adams. Boston: Beacon Press.

Tillich, Paul. What is Religion? Edited and with an Introduction by James Luther Adams. New York: Harper & Row, 1969.

Weber, Max. Sociology of Religion. Translated by
Ephraim Fischoff, Vol. III of Sociology of Poli-
tics and Religion. Edited by James Luther Adams.
Boston: Beacon Press, 1963.

Wieman, Henry N. The Directive in History. Edited
by James Luther Adams. The Phoenix Series.
Boston and Glencoe: Beacon and The Free Press,
1949.

5. Translations by Adams

Barth, Karl. "An Introductory Essay." Translated by James
    Luther Adams. The Essence of Christianity. By
    Ludwig Feuerbach. New York: Harper Torchbook,
    1957, pp. x-xxx.

Benjamin, Walter. "The Concept of History." Translated
    by James Luther Adams and Olric Prochazka. 1955
    (mimeographed).

Dehn, Gunther. "The Angels and the Authorities." Toward
    the Understanding of Romans 13:1-7." Translated
    by James Luther Adams. Andover-Harvard Library,
    Harvard Divinity School (typewritten). The original
    essay in German appeared in Theologische Aufsatze.
    Karl Barth zum 50 Geburtstag. Munchen: Kaiser
    Verlag, 1936.

Fromm, Erich. "The Dogma of Christ." Translated by
    James Luther Adams. Essay in volume of the same
    name. New York: Holt, Rinehart & Winston,
    1963, pp. 1-95.

Philip, Andre. "Christianity and Peace." Translated by
    James Luther Adams. Protestant Digest, No. 8
    (1939), 16-31.

"A Sad Document." A pro-Nazi comment on Karl Barth's
    letter to Professor Hromadka. Translated by James
    Luther Adams. Protestant Digest, I, No. 2 (1939),
    88-89.

Siegfried, Theodor. "Rudolph Otto, Theologian: An
    Apostle of the Kingdom of God." Translated by
    James Luther Adams. The Inquirer, London, No.
    4971 (October 9, 1937), pp. 485-86. Also in The
    Christian Register, CXVI, No. 42 (1937), 696-98.

Tillich, Paul. "Answer to an Inquiry of the Protestant
    Consistory of Brandenburg." Metanoia, III, No. 3
    (1971), 10-12, 9, 16. Translated by James Luther
    Adams. The original is to be found in Gesammelten
    Werken von Paul Tillich, Band 13. Stuttgart:
    Evangelisches Verlagswerk.

_____. "The Class Struggle and Religious
    Socialism." Translated by James Luther Adams.
    Meadville Theological School Library and Andover-

Harvard Library, Harvard Divinity School (typewritten).
The original essay in German appears in Religiose
Verwirklichung, Chapter 9. Berlin: Furche-Ver-
lag, 1930.

Tillich, Paul. "E. Troeltsch: Historismus und Seine
Probleme." Review of Historismus und Seine Probleme by Ernst Troeltsch. Translated by James
Luther Adams. Journal for the Scientific Study
of Religion, I, No. 1 (1961), 109-14.

_____. "The Philosophy of Religion." Trans-
lated by James Luther Adams, Konrad Raiser, and
Charles W. Fox. Contained in What Is Religion?
Edited by James Luther Adams. New York: Harper &
Row, 1969, pp. 27-121.

_____. The Protestant Era. Translated by
James Luther Adams. Chicago: The University of
Chicago Press, 1948.

_____. "The Religious Symbol." Translated
by James Luther Adams and Ernst Fraenkel. Journal
of Liberal Religion, II, No. 1 (1940), 13-33.

_____. Review of Ideology and Utopia, by
Karl Mannheim. Translated by James Luther Adams.
Andover-Harvard Library, Harvard Divinity School
(typewritten). The original appeared in Gesell-
schaft, VI, No. 10 (1929), 348-55.

Visser t'Hooft, W. A. "The Protestantism of Rembrandt."
Translated by James Luther Adams and J. B. Allin.
Protestant Digest, I, No. 5 (1939), 79-85.

6. Other Sources Besides Adams

Ahlstrom, Sidney. A Religious History of the American People. New Haven: Yale University Press, 1972.

Bennett, John C. "Voluntary Associations in the Post-Christendom Church." Address delivered at James Luther Adams' Festschrift celebration, Harvard Divinity School, November 12, 1966 (transcribed).

Berger, Peter. A Rumor of Angels. Garden City: Doubleday Anchor, 1970.

Bernard, M. G. and Reardon, Adam, eds. Liberal Protestantism. London: Charles Black, 1968.

Braaten, Carl. "Paul Tillich and the Classical Christian Tradition." A History of Christian Thought, Paul Tillich. Edited by Carl Braaten. New York: Harper & Row, 1972, pp. xiii-xxxiv.

Brill, Earl H. The Creative Edge of American Protestantism. New York: Seabury Press, 1966.

"'By Their Groups Shall Ye Know Them': Tributes to James Luther Adams." Kairos, II, No. 1 (1976), 3-5.

Carney, Frederick S. "James Luther Adams: The Christian Actionist as a Man of Culture." Perkins Journal, XXVI, No. 1 (1972), 14-16.

Carter, Paul. The Decline and Revival of the Social Gospel: Social and Political Liberalism in America. New York: Archon Books, 1971.

Cauthen, Kenneth. The Impact of American Religious Liberalism. New York: Harper & Row, 1962.

"The Church and the Present Situation." News Digest of the International Association for Liberal Christianity and Religious Freedom, No. 66 (1969), pp. 20-22.

Faber, H. "A Short History of the IARF." Proceedings of the International Association for Liberal Christianity and Religious Freedom. 16th Congress, August 1958, Chicago. The Hague: IARF Headquarters, 1958, pp. 126-31.

"From Hitler to Chicago, He [James Luther Adams] Found Bias." Chicago Daily News, December 2-3, 1972.

Gilbert, Richard S. Review of On Being Human - Religiously, by James Luther Adams. Edited by Max L. Stackhouse. Kairos, II, No. 1 (1976), 11.

Gilkey, Langdon. "Social and Intellectual Sources of Contemporary Protestant Theology." Religion in America. Edited by William G. McLoughlin and Robert W. Bellah. Boston: Houghton-Mifflin, 1968, pp. 137-66.

Gustafson, James. "Christian Ethics." Religion. Edited by Paul Ramsey. Englewood Cliffs, N.J.: Prentice-Hall, 1965, pp. 287-354.

Handy, Robert T. A Christian America. New York: Oxford University Press, 1971.

Harrison, Paul. Authority and Power in the Free Church Tradition. Princeton: Princeton University Press, 1959.

Hartshorne, Charles. "Redefining God." Contemporary American Protestant Thought: 1900-1970. Edited by William R. Miller. Indianapolis: Bobbs-Merrill, 1973, pp. 315-22.

Hermann, Robert. "They're a peril and they're an opportunity." The National Observer, III, 10 (1964), 1, 16. Interview with James Luther Adams on medical transplants.

Holl, Karl. "The History of the Word Vocation (Beruf)." Address delivered to the Prussian Academy of Science, January 24, 1924. Translated by Hebert F. Peacock (mimeographed).

Holmes, Frank O. and Schacht, Robert H. Jr. "The Greenfield Group--Its Beginnings and History." The Christian Register, CXXVII, No. (1948), 45-48, 63.

Hunt, James D. "James Luther Adams and His Demand for an Effective Religious Liberalism." Unpublished Ph.D. dissertation, Syracuse University, 1965.

Hunt, James D. "James Luther Adams as a Student of
    Tillich." Journal of the Liberal Ministry, VI, 3
    (1966), 184-90.

_____. "Voluntary Associations as a Key to
    History." Voluntary Associations: A Study of
    Groups in Free Societies. Edited by D. B. Robert-
    son. Richmond: John Knox Press, 1966, pp. 359-73.

Kaufman, Gordon. "Theological Historicism as an Experi-
    ment in Thought." The Christian Century, LXXXIII
    (March 2, 1966), 268-71.

Macquarrie, John. "The Essence is Within." Review of
    Paul Tillich's Philosophy of Culture, Science,
    and Religion, by James Luther Adams. The New York
    Times Book Review, February 13, 1966, pp. 12, 14.

_____. Twentieth Century Religious Thought.
    London: SCM, 1963.

Meiklejohn, Donald. Review of Voluntary Associations:
    A Study of Groups in Free Societies; Essays in
    Honor of James Luther Adams. Edited by D.B.
    Robertson. Ethics, Vol. LXXIX, No. 2 (1969),
    165-66.

Merton, Robert K. "Karl Mannheim and the Sociology of
    Knowledge." The Journal of Liberal Religion, II,
    No. 3 (1941), 125-47.

Meyer, Donald B. The Protestant Search for Political
    Realism 1919-1941. Berkeley: University of
    California Press, 1961.

Miller, Robert. American Protestantism and Social Issues.
    Chapel Hill: University of North Carolina Press,
    1960.

Miller, William R., ed. Contemporary American Protestant
    Thought: 1900-1970. Indianapolis: Bobbs-Merrill,
    1973.

Miller, Samuel. "Dean's Report, 1962-1963." Report of
    the Divinity School to the President of Harvard
    University. Pamphlet, Cambridge, 1963, pp. 8-9.

"The Mission of Western Religious Liberalism." News
Digest of the International Association for Liberal
Christianity and Religious Freedom, No. 66 (1969),
pp. 28-29.

Muelder, Walter G. "James Luther Adams as Theological
Ethicist." Andover Newton Quarterly, XVII, No. 3
(1977), 186-94.

Pauck, Wilhelm. The Heritage of the Reformation. Revised. New York: Oxford University Press, 1971.

Pennock, J. Roland, and Chapman, John. "Preface."
Voluntary Associations. Edited by J. Roland Pennock and John Chapman. New York: Atherton, 1969,
pp. vii-ix.

Pickering, George W. "Voluntarism and the 'American
Way.'" Journal [of Current Social Issues], IX,
No. 1 (1970), 4-9.

Potter, Ralph B., Jr.; Potter, Jean; and Hunt, James D.
"A Bibliography of James Luther Adams." Voluntary
Associations: A Study of Groups in Free Societies.
Edited by D.B. Robertson. Richmond: John Knox,
1966, pp. 375-95.

Robertson, D. B., ed. Voluntary Associations: A Study
of Groups in Free Societies. Richmond: John Knox,
1966. Essays in honor of James Luther Adams.

Sabel, Charles F. "Divinity School: No 'Spectator
Religion.'" The Harvard Crimson, November 12,
1965, pp. 3-4.

Selznick, Philip. TVA and the Grass Roots: A Study in
the Sociology of Formal Organizations. Berkeley:
University of California Press, 1949.

Shinn, Roger L. "Theological Ethics: Retrospect and
Prospect." Theology and Church in Times of Change.
Edited by Edward Leroy Long, Jr., and Robert T.
Handy. Philadelphia: Westminster, 1970, pp.
117-41.

Smith, H. Shelton; Handy, Robert T.; and Loetscher,
Lefferts A. American Christianity: An Historical
Interpretation with Representative Documents,
Vol. II, New York: Charles Scribner's Sons, 1963.

Smith, James W. and Jamison, A. Leland, eds. The Shaping of American Religion. Princeton: Princeton Press, 1961.

Soper, David W. "James Luther Adams: A Theology of History and Hope." Men Who Shape Belief: Major Voices in American Theology, Vol. II. Philadelphia: Westminster, 1955, p. 15-29.

Stackhouse, Max L. "Editor's Introduction." On Being Human - Religiously. James Luther Adams. Boston: Beacon Press, 1976, pp. xi-xxx.

_____. "James Luther Adams: A Biographical and Intellectual Sketch." Voluntary Associations: A Study of Groups in Free Societies. Edited by D.B. Robertson. Richmond: John Knox, 1966, pp. 333-57.

Tillich, Paul. "Foreword." Voluntary Associations: A Study of Groups in Free Societies. Edited by D.B. Robertson. Richmond: John Knox, 1966, pp. 5-6.

_____. Perspectives on 19th and 20th Century Protestant Theology. Edited by Carl Braaten. New York: Harper & Row, 1967.

_____. Systematic Theology. Three Volumes in One. New York: Harper & Row, 1967.

Weber, Max. "Proposal for the Study of Voluntary Associations." Translated by Everett C. Hughes (mimeographed).

Wells, Clarke. "Festival in the Church for JLA." Poem. Kairos, II, No. 1 (1976), 1.

Williams, Daniel, Day. "The New Theological Situation." Issues in American Protestantism. Edited by Robert L. Ferm. Garden City: Doubleday Anchor, 1969, pp. 397-418.

Williams, George H. "James Luther Adams and the Unitarian Denomination." Andover Newton Quarterly, XVII, 3 (1977), 173-183.

Williams, George H. "A Tribute to James Luther Adams."
     Godbox, II, No. 3 (1967-68), 22-31.

Williamson, Joseph. "The Christian Life: An Interview
     with James Luther Adams." _Colloquy_, V, 9
     (1972), 11-17, 46-47.

APPENDIX

Legend: A hyphen after a date means that
          Adams still belongs to the asso-
          ciation.

          ff. after a date means that Adams'
          membership is undetermined as to
          termination of association.

          Associations and activities are
          chronologically arranged.

APPENDIX

Organizational Activities and Associations
of James Luther Adams

1927-34   Ordained: Second Church, Salem, Massa-
                 chusetts. Served there as minister
                 until 1934.

1928-   One of the organizers and a continuing
                 sponsor of the Greenfield Group,
                 Eastern Unitarian Ministers' Study
                 Group holding semi-annual conferences.
                 It was named the Greenfield Group in
                 1934.

1930-35   One of "The Religious Associates" of the
                 Congress of Industrial Organizations
                 (CIO).

1930ff   Member, Unitarian Fellowship for Social
                 Justice.

1930ff   One of the founders of Greater Boston
                 Marriage Study Association.

1933-34   Editor, Christian Register.

1934-35   Minister of the First Unitarian Society,
                 Wellesley Hills, Massachusetts.

1934-36   Co-initiator and member of the American
                 Unitarian Association Commission of Ap-
                 praisal, which brought about a denom-
                 inational reorganization.

1935-   Member, Unitarian Universalist Christian
                 Fellowship. Vice President, 1977-.

1936, 1938   Lecturer, International Association for
                 Religious Freedom and Liberal Christ-
                 ianity, The Netherlands.

1937-57   Professor at Meadville Theological Semin-
                 ary and then also at University of Chi-
                 cago Federated Theological Faculty
                 (beginning in 1943).

209

1936-56	Member, First Unitarian Church, Chicago. Chairman of the Board of Trustees, 1954.
1937-56	Member, Apollos Club. Member of Board of Directors, 1954.
1938-48	Associate Editor, The Protestant.
1939-44	Editor, Journal of Liberal Religion.
1940ff	Member, Religion and Labor Foundation.
1942-45	Member, Middle West Theologians Ecumenical Group.
1942-56	Chairman, Independent Voters of Illinois. Member of the Board of Directors most of the time. Chairman for three terms.
1942-45	Member, Chicago Ecumenical Discussion Group.
1943-54	Consultant, Chicago Council Against Racial and Religious Discrimination.
1943-57	Professor of Religious Ethics, University of Chicago. Chairman, Department of Ethics and Society.
1944-48	Member, Nominating Committee, American Unitarian Association.
1945-47	Member, Unitarian Commission on Planning and Review.
1945	With Lee Szilard and some sixty professors, Adams released the first public protest against the atomic bombing of Hiroshima and Nagasaki.
1945-55	Member, Advisory Board, American Christian Palestine Committee.
1945-	Member, American Association of University Professors.
1945-46	Member, Congress of Racial Equality.

210

1945-54	Advisory Board, Chicago Chapter, American Civil Liberties Union.
1945-62	National Theological Discussion Group, College of Preachers, Washington Cathedral, Washington, D. C.
1945-47	Member of the American Unitarian Association Commission on Planning and Review.
1945-57	Member, Advisory Board, Chicago Chapter of the American Civil Liberties Union. Chairman of Church and State Committee, 1966-68.
1947ff	Member, Hyde Park Community Conference.
1948-	Member, American Sociological Society.
1950ff	Member and Officer, Christian Action, Chicago Chapter.
1950-58	Associate Editor, Faith and Freedom (British).
1950-56	Vice-President, Chicago Chapter, Protestants and Others United for Separation of Church and State. Member of National Advisory Board.
1951-56	Co-editor, Journal of Religion.
1952	Lecturer, International Association for Religious Freedom and Liberal Christianity, Oxford, England.
1952-56	Member, Prairie Group, Unitarian Ministers' Study Group, Middle West.
1952-56	Chairman, Advisory Board, Beacon Press, Boston. Member of the Board as well.
1952-57	Member, American Committee for Cultural Freedom.
1953-	A founder and member, Society for the Scientific Study of Religion. President, 1957-58.

1954-	Member, Legal Defense and Education Committee, National Association for the Advancement of Colored People.
1954-	Member of the International Council of La Societe Europeenne de Culture. Annual columnist, Comprendre, publication of the organization.
1957-68	Member of the Massachusetts State Board of the American Civil Liberties Union. Chairman of· Church and State Committee, 1966-68.
1957-69	Massachusetts State Board, Americans for Democratic Action.
1957-	First theologian to be a member of the Society for Political and Legal Philosophy.
1957-68	Edward Mallinckrodt, Jr., Professor of Divinity, Harvard Divinity School.
1958	Fellow, American Acadeny of Arts and Sciences.
1958-	Member, American Theological Society. President, 1972-73.
1958	Attended and lectured at conferences in Japan and India: International Association in the History of Religion, Tokyo and Kyota; World Center for Buddhist Studies, Rangoon; The Theological College, Bangalore.
1960	Arminius Symposium, The Netherlands.
1960-65	Massachusetts State Board, American Association for the United Nations.
1960-65	Member, State Board, American Association for the United Nations.
1961	Colloquium on the Nature of Man, American Unitarian Association Speaker.

1961-64	Member, Coordinating Council, American Unitarian Association Commission on the Free Church in a Changing World.
1962	Observer, Vatican Council II, for the International Association for Liberal Christianity and Religious Freedom.
1964-68	Member, Advisory Committee, Council on Population Studies, Harvard University. Initiated Department for Population Studies at Harvard Divinity School.
1965-69	Chairman of the Advisory Committee of the Unitarian Universalist Association Department of Social Responsibility.
1966-68	Chairman, Committee on International Organizations, American Academy of Arts and Sciences.
1967-68	Member, American Society for Christian Ethics.
1968-72	Distinguished Professor of Social Ethics, Andover Newton Theological Seminary.
1969	Member of the Board of Directors of Fellowship for Racial and Economic Equality. Chairman of the Board, 1971-75.
1971-	Vice-President, Association for Voluntary Action Scholars.
1971-	Minister of Adult Education, Arlington Street Church, Boston.
1971-73	Chairman of the Board, Society of the Arts, Religion and Contemporary Culture.
1972-76	Professor of Theology and Religious Ethics, University of Chicago, and Distinguished Scholar in Residence at Meadville/Lombard Theological School.
1973-	Editorial Board, Journal of Religious Ethics.

1974-   Executive Committee, North American So-
            ciety for Tillich Studies.

1974-   Board of Associate Editors, Journal of
            Voluntary Action Research.

1977-   Executive Committee, Council on Religion
            and Law.

            Member, National Advisory Board, Northern
            Student Movement (no dates).

Sources: University of Chicago, Faculty Biographical Data,
            1954.

            Max Stackhouse, "James Luther Adams: A Bio-
                graphical and Intellectual Sketch," p. 352.

            Curriculum Vitae (Harvard Divinity School).

            "James Luther Adams/UU Chronology." Andover
                Newton Quarterly, XVII, 3 (1977), 184-85.

            James D. Hunt, "James Luther Adams and His
                Demand for an Effective Religious Liber-
                alism."

ABOUT THE AUTHOR

The son of Margaret Lally Wilcox and Herbert Wilcox, the author grew up in New York City. Educated in parochial and public schools, he joined the Roman Catholic religious community of the Marist Brothers. Together with other candidates for the religious community, he attended Marist Preparatory School, Esopus, N.Y. After making his initial commitment and receiving religious training, he attended Marist College in Poughkeepsie, N.Y., from which he graduated, magan cum laude, in 1961. During the next five years, he taught a variety of subjects in several Marist high schools.

In 1963, Dr. Wilcox began a Master's degree in religious education at Fordham University, a degree completed in 1966, while teaching at Cardinal Hayes High School, Bronx, N.Y. He began teaching courses in theology at Marist College in the spring of 1967, where he continued lecturing,until he received a Fulbright Fellowship in 1968 to study the relationship between religion and sociology at the University of Nijmegen, The Netherlands. Upon returning to the United States in 1969, Dr. Wilcox commenced the course of study leading to the doctoral degree in Christian ethics at Union Theological Seminary, New York City. While pursuing this degree he served as tutor at Union and taught Christian ethics at Fordham, Fairfield, and Pace Universities. In 1974, he took a full-time position in the religious studies department at Manhattan College, Riverdale, N.Y. Dr. Wilcox continues to teach there, specializing in sexual and social ethics.

At the present time, the author lives in Dobbs Ferry, N.Y., with his wife, Suzanne Dale, whom he married in 1974.